Business Explained
FINANCE, INFORMATION AND BUSINESS

MALCOLM SURRIDGE
Senior Lecturer and Assistant Director of External Affairs, Great Yarmouth College; Senior Examiner AEB A Level Business Studies

TONY BUSHELL
Principal Lecturer in Business and Management Studies, City College, Norwich

PHILIP GUNN
Head of the School of Management, Great Yarmouth College; Assistant Chief Examiner AEB A Level Business Studies

Collins Educational
An imprint of HarperCollins*Publishers*

Dedication
To Rosemary, Diana and Sheila

Malcolm Surridge, Tony Bushell and Philip Gunn assert the moral right to be identified as the authors of this work.

Published by
Collins Educational Ltd.
An imprint of HarperCollins*Publishers*
77-85 Fulham Palace Road
Hammersmith
London W6 8JB

First published in 1993
Reprinted 1994

British Library Cataloguing in Publication Data is available on request from the British Library

ISBN 000-322-3132

Typeset by Dorchester Typesetting Group Ltd
Cover designed by Ridgeway Associates
Printed by Scotprint Ltd, Musselburgh

FINANCE, INFORMATION AND BUSINESS

Also in the HarperCollins Business Explained Series

The Business Environment
Malcolm Surridge, Tony Bushell and Philip Gunn

People, Marketing and Business
Malcolm Surridge, Tony Bushell and Philip Gunn

Contents

ACKNOWLEDGEMENTS

A number of people have been of great assistance in the production of this book. We are most grateful to Murray Lauder for reading and commenting upon the whole manuscript. His ideas were invaluable and improved the manuscript in many ways. We are very grateful to Martin Liu of HarperCollins for his thorough and professional work in helping to prepare this book for publication. We also wish to thank David Chell, Clare Gunn and Kevin Gunn for reading and offering comments upon specialist parts of the manuscript. In spite of their help we are, of course, entirely responsible for any errors or omissions which may remain.

We wish to record our thanks to Barbara Francis for her suggestions as to sources for the various materials necessary to write this book. We are indebted to the many businesses, big and small, who offered materials for publication in the book. Without their co-operation the end result would have been much poorer.

Finally, we wish to acknowledge the following examination boards for permission to reproduce questions from past examination papers: Associated Examination Board, Northern Examination and Assessment Board, and Cambridge Local Examinations Syndicate. Any answers or hints of answers are the sole responsibility of the authors and have not been provided by the Boards.

Every effort has been made to contact all copyright holders, but if any have been inadvertently overlooked the publisher would be pleased to hear from them and to make the necessary arrangement at the first opportunity.

Study Skills

▷ ▷ **QUESTIONS FOR PREVIEW** ▷ ▷

1. *How can I organize myself to study effectively?*
2. *How can I become more aware of business that exists around me?*
3. *What do examiners expect in answers to business studies questions?*
4. *What other sources of information about business studies exist?*
5. *How is the Business Explained series organized and how can it help me to study the subject?*

Effective Study

MANY of you who are about to start an A level, BTEC or similar course in business studies will have had relatively little experience of taking more advanced courses where much is expected of the student outside the classroom. It is broadly true to say that the higher the level at which you study the more work the student is expected to undertake outside the classroom or lecture theatre. Do not be daunted! By organizing yourself and your time you can develop the skills and techniques which are essential for success at this level.

Probably the first thing you need to sort out is somewhere to study. You will need a desk or table to work on and possibly some shelves for your books. It should also be somewhere you can work without disturbance – well away from distractions!

You need to organize your week so as to allocate regular times for study. It makes sense to use the same times each week so that you and your family and friends become used to the arrangement. This might seem unnecessarily formal to you but it is essential that you work steadily throughout your course. You cannot expect to do well by leaving everything to the last minute. Indeed, the growing emphasis on coursework will make such an approach impossible.

The actual studying you undertake may take a number of forms. Business studies is a unique subject in that it is going on around you all the time. Pick up a newspaper or magazine and it will inevitably contain a number of advertisements. Similarly, your favourite TV programmes may be interrupted by advertisements. As your knowledge of the subject increases, you will discover that you can learn much about the firm and its competitors from the way and place it advertises. Equally, as you walk down your local high street you find a lot of evidence of business taking place. Delivery vans and lorries will be regularly seen and many famous retailers such as Marks & Spencer and W H Smith will have branches. Business studies will help you to understand why they have chosen such a location and why some businesses succeed and others fail.

You can learn a lot about business from talking to relatives or friends who are at work. You may care to ask some of the following questions:

- What do you like most and least about your job?
- What does your business (organization) do?
- Where and how does it advertise?
- Do you work mainly with machinery or with people?
- How large is your business? How do you measure the size of it?

- Are there trade unions where you work?
- Has the business changed a lot over the last few years?
- Do you use computers a lot in your work? If so, in which department – production, design, administration?
- With which other businesses do you do business?

Examples of business studies in action are all around you: make the best use of the examples and evidence offered to support your classroom study. You will gain marks in examinations and coursework by being able to quote relevant, real-life examples.

Writing Answers

Your teacher or lecturer will set you essays, case studies and possibly coursework throughout the course. It is important that you do as well as possible when completing this work, particularly where the marks you score contribute to your final, overall grade.

When tackling essays or other coursework you should resist the temptation to leave everything until the last moment. A successful piece of written work requires careful preparation. You will need to research your answer by using class or lecture notes and texts such as this one. You may also follow up references given in the books you read. Finally, but importantly, you may use quality newspapers and periodicals, such as *The Economist,* to give relevant up-to-date examples in support of your answers. Again, examples from the real world around you should prove valuable. With this material to hand, you should carefully plan your answer before you commence writing.

A level in particular requires more than a simple regurgitation of facts. Marks for factual content alone probably represent less than 30 per cent of the total available. It is what you do with your knowledge that will determine how good a mark you score.

Examiners are looking for evidence of *analysis* in your answers. This means that you must be able to apply your factual knowledge to unfamiliar situations presented to you by the examiners. For example, you may be given a case study describing a large firm which is experiencing communications problems. You might be asked to explain why this firm experiences problems and to recommend some solutions. You may use your notes on barriers to communication as a guide but you will also need to *apply* them to the firm in question, thus analysing that firm's particular problems.

Most questions will also require some *evaluation.* This involves judgement or assessment. So, continuing with our example from the previous paragraph it may be necessary to identify (justifying your choice) the major barrier to communication or perhaps the most likely cure.

Analysis and evaluation are important components of answers to most types of question and not just case studies. Your teacher or lecturer will be able to help you develop the necessary technique to write well balanced answers.

When the piece of work is returned to you it is important that you read carefully your teacher's or lecturer's comments in order to eliminate weaknesses and improve future performance.

Using the Business Explained Series

This series of book comprises three titles:

- Finance, Information and Business
- The Business Environment
- People, Marketing and Business

It is designed to make business studies both understandable and enjoyable. By adopting the language and approach that we have, we have aimed to provide a rigorous treatment of the subject whilst not confusing you, the reader.

The series has been written for a typical student who is following an A level, BTEC, GAVQ or similar course in business studies. In particular, consideration has been given to students who will be working alone. Much of your studying will take place outside the classroom and these books are intended to act as a support to the teaching that you receive.

The three books in the series can be read in any order. We have deliberately avoided writing the books in any sequence. Not only can you begin with any book, but with any chapter. If you encounter business terms with which you are unfamilar then simply look them up in the Dictionary at the end of each book.

We recommend two ways in which you may use this book apart from as a class text.

Method A

Reading about business studies in this book and others, as we saw earlier, is an important part of your studies. It will help you to strengthen your knowledge of the subject and its techniques. You may wish to read a topic area prior to your teacher covering it in class. Indeed you may be asked to do so! Alternatively, it could be that you choose to read such an area after you have been taught it.

At the end of the chapters we have included an Exam Preparation Section. This will allow you to practise the skills you are attempting to acquire and to assess how well you understand the subject matter. Because many examination boards are now using case studies most chapters contain at least one to allow you to familiarise yourself with this style of question.

We have also included regular Key Points which act as a summary of the principal elements covered in the preceding section. When you reach the end of each chapter you should reread the points for preview and confirm that you now understand them.

Method B

Throughout your course, your teacher or lecturer will set you essays, case studies or similar questions. You will be able to use this book in several ways to help with such assignments. It will, of course, provide you with much of the information needed to answer questions set on A level, BTEC, GNVQ and similar courses. In addition, you may also make use of the references offered at the end of each book.

Finally, you would be well advised to look at some of the past examination questions and the suggested solutions at the back of the books. This should give you valuable guidance on what your teacher (or the examiner) is looking for when setting questions.

As the examination approaches your studying should become more intensive with the main emphasis on the revision of material covered earlier. In the meantime the best of luck with the course!

CHAPTER 1

Introduction to Business

▷ ▷ QUESTIONS FOR PREVIEW ▷ ▷

1. *What do we mean by the term 'business'?*
2. *In what sense are businesses dynamic and how do they interact with society?*
3. *Why can businesses be described as integrated systems and how should they plan their activities?*
4. *What forms of business exist in the UK?*

What is Business?

A DICTIONARY and Thesaurus give many meanings of the noun 'business':

- A trade or profession – for example, 'What business are you in?'
- The purchase and sale of goods and services – for example, 'Smith and I do business together'
- A commercial or industrial establishment – for example, 'This business employs 400 people'
- Volume of commercial activity – for example, 'Business is good at the moment'
- Commercial policy – for example, 'Overcharging customers is bad business'

Other meanings exist, but they are not relevant here. So you can see the problem that needs to be cleared up before we start a study of business. What do we mean when we use the term 'business' in this book?

It is essential that our study examines all the internal and external pressures that affect the many organizations from which we earn or receive money, and all the organizations with which we spend our money either voluntarily or by compulsion. Therefore, in general we mean 'commercial or industrial establishments' like ICI, Marks & Spencer, Abbey National Building Society or Commercial Union Insurance.

But we cannot exclude local government which places planning and development restrictions on businesses, or national government which passes laws that affect every business, and collects taxes on profits and VAT on purchases. Trade unions influence the pay and conditions that employers provide, and pressure groups can cause firms to alter the way they make or package their products. Similarly, we must consider the impact of international organizations such as the European Community and the International Monetary Fund. This book, together with the two others in this series, will consider all the forms of business which exist, what comprises these businesses and the external influences to which they are subject.

So when we think about 'business' in this book, we mean commercial and industrial establishments and everything that affects them.

Business studies is not a single, tidy subject with its own body of knowledge and its own language. Rather, it is a blend of many specialist subjects. Economics is the basis of business studies and provides a firm foundation upon which to build. Money (as represented by finance and accounting) is the language of business, and needs to be controlled and kept secure. People make business, and their behaviour must be understood and influenced when possible. Laws control business and protect society from its worst excesses. Communication is the lifeblood of business and pervades every aspect of it. Mathematics and statistics are the key to understanding, describing and solving many of the problems faced by businesses. We do not need to study each of these in as much depth as a specialist might – we need a working knowledge of each, and to understand the interaction of each of them with the others. The good student of business studies understands the components which comprise business studies and the way in which the elements fit together to provide an integrated approach to the subject.

For example, a company thinking about developing a new product or service ought to consider if there will be sufficient demand for it, and whether the level of demand would be affected by price (*economics*). Can the company afford to produce it and make a profit at the price customers would be willing to pay (*finance*)? Has it got people with the right skills and expertise to design and make the good (*people*)? Is the product covered by any special legal regulations as the upholstery or toy industries are (*law*)? Ought the company do some marketing research to find out what people think before they spend too much money (*mathematics* and *statistics*)? In everything mentioned here, the company will be giving and gathering information and ideas all the time (*communication*).

If any one of these activities turns up a problem, it will affect all the others. For example, if the law says that only flame resistant foam may be used in the product, it may put up the costs, the price may have to be raised to cover it, that may mean fewer customers and less income, which may mean the company cannot afford to employ expert staff, so it may have to drop the whole idea.

ACTIVITY 1.1

Your cousin is about to set up in business as a window cleaner. In conversation with him, you mention the elements which make up business and remark that he will be affected by them all once he starts trading. He is surprised and asks for examples which relate to his business.

Using the six headings outlined earlier, give examples of how he will call upon skills or knowledge from these subject areas in running his business.

Classifying Businesses

Another difficulty facing you is the very wide range of activities that can be described as business. If you look at the *Yellow Pages* trade directory, there are over 2700 trade classifications, starting with 'Abattoir equipment' and ending with 'Zoos'. We need a much more general structure to allow access to the subject.

The most common and accepted classifications take three stages in the production of goods and services:

- Primary activities
- Secondary activities
- Tertiary activities

Primary Activities

Most commodities or goods that we buy start their life as raw materials in the ground, the seas or the fields.

All the activities concerned with extracting ores, oil or other basic materials; growing grain, fruit and vegetables; breeding animals for meat and fishing are called primary activities, and this part of the production chain is called the primary sector. The industries that make up this sector include mining and quarrying, agriculture, forestry and fishing.

Secondary Activties

Converting these raw materials into useful products, either by manufacturing or processing, is called secondary activity. For example, converting iron ore into steel, and then using the steel for manufacturing cars; or purifying water and pumping it to homes for drinking; or milling wheat to make flour, and then baking it for bread – all these are secondary activities, and together these industries constitute the secondary sector.

Tertiary Activities

Distributing these goods to make it convenient for the consumer to buy them – transportation, wholesaling, retailing, direct mail – are tertiary activities. So, too, are all the supporting services to industry: banking, insurance, travel, street lighting, refuse collection and any other supporting activities (such as holidays, health services, education and training). All these make up the tertiary sector.

SUB-DIVISIONS

There are many sub-divisions to these general categories. Farming can be sub-divided into arable (crops) and dairy (cattle), and these can be sub-divided again into types of crop and types of cattle. We could carry on sub-dividing until we are back to the 2700 classifications found in the *Yellow Pages*. But the three main sectors we have described above are enough for our purposes.

ACTIVITY 1.2

Look in your daily or local newspaper and turn to the pages where jobs are advertised. Select ten advertisements and categorize the firms that placed them according to whether they are in the primary, secondary or tertiary sectors. Why do you think that firms from certain sectors of the economy placed most of the advertisements – particularly if you looked in a national newspaper?

The Size of Businesses

Another difficulty we have to deal with is the variation in the size of different businesses and the scale of their operations. For example, the Ford Motor Company is a business that manufactures cars on a very large scale in many countries of the world. Rolls Royce manufactures a small number of exclusive cars in the UK for a particular type of customer. Dennis Beeston & Co service and repair cars for a small number of customers in Bradwell, near Great Yarmouth. The one thing they have in common is that they are businesses to do with motor cars – but there is little else.

There are many ways to measure the size of businesses. Probably the most commonly used is the value of turnover or sales, although the number of employees is also used on occasions. Can you think of any alternatives?

Look back now at your answers to Activity 1.2. Do you think that there is any relationship between the size (and probable wealth) of firms and where they advertise for employees? Might this have biased your mini-survey?

The Dynamic Nature of Business

Another aspect of business that we must take into account is the fact that it is dynamic. It is always changing in response to changes within it, and in response to changes outside it. It has an energy of its own that affects its environment, just as its environment has energy that affects the business. In other words, businesses and the environment in which they operate affect one another.

A writer on psychology, Kurt Lewin, described this idea as 'a field of forces' that create a balance between opposing forces. Imagine a balloon that has been inflated. It is the shape and size that it is because the pressure (forces) inside is exactly equal to the forces outside. If you increase the forces outside without an equal response from inside, the balloon will get smaller. The opposite is also true. If you increase the forces inside the balloon without an equal response from outside, the balloon will get bigger. This idea is very useful in helping us to understand what might happen to a business, or to businesses in general, as the environment in which they exist changes. We can call this the 'concept of balancing forces'.

The energy inside a business comes from the people who manage and work in it. When a team of people are working together in harmony, committed to the same aims and objectives and all pulling in the same direction, it is likely that it will be creating forces which will affect its environment. For example, if it develops a new and revolutionary product that the consumers want, and none of its competitors have responded to this new 'force', almost certainly it will get larger and the competitor will get smaller as a result. Similarly, if the company invests in new technology, and as a result reduces its costs, it can either lower its prices to gain a bigger share of the market (thus taking business away from its competitors) or it can make more profit to finance further growth.

We will study the various internal forces that make businesses dynamic. Whether a company grows or contracts depends upon its ability to respond to the changes in internal and external forces.

Business Within Society

People in society demand goods and services for a number of reasons. For example, we need food

KEY POINTS 1.1

- **'Business' in this book means commercial and industrial establishments and everything that affects them**
- **The study of business calls upon knowledge from many disciplines**
- **Businesses can be classified by describing where they come in the production chain: primary, secondary or tertiary**
- **The size of a business can vary enormously even between firms in the same industry**
- **There are a number of ways in which the size of a business can be measured**

and drink in order to survive. It is very difficult nowadays for an individual or family in the UK to provide for themselves all that they want in the way of basic needs. So they depend upon businesses to supply their needs. Also, we need good health care to keep us fit and free from disease. Not many of us are expert enough to do this for ourselves. We also need recreation and leisure pursuits to help us relax and enjoy friendship.

Another reason is because we have very high expectations. As a very affluent society, we do not see our needs in terms of survival, but in terms of our standard of living. And this standard is set not in relation to necessities, but in relation to how much other people have. Today's luxuries become tomorrow's necessities. Televisions and cars are good examples of this. How many people do you know who do not have a television? Politicians and the media make comparisons between what we have and what others have so that our expectations are never allowed to rest.

ACTIVITY 1.3

Make a list of all the goods and services you have used today. Now tick those services which you think you could provide yourself. Why do you choose not to produce for yourself the goods and services which you have not ticked?

In response to this demand, appropriate means of supply develop. These may be businesses which produce goods in response to the demand in order to make a profit, or the government of the day providing the health care required. It is almost certain that if a demand exists, a means of supply will respond. So business is shaped by the demands of society.

However, you can probably quote many examples of business shaping society. For example, do you think that 'Coke is it!' whatever 'it' is? Yet, worldwide, more people buy this soft drink than any other. The power of advertising can and does create expectations that influence our society. The temptation to improve our looks or to become more attractive to the opposite sex, as promised in many advertisements, is too great for many of us, and we buy the product whether or not the promise is realistic. Advanced economies become more advanced. Developing economies try to grow by serving and competing with them. Some will provide raw materials while others, like the textile industries in Korea and Taiwan, use cheap local labour to produce low-price goods. Some of them get into debt to such a degree that they use their new wealth to pay the interest rather than improving the standards of living in their own country. Poland and Mexico actually got to the stage where they could not even pay the loan interest. Western businesses are shaping the societies of the developing nations as well as their own.

Our standard of living is greatly influenced by job opportunities. The more successful business is, the more jobs there will be (if we assume that technology does not take over!). This in turn influences the amount of money that is spent on goods and services. Failure of business can have the opposite effect. When British Steel closed down a major factory at Corby, it had a disastrous effect on the local community because the firm had been the major employer and purchaser in the town.

During the 1980s, many incentives were offered to businesses to start up, grow and become more efficient. The spirit of enterprise was encouraged by the Conservative government under Margaret Thatcher. The philosophy of the free market economy has given businesses a much greater influence in the shaping of society than previously: and, almost inevitably, they shape society to demand more of their goods and services.

As demand grows, more raw materials are used and more waste is generated. Lewin's concept of

KEY POINTS 1.2

- **Businesses shape and respond to their environments**
- **The internal and external environments of business interact with one another**
- **Our society demands a wide range of goods and services, few of which we can produce for ourselves**
- **Our changing demands and rising expectations have implications for businesses**

balancing forces warns us that as one force alters, it affects the other variables in the environment.

Should businesses be allowed to behave in such a way as to risk these undesirable consequences? Is it ethical or not to pursue profit at all costs? It is possible to control some aspects of business behaviour by law, but it is not possible to cover all eventualities. Should some moral responsibility, therefore, be borne by owners and managers? There is no ethical code for managers as there is for, say, doctors and other professions, so how can they be controlled?

Business as an Integrated System

- Which comes first, the chicken or the egg?
- Which comes first, the product or the customer?

CASE STUDY

(The Negative Version)

John returned home from work looking more frustrated and fed up than usual. He hardly said a word to his wife and family, sat down and drank his cup of tea without looking up. Going through his mind were things that had happened at work that day: things like the decision by his boss to change production from 500-gramme packets to 400-gramme packets without consulting him. He could have told the boss that the 500-gramme packets were an urgent run for their best customer, but he had not been asked. It seemed to John that the only way to run the job properly was to run it himself – but how could he with a boss who does not consult.

His wife Jenny sat down beside him and asked him what was wrong. John explained his frustration as he had done many times before, only this time Jenny sensed that it was about time he did something about it.

'Why don't you set up on your own?' Jenny asked. 'You will never be happy working for somebody else. Take the bull by the horns before it's too late. You've got skills and experience and lots of energy. I'll support you.'

'It's not as easy as that,' replied John. 'What could I do? Where would I get enough money? Who would buy from me?' At the same time John found the idea of being his own boss very attractive. Perhaps it would be worth making a few enquiries, he thought.

(The Positive Version!)

John came home from work very excited. He could not wait for the children to go to bed so that he could discuss his decision with his wife, Jenny. At last they sat down with a cup of tea, and John said, 'Jenny, I'm going to set up in business with two of the lads from work. We know we've got the skills and experience, it's just a matter of deciding exactly what we're going to make and sell. How do you feel about joining us and running the marketing side of the business? You'd be brilliant.'

Jenny smiled. She had often thought about running their own business. It seemed a very attractive proposition, but too many people started their own business only to fail within a very short time.

'On one condition,' she said, 'and that is that we do everything properly: don't rush in and don't take unnecessary risks.'

'That's right,' agreed John, 'we'll take it one step at a time and plan carefully before we take any action.'

The conversation went on into the night, and the main outcome was that they would take the best advice they could find at each step along the way.

QUESTIONS

1 Why do you think that John and Jenny are more likely to succeed with their business in the second case than in the first? You should give as many reasons as you can.

2 If John and Jenny asked for your advice about their intended business in the first case study, what would you advise them to do?

A business can be run by one person. That person can do everything: the production of the good or service, the accounting, the selling, the delivering and any after-sales service. This person will be very busy, too busy to become an expert at any of the tasks in the business. She or he will be talking to a customer one minute, paying a supplier the next, making the product the next minute, answering the phone, trying to find time for a cup of tea and so on. All these jobs are essential to the success of the business, no one being more or less important than another.

In a medium-sized company, there will be enough selling activity to justify the full use of one or more person's time. It will become a specialist department where real expertise can be developed. Similarly, several people may make the product in such a way that it is more efficient and less costly. A specially trained accountant may take care of all financial matters and ensure that the company keeps spending in line with income. Perhaps a special section is set up to employ the right sort of person for each job, train them, make sure that the workplace is safe and that the company looks after its staff well. Each of these *functions* is important to the success of the business.

As with the one-person business, all these activities are going on all the time, non-stop, day-in and day-out. But in the case of the medium-sized business, no one person knows everything that is going on at any one time. There is a need for planning and co-ordination to keep everything pulling in the same direction.

A good example of this need for planning and co-ordination may be seen in your school or college. The National Curriculum requires that certain subjects are taught to all students and that some of those are taught across the curriculum (Information Technology, for example). Teachers and lecturers will attend training days and staff meetings in order to plan how this will be achieved and to ensure that everyone is doing what is required of them.

An example from industry might include every department in a company. If the people doing the selling learn that there is going to be an increase in demand for the company's product, they need to tell production to make more. Production need to buy more raw materials in time to have the goods ready when the customer wants them. If production needs more workers to make the goods, the personnel section will need to find, employ and train enough people. The accountant must ensure that the company has enough money available to pay for the additional raw materials and wages. And someone must make certain that all these interdependent activities happen at the right time to avoid holding anyone else up – particularly the customer.

You can see how complicated business can be in a medium-sized company. Just think how much more complicated it can be in a very large company, with several factories and many different products. Or a multinational company like Ford or Unilever. Or a large government department, or a worldwide charity.

All the various activities that are continuously going on affect each other. We can apply Lewin's concept of balancing forces to these internal activities – as one alters, so it affects others, and they must respond or the business will go out of balance.

A business is like a stewpot. There are a lot of ingredients and each one affects the flavour of the dish. If one is missing, or there is too much of another, the flavour will be different, and perhaps not very nice.

In our study of business, we have to understand how each of the functions operate, how they contribute to the well-being of the whole business, how each one influences and affects the others, and how to keep them all in balance. We must also see the business in its environment. How it affects the environment and is affected by it is very important.

Business Plans

Before starting any business it is essential that plans are drawn up. Small businesses have a very high mortality rate: only 20 per cent survive the first five years. A major reason for this is that the new owners of businesses do not fully understand all the aspects of running a business, or the environment in which their business is to operate, or both!

It is important to research the market to make sure that buyers exist for the good or service that is to be sold and to get some idea of the prices that should be charged. Hopeful entrepreneurs should then calculate carefully the costs of supplying the good or service in order to find out whether a profit can be made.

The process of planning a business is important. It helps to draw attention to aspects of the business which might be unsuccessful or difficult and to skills which the entrepreneur may not possess.

A good business plan will help an entrepreneur to obtain finance. Bank managers are likely to be more impressed by a carefully prepared plan than by a simple expression of a business idea – no matter how great its potential.

A good business plan will contain some or all of the following:

Figure 1.1 – ***A Business Plan Checklist***

Objectives:
What are your personal objectives?
What are your business objectives?
Are they specific?
Have you thought of the consequences?

The business:
History if already established.
Accounts for previous years's trading.
Present financial position.

Management:
Experience of proprietors/managers.
Responsibilities of managers.
Is the team complete or is further recruitment necessary?

Market:
How large is it?
Is market research possible/available?
What is the competition?
What advantages do competitors have?
What advantages does your product/service have?
What are the distribution channels?
What advertising or marketing will you need?

Products:
Do they meet customers's needs?
Have they been tested, including production methods?
How have costs been calculated?

Pricing:
How have prices been arrived at?
Are they competitive?

Suppliers:
Are adequate supplies available?
Is quality known to be acceptable?
What credit is available?

Physical resources:
What premises are available?
Are they adequate?
What is the cost?
What machinery/vehicles are required?

Source: Barclays Bank plc

- A full account of the entrepreneur's business experience and qualifications
- A clear statement as to what product or service is to be sold and the intended target market. How is it different from other goods or services that are already being sold on the market?
- An assessment of the costs that the business will incur in starting production and continuing over the first year or so. These should be broken down into monthly payments so that periods of financial difficulty can be identified and planned for
- The amount of capital that the owner of the business has contributed; the amount that she or he has borrowed (or wants to borrow) from others, and the rates of interest that the business is already commited to pay
- Details of the place in which the product is to be produced and sold (this might be a factory, office or shop). Does the business own part or all of it, or is it rented?
- The aims and objectives of the business. What are the intentions of the entrepreneur with regard to her or his business? Does she or he hope for rapid growth or slower growth, concentrating on a particular segment of the market. In other words, what is the overall aim of the business? What objectives will be pursued in order to achieve this overall aim?

KEY POINTS 1.3

- **It is unlikely that one person can carry out all the activities necessary to operate a business**
- **Planning and co-ordination are essential for business success**
- **The many components of business all interact and contribute to the operation of that business**
- **Business plans highlight areas of weakness and can help avoid problems before they occur**

Finance, Information and Business – About This Book

The first four lines of Rudyard Kipling's poem *The Elephant's Child* are often quoted in business to remind people of the need for information. These lines are:

I keep six honest serving-men
(They taught me all I knew)
Their names are What and Why and When
And How and Where and Who.

There are probably a number of questions which we can think of, the answers to which provide very valuable information. For example, if we start with Kipling's 'serving-men':

- *What* profit did we make last week?
- *Why* was the profit less than we planned?
- *When* will sales pick up?
- *How* can we reduce the cost of production?
- *Where* can we purchase the best materials?
- *Who* should we employ to do the work?

In order to be valuable, the answers must also be timely, understood and useful.

Information has no value if it is not available when required. In some businesses, knowledge of the profit made during a year's trading is not known until nine months after the end of the year. Such information may be useful to the Inland Revenue in order to calculate the taxes due, but it is not useful to the business manager who needs to change plans if profits are not good.

Sometimes information is presented in a format which is not understood by the recipient. This could be because of bad English, unclear diagrams, or by using words or mathematics which are new to the recipient. Information relies on good communication systems in order to transfer meaning. Often large amounts of data need to be processed in order to change the data into information which can be more easily understood. The ages of one hundred people can be processed to give the average age of the people; this may be a very useful piece of information if the need is to compare one group of people with another group.

That information has to be *useful* sounds obvious, but often people generate information which is not needed. This is a waste of time and money. When computers first appeared in business, many, many pages of printed computer output were generated which were not read by anyone. This could hardly be called information. Hopefully, such output is now obsolete in any efficient system.

ACTIVITY 1.4

Visit a small business, such as a local store, and find out the important *information* needed by all the staff. List these needs under different categories, such as information about money, information about customers, information about stock or materials, and information about sales.

As a result of your investigations have you found that the needs of any one information category are higher than any other? What conclusions do you draw if this is indeed the case?

Is a computer being used to help process data in the business? If not, do you think that one might be helpful, if only to save time? Do you find that staff are generally happy about the information that is available? If they are not, what suggestions do they have to improve matters?

This book primarily examines the quantifiable information needs of a business – that is, information which can be clearly defined, measured and recorded for a stated purpose.

Chapter Two examines the types of business organization to show that different types of business have different information needs, because they have different objectives.

Chapters Three, Six and Seven examine the financial information aspects of businesses in terms of 'Where does the money come from?', 'How much will it cost?' and 'Should I invest in a new factory?'. In business jargon this is sometimes referred to as the 'bottom line'. This saying is derived from the accounting systems where the last line on the page of accounts showed the total cost or profit for the period. The 'bottom line' implies that only the profit is important and that the means justify the ends. This is an out-of-date business philosophy among today's business leaders. 'Delighted customers' is now the slogan of many quality businesses who realize that happy customers will eventually lead to business success.

Chapter Four looks at the mathematics of business and the data processing methods available to generate information. The analytical methods for processing numbers are not always easy to understand if the purpose for undertaking the routine is not clear. Many students in the past were taught mathematics as a series of problems to solve with little or no application to real life. The modern approach is to show that business needs information on a variety of issues, not least on the quality control of processes. 'Is the process giving a good, consistent and reliable output?' is a question requiring a statistical approach rather than an emotive one. Measuring variability, understanding the causes and trying to minimize it are suggested by the management thinker Edwards Deming as being the essential steps in improving business efficiency.

Chapter Five considers the information needs of operations managers, whether they are in a production or a service environment. 'How are products made?', 'How are processes planned and controlled? and 'How can we improve the service?'. The answers specify methods, time and resources required which are clearly recorded and measured.

Finally, Chapter Eight shows how computer systems are used to generate, process and store information. The computer is revolutionizing all aspects of business, and is freeing valuable human brains from mundane tasks such as adding up numbers and calculating weekly wages. The computer will allow people to concentrate on more important issues, such as new product ideas, improving industrial relations and preparing marketing plans. The potential for the computer in supplying business information is tremendous, and technologists working with the most advanced business systems will agree that in ten years's time, today's computer and information output will be laughed at.

KEY POINTS 1.4

- **Information is only valuable if it is delivered on time**
- **Information is essential for planning and controlling a business**
- **Information is often improved by processing data**
- **Information transfer requires good communication systems**
- **Information has to be useful**

CHAPTER 2

The Structure of Business

▷ ▷ QUESTIONS FOR PREVIEW ▷ ▷

1. *What are the advantages and disadvantages of organizing a business as a sole trader or partnership?*
2. *What benefits do shareholders and businesses receive from having company status?*
3. *How are companies organized and managed?*
4. *What other structures can private sector businesses adopt?*
5. *In what ways can businesses be organized and operated by the public sector?*

THERE ARE many different types of business, and each type has a different reason for being in existence. This chapter examines the different businesses and the information needed for setting them up and running them.

Non-Corporate Businesses

If you walk down your high street or look through your local copy of *Yellow Pages,* it will be clear that a range of businesses operate: they have different names and are of different sizes. Small organizations may deliver your newspapers or tidy your garden, whilst much larger businesses may build your house or car. The law recognizes that businesses can take a number of different forms. One-person businesses may run local corner shops, but a vastly different arrangement is necessary for some of the UK's largest firms, such as ICI and British Telecom. Sole traders and partnerships are non-corporate businesses, which means that the business cannot be separated from the people who own it. The business is not a separate legal 'body'.

Sole Trader

Many businesses are owned by a single person. Although that person may hire help in running the business, he or she is solely responsible for the organization and receives all the profits, if it makes any!

They are simple and cheap to set up with few legal formalities. They are also straightforward to run and flexible. Because only one person is involved in taking any decisions, the business can respond quickly to changes in customer requirements. For example, a small local builder may be more able to build to individual customer needs than a national building firm which constructs large numbers of standard houses.

A difficulty which is common to most sole traders is a shortage of capital – that is, funds for investing in and improving and/or expanding the business. Banks may be unwilling to lend to small businesses with few assets of value to serve as collateral and a single owner is unlikely to have sufficient savings to finance completely the business. Such businesses raise their funds from a variety of sources, including family and friends.

People who choose to set up their businesses as a sole trader face a significant disadvantage: they suffer from unlimited liability. This means that if their business were to fail then they might have to sell their private possessions (for example, their houses or cars) in order to pay the business's debts. This is because the law does not recognize that sole trader's business affairs are separate from their personal finances. You will see that this means those people who establish their businesses as sole traders take a risk but hope to make profits. Unfortunately, about 80 per cent of sole traders fail within the first five years of business.

Sole traders are the most common type of business in the UK. It is quite likely that your local newsagent, hairdresser and plumber are sole traders.

Partnerships

Partnerships comprise between two and twenty people who contribute capital and expertise to a common enterprise. Only in special circumstances can the number of partners exceed twenty. The legal rules under which partnerships must be established were set out in the Partnership Act 1890.

It is usual when setting up a partnership to draw up a Deed of Partnership, which is a legal document stating how much capital has been contributed to the business by each partner, the share of profits they shall receive and rules for electing new partners. In the absence of such a deed the 1890 Act states that profits (if any are made) should be shared equally between the partners.

A partnership offers a number of advantages to businesses. It is likely that a group of partners will be able to raise more capital than an individual sole trader. Partnerships also benefit from a greater range of expertise. They are more likely to succeed if partners have different ranges of experience and ability. For example, we commonly find partnerships in the professions, such as accountants, solicitors and estate agents. A partnership of estate agents might have experts in residential property as well as in industrial and agricultural property. It could be that some of the partners are 'sleeping partners' – that is, they contribute capital to the business but take no part in the running of it.

Partnerships reduce the pressure on the owners of the business. Unlike sole traders, partners can cover for one another in the event of illness and holidays. Decisions can be taken jointly.

However, they do suffer from a number of disadvantages. There is a limit to the amount of capital that even twenty partners can raise. Partnerships are often short of capital, particularly when expansion is being considered. As with sole traders, most partnerships suffer from unlimited liability with all the consequent risks for partners's private possessions. The exceptions are limited partnerships which can exist so long as at least one partner has unlimited liability. Obviously, the one or more partners who carry unlimited liability bear a high degree of risk. Moreover, partners are notorious for arguing! Minor disputes are common, but more serious disputes can result in the dissolution of the partnership. This is a significant disadvantage to this form of business.

Corporate Businesses

Companies are corporate businesses and are commonly found in all areas of activity: in agriculture, manufacturing and services (such as banking or insurance). They can be recognized by the abbreviations 'plc' or 'Ltd' after the name of the company. 'Ltd' stands for 'Limited' and is affixed to a private company; 'plc' stands for 'public limited company' and is affixed to a public company. The differences between these two types are considered later in this section.

Companies are regulated by a series of Companies Acts that were passed between 1948 and 1985. The 1985 Act consolidated the earlier ones and currently regulates the activities of companies. It was amended in 1989 to achieve the

KEY POINTS 2.1

- **Many small businesses are owned by a single person and are termed sole traders**
- **Sole traders are at risk because they are frequently short of capital, can face intense competition and may be poorly managed**
- **Partnerships normally have up to twenty owners and thus have access to more capital and expertise**
- **Sole traders and most partnerships suffer from unlimited liability. This means that all the owners's personal possessions can be at risk**

harmonization of company law necessary to create the European Community's (EC) Single Market.

The 1985 Act covers many matters concerning the management and operation of companies. For example, it defines what comprises a public company (and hence distinguishes between public and private companies); it sets out the regulations necessary to form a company; and along with the Business Names Act 1985, it controls the names a company can adopt. It also covers the raising of finance and the amount of information which has to be disclosed in company accounts, which varies according to the size of the company (with larger companies having to disclose more!).

Companies are different from the other forms of business we have discussed so far, in that they are regarded as separate legal entities. The law recognizes that they are separate from the people who own the company who are the shareholders. Shareholders own the company because they buy parts (or shares) of that company (thus providing its capital) in the hope of making a profit.

Because the law regards the company as a legal entity, rather like a person, companies can do many things that an individual can do. For example, companies have the right to sue and to be sued; and they can enter into contracts. The exact powers that any company has are set out in its Memorandum of Association. We shall look at this document in more detail later in this chapter.

Figure 2.1 – ***Legal Position of Companies***

Zeebrugge trial may last five months

A JURY at the Old Bailey was warned yesterday to expect a trial lasting between three and five months as P & O European Ferries and seven of its former employees denied the manslaughter of a victim of the *Herald of Free Enterprise* disaster.

The prosecution – only the second in legal history to accuse a company of corporate manslaughter – alleges in separate sample charges that each of the eight defendants alone unlawfully killed Alison Gillard, 27, a passenger who died when the vessel capsized outside Zeebrugge harbour on 6 March 1987, with the loss of 193 lives.

The seven men pleaded not guilty from the dock. The company, formerly Townsend Car Ferries Ltd, pleaded not guilty in writing.

Source: adapted from the *Independent*, 12 September 1990

The newspaper cutting in Figure 2.1 illustrates the legal position of companies. They are separate from their owners and can be the subject of legal action. You should note that it is the company that is being sued, not its owners.

The legal status of companies offers a major benefit to its shareholders. The shareholders are granted the protection of limited liability. This means that shareholders can invest in the business secure in the knowledge that all that they are risking is their investment. Thus, if a company fails then the shareholder's personal possessions are not at risk: the shareholder cannot be called upon to contribute more than his or her full original investment.

All registered companies can benefit from this privilege under the Limited Liability Act 1855. This Act had become necessary by the middle of the nineteenth century because businesses were growing in size and requiring larger amounts of capital. However, prior to the Limited Liability Act, investors were unwilling to put funds into businesses if it meant risking their entire personal fortunes.

Nowadays there are two methods by which shareholders's liability is limited:

a Limitation by shares
Here shareholders's liability is limited to the nominal value (this is the face value which is written on the share certificate) of the shares they have purchased. There can be no further call on their personal wealth. Most companies use this method of limitation of liability.

b Limitation by guarantee
Here each member's liability is restricted to the amount he or she has guaranteed to pay in the event of the company being wound up. This is rarer and is used mainly by companies not seeking to make profits as well as by some well-known organizations (for example, the Institute of Directors). Under this system members are only liable for the amount stated in the Memorandum of Association.

Most companies raise at least some of their capital by issuing shares in the company. In effect, they sell a 'share' in the company and use the funds raised to finance their activities. Persons who buy these shares are called shareholders and are the owners of the company.

Types of Shares

Ordinary Shares

Companies can issue a number of different types of shares to raise the capital necessary to run their businesses. Probably the most common type is the ordinary share, sometimes called equity shares. These carry a high degree of risk because a share of the profits paid to the shareholders (known as a dividend) is not guaranteed on these shares. If the company concerned makes a large profit, then the ordinary shareholders may receive a handsome dividend. However, in less profitable years ordinary shareholders may not receive any dividend.

Shareholders can receive another type of return on their investment. This occurs if the value of the shares themselves rise. It is obviously beneficial to have an asset which is rising in value. Since the dividend on ordinary shares depends upon the profitability of the company, ordinary shares tend to fluctuate considerably with the company's fortunes, and offer the chance of a so-called capital gain. Because of the high degree of risk carried by these shares, they give the shareholder the right to vote at company meetings (such as the Annual General Meeting).

A special type of ordinary share also exists. These are founders's shares and are usually bought by the establishers or founders of a business when they sell it. This is taken as a sign of goodwill and confidence in the business. They receive a share of the company's profits after the ordinary shareholders have received a certain amount.

Preference Shares

The second major type of shares that exist are preference shares. These receive a definite rate of return as a dividend (say 5 per cent) of the face value of the shares, but only if sufficient profits are made. If the company makes very large profits then preference shareholders still only receive their fixed dividend. Should a company sell off all its assets and close down, preference shares often have the right to be paid in full at face value before payment is made to ordinary shares. On occasions, companies may issue cumulative preference shares. These allow dividends to be accumulated, so that if insufficient profits are earned in one year to pay the full, fixed dividend then the balance of the payment becomes due the next year. Because most preference shares receive a fixed return or dividend, they do not tend to fluctuate with the level of company profits as do ordinary shares.

However, preference shares are not popular with companies nowadays. The major reason for this is that dividends, even though they are fixed, do not count as a charge against the profits of the company when calculating liability for corporation tax. Thus, companies cannot reduce their tax liability by issuing them.

Debentures

Finally, companies can raise capital by selling debentures. These are really loans rather than shares because they carry a fixed rate of interest which is payable to debenture holders whether or not any profits are made. They represent a very low risk to the debenture holder because the company issuing the debenture is committed to making the interest payment. Debentures are mainly purchased by people seeking a secure investment. However, due to the low level of risk, debenture holders do not have any voting rights.

ACTIVITY 2.1

The top ten UK businesses are set out in Figure 2.2 according to their market capitalization – that is, the total value of their equity shares at the current market value of each share. For example, a business which has issued a total of 1 000 000 shares, each of which are currently valued on the Stock Market at £5 each, would have a market capitalization of £5 million.

Market capitalization is not the only measure of size. Think of three other ways of measuring the size of companies. Do you think that market capitalization is the best measure? If not, which other measure is?

Figure 2.2 – ***Market Capitalization***

Company	Market capitalization (£bn)
Glaxo Holdings	23.388
British Telecom	22.149
Shell	17.072
British Petroleum	14.769
British American Tobacco Ind.	12.001
Guinness	11.698
SmithKline Beecham	11.311
Hanson	11.248
British Gas	11.155
Grand Metropolitan	10.440

Source: Extel Financial Limited (quoted in the *Sunday Times*, 31 May 1992)

Forming a Company

Anyone wishing to form a company in the UK will find that the law requires them to follow a set procedure. The people involved in setting up a company (known as the 'promoters') have to apply for registration to the Registrar of Companies in Cardiff. The Registrar will require details regarding the nature of the company, how it will be organized and the rules governing its methods of operation.

The promoters must send several documents to the Registrar of which the two main ones are:

- The Memorandum of Association
- The Articles of Association

The Memorandum of Association

This document is mainly concerned with the establishment of the new company's reasons for being in business and information about the name and contact address. It will include the following:

- The proposed company's name
- The company's registered address
- The amount of capital the company wishes to raise
- The company's objective in trading. Generally, companies construct this clause in vague terms so as not to restrict their future expansion, if required
- For public limited companies (see below), a statement that they are public and are offering their shares for sale to the general public
- A statement to the effect that the shareholders's liability is limited

The Articles of Association

The Articles of Association of a company consist of a series of regulations governing the conduct of the company's business and the internal management of the company. They form an agreement between the company and its members, defining their respective rights and duties. The areas covered by this agreement include:

- The nominal capital (the total face value of all the shares a company is allowed to issue)
- The directors's names
- The frequency of, and procedures for, shareholders's meetings
- The distribution of profits
- Shareholders's voting rights
- Directors's duties and responsibilities
- Arrangements concerning the appointments of directors
- Transfer of shares

Additionally, the promoters must provide a statement of the company's capital, the names of the company's directors and a signed statement that the provisions of the Companies Acts have been met.

Once all these documents have been sent to the Registrar of Companies the promoters will then receive a Certificate of Incorporation. This gives the company independent legal status and entitles it to commence trading.

Private and Public Companies

There are two types of company that exist in the UK: private limited company and public limited company. The 1985 Companies Act defines public limited companies. Those that do not fall within this definition are deemed to be private limited companies and are identified by the letters 'Ltd' or 'Limited' after the name.

Private Limited Companies

Private limited companies are generally smaller than public companies. They can have any number of shareholders in excess of two. The greater the number of shareholders this type of company has, the larger the sums of capital that can be raised. However, more shareholders means that individual shareholders receive a lesser proportion of the profits, if any are made.

Private companies are not allowed to sell their shares on the Stock Exchange, the main market in which shares are bought and sold. Indeed, such companies are not allowed to offer shares to the general public.

The law does not require private companies to disclose as much information as public ones when publishing their accounts. Private companies are found in most areas of the economy and can vary from a small family business to large, nationally known companies (such as the Virgin Group).

Public Limited Companies

Public limited companies, which have the letters 'plc' affixed to the company name, are larger and generally better known. They are likely to have more shareholders, though they also have a theoretical minimum of two. They enjoy the privilege of having their shares sold on the Stock Exchange which enables them to reach a wide group of people and institutions and to raise large amounts of capital. People and institutions are more willing to buy their shares in the knowledge that there is a safe and efficient market in which to sell them at a later date. Their authorized share capital must be a minimum of £50 000 (of which 25 per cent must have been 'paid up' or received by the company) and they must be registered as a public company.

Public companies are unable to borrow or commence business until they have received a Trading Certificate from the Registrar of Companies. Once public companies begin trading they can apply to have their shares traded on the Stock Exchange. This will be given when the business has demonstrated that the trading rules of the Stock Exchange have been met. Partial satisfaction of these rules, in many cases because of the short time a new company has been in existence, may mean that the company is restricted to the Unlisted Securities Market (USM), which is the market for shares of public companies not included in the official list for the main market.

In Figure 2.3, the share prices are shown together with the changes from the previous day's trading prices. The 'Net div' is the last dividend paid per share expressed as a percentage of the share printed value. The 'Yld %' is the last dividend paid as a percentage of the share trading price. 'P/E' is the price earnings ratio, which is the ratio of the trading price of share divided by the total profit earned by the business per share issued.

For example, say a business with 10 000 000 £1 shares earned profits after tax of £2 000 000 and the trading price of each share was 145p. The company declared a dividend per share of 5p.

Net dividend	=	5p/£1 = 5%
Yield %	=	5p/145p = 3.44%
P/E	=	145p/20p = 7.25
Earnings per share	=	£2 000 000/10 000 000 shares = 20p

Figure 2.3 – ***Share Prices***

1992 High	1992 Low	Company	Price (p)	+/–	Net div	Yld %	P/E
150	115	BWI	149	† +3	...	6.0	14.9
61½	52	Babcock	59	+½	3.0	6.8	9.6
6¼	4¾	Bailey (CH)	5¼	...	...	...	...
238	203	Baird (Wm)	238	+9	8.9	5.1	∞
1037	812	Barlow Rand	912	–12	...	3.7	12.8
45	23	Barrett (H)	32	...	2.0	8.3	74.0
62	51	Baynes (Charles)	60	...	1.3	3.0	16.0
25	15	Beauford	16	...	1.8	15.4	∞
18	5½	Beckenham ♠	10	...	...	...	...
28	23	Bedford (W) ♠	23	...	...	...	...
533	444	Bespak	530	...	...	2.3	25.0
187	170	Bibby (J)	178	...	9.7	7.3	9.0
119	84	Billam (J)	111	+2	4.2	5.1	6.2
36	28	Bilston Bttrsea ♠	36	...	...	...	...
77½	47	Bimec Ind	55	...	...	3.6	10.6
37	23	Black Arrow	23	...	21	12.2	7.8

Source: Times, 17 April 1992.

ACTIVITY 2.2

Study the Stock Exchange quoted share prices in a range of provincial or national daily papers. Share prices are quoted on Tuesdays through to Saturdays for business on the previous day. The Stock Exchange does not operate on Saturdays or Sundays. You will notice that different newspapers contain more business names than others. This is because businesses are charged by the newspaper for printing their share prices. Some businesses find the cost of this service to be too high.

You will also notice that the businesses are separated into different classifications, such as 'Banks', 'Industrials', 'Printing', etc. These titles are by no means universal, but enable you to find the name of a business quickly and to compare the share price with other similar businesses.

Select one of the business categories, such as 'Water', and calculate the average percentage increase or decrease in the share prices over a week. For example, if a category comprised only three names and these share prices changed by +12 per cent, −10 per cent, and +16 per cent respectively, the average change would be (12−10+16)/3, or 6 per cent. Compare your answer for this category with the same calculation for another category.

What conclusions can you draw by comparing these two different categories?

Returning to Private Company Status

Over recent years a number of companies, such as Richard Branson's Virgin Group and Andrew Lloyd Webber's Really Useful Music Group, have given up public limited company status to return to being a private limited company. This entails a group of shareholders buying a large majority of shares in order to force through the change. What factors could prompt a move of this nature?

Such a reversal does release the company from the adverse side effects of variations in their share price on the Stock Exchange. A company's share price can decline because of rumour or speculation, or simply because of a temporary loss of confidence in the particular industry or economy. While this occurs the prosperity, value and stability of the company may be unaffected, but acquiring credit or finding a buyer for products or services may become more difficult. This is because of fears that there is a chance that the business may not be able to pay its bills. Some companies welcome freedom from this constraint. Such a move also limits the likely impact of external organizations on a company. For example, the company would no longer be under the control of the Stock Exchange Council and, importantly, the company would be less vulnerable to media speculation as to the state of the business.

Some companies have chosen to revert to private limited company status because it allows

KEY POINTS 2.2

- **Companies enjoy the privilege of limited liability, protecting investors and encouraging investment**
- **Companies can raise capital by issuing a variety of shares of which ordinary shares are the most common**
- **Companies are regarded as separate legal entities and have the power to enter into contracts and take legal action**
- **To establish a company it is necessary to send a number of documents to the Registrar of Companies**
- **Public companies are usually larger than private ones and their shares are traded on the Stock Exchange**
- **In recent years a number of public companies have reverted to private limited company status**

them to concentrate on attaining their long-term aims, such as growth or the domination of their market. Thus, they may be able to seek long-term as opposed to short-term profits. As a public limited company the organization is under pressure from shareholders to achieve short-term success to boost dividends and share values.

In many economies, notably Germany and Japan, share ownership is concentrated in the hands of industrial investors who understand and accept the principle of waiting for long-term returns.

The ability of a company to revert to private company status will depend upon whether those shareholders concerned can raise sufficient capital to carry through their plans. Clearly, interest rates will play a role here. So will the state of the market: following the Stock Market crash of 1987 a number of companies became undervalued as a result of falling share prices, which encouraged some shareholders to implement plans to revert their company to private status.

Managing Companies

We noted earlier that it is relatively easy to organize the management structure of a business that is a sole trader. The owner has to carry out all the functions (marketing, managing the accounts, etc) necessary to operate such a business and will purchase specialist skills when required. A partnership faces similar circumstances: some of the partners may be specialists and the functions will be divided up according to such specialisms. The same arguments apply to many private limited companies that are small businesses with just a few shareholders, managers and employees. In these smaller organizations, the owners and managers have to be 'jacks of all trades' and turn their attention to a number of management functions.

Larger private and most public companies are likely to be organized more formally. We saw earlier that companies, both public and private, are owned by their shareholders. A private company that is a small family-owned business may only have a handful of shareholders, all of whom are individuals. The UK's largest public companies have thousands of shareholders: some are individuals whilst others, and in many cases the majority, are institutions such as banks and insurance companies which have large amounts of funds to invest.

The group that effectively controls the company is the board of directors. This comprises full-time directors who work exclusively for that company and take responsibility for major functions within the company such as marketing and finance. In addition, most boards contain some part-time or non-executive directors who will offer specialist advice and/or enhance the company's prestige. A large number of Members of Parliament are on the boards of major public companies giving the board specialist advice on legal, political or related matters as well as greater respectability.

Figure 2.4 shows a general 'chain of command' in a business. The shareholders with voting rights will elect a chairperson of the board of directors and give approval to the appointment of individual directors. The board will approve the appointment of a chief executive who is often a director, and in some cases is also the chairperson. Hence, in some businesses you may find Mr X is chairperson and managing director. The chairperson of the company leads the board of directors and guides it towards the key decisions that it has to take.

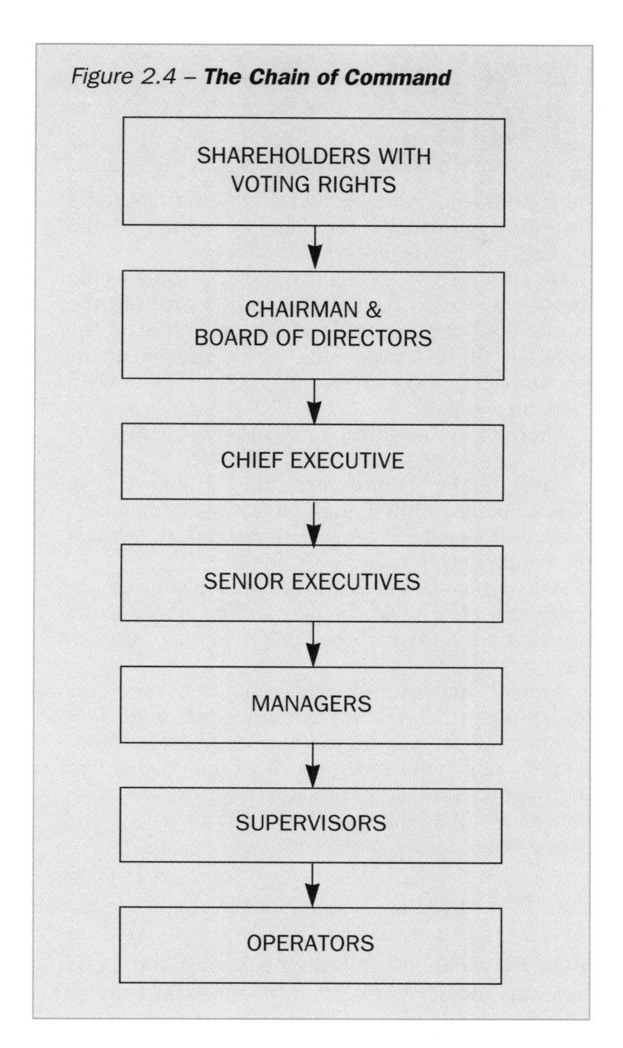

Figure 2.4 – ***The Chain of Command***

The chief executive has reporting to him or her a number of senior executives who are often directors in their own right (for example, a marketing director). Senior executives have reporting to them a number of managers usually responsible for weekly or monthly operations (such as the sales manager). Beneath the manager are supervisors who tend to be responsible for the daily or weekly activities (for example, a sales supervisor). Under the supervisors are the operators who carry out the daily activities of the business (such as a salesperson).

Some of the directors may be major shareholders in the company concerned, but most will not. Directors are elected at the company's Annual General Meeting (AGM). You will recall that the Articles of Association has to include details of the company's meetings. The AGM allows shareholders some control over the company's affairs. The board has to present a report outlining the company's activities since the last meeting. The shareholders then have the choice of whether or not to re-elect the existing board of directors.

In most large companies there is a divorce between control and ownership. Shareholders, in spite of their annual 'say' in the company's affairs, have little control over day-to-day affairs. Few individual shareholders bother or go to the expense of attending an AGM, and therefore control effectively lies with the board of directors. Individual shareholders also have little power because they only have one vote per share. At AGMs they can easily be outvoted by institutions, such as insurance companies and pension funds, who own huge amounts of shares and therefore have great voting power. In effect, although all shareholders own the company, it is a few large shareholders who dictate policy and directors who carry it out.

Boards take important, long-term decisions such as whether or not to produce new products or to enter new markets; whether or not to buy a new factory or, in different circumstances, whether to employ or sack groups of workers. They will decide how to raise finance and what to do with profits if they make any. Above all, they will aim to ensure that the company flourishes and thus protect their own jobs!

ACTIVITY 2.3

Consider your school, college or the business which you might be closely involved with. Using Figure 2.4 as a guide, construct the levels of authority from the top to the bottom.

What are the significant differences, if any, between the diagram shown in Figure 2.4 and your diagram? Can you put names to all the positions you have located?

Advantages and Disadvantages of Companies

Establishing a business as a company has both advantages and disadvantages. It may suit some enterprises but not others. A private limited company is cheap to establish and is applicable to many business situations. Family businesses commonly organize their business this way and by so doing can retain control by holding a majority of the shares. Larger businesses which require greater amounts of capital are likely to choose public limited company status. However, as we noted earlier, some businesses (such as solicitors) are prevented by their professional bodies from organizing as companies.

The major advantage for shareholders is that they have limited liability. The company itself

Figure 2.5 – ***The Problems of Starting a Small Limited Company***

The failings of starting a firm

MANY small businessmen are unwittingly opting for bigger tax bills and more red tape – by setting up limited companies for themselves.

Lured by the prestige of a company directorship, the financial protection of limited liability, or vague ideas of saving tax, they are unaware that the goal posts have been moved.

Following the 1986 Insolvency Act, a company directorship is a heavy burden. A director may be guilty of wrongful trading if the company remains in business when he knows – or ought to know – it is heading for insolvency. Gone are the days when directors could walk away from a corporate failure.

And while incorporation was once seen as the only way to avoid income tax at up to 98%, the present top rate of 40% is not so far adrift from corporation tax at 25%-33%. Indeed, with companies now liable to a 10.4% payroll tax in the form of National Insurance on all remuneration paid to directors and the steep hikes in the charge on company cars, the tax balance has swung against incorporation.

Were that not enough, the Revenue has launched a purge against directors of small firms taking company money for private expenditure.

Penalties

Where any such withdrawal has not been subjected to PAYE income tax and National Insurance, it will be regarded as a loan to the director which triggers two tax charges.

He is treated as receiving a benefit, equal to the interest he would have paid had he borrowed the money, and this is taxable at his top rate. And the company must deposit 33% of the sum taken by the directors, although this will be refunded when the loan is repaid.

There can be swingeing penalties and interest if the proper procedures are not followed.

And finally, there are the administrative requirements. Although a new company may purchase 'off the shelf' for less than £200, this is just the beginning.

Audited accounts must be filed each year at Companies House where they will be available for inspection by any member of the public – including competitors.

Annual returns must be submitted reporting directorships, shareholdings and other important company data. And there are also a host of Companies Acts requirements concerning issues like the maintenance of a company register, the holdings of meetings and the issue of shares.

Source: Mail on Sunday, 24 May 1992

benefits because they can employ specialists such as lawyers and accountants and they can operate on a larger scale and achieve economies of scale. In addition, banks are often more willing to lend to companies as opposed to partnerships or sole traders because they have more assets to act as collateral and pose less of a risk. Companies benefit from their size in a number of other ways: they can offer better salaries and conditions and attract better employees; and they can produce on a larger scale at a lower cost per unit and so win more sales. They can also afford to market their products fully.

However, choosing to trade as a company also has disadvantages. (Figure 2.5 outlines the problems of starting a small limited company.) The

KEY POINTS 2.3

- **Two types of company exist: public and private companies**
- **Shareholders in companies can enjoy limited liability**
- **Public companies are generally far larger than private companies**
- **Usually different groups own and manage public companies**
- **Setting up a company involves fulfilling certain legal requirements**

law requires that companies make some of their financial details available to the general public. In many instances this is beneficial to competitors. Trading as a company also involves the payment of some fees and can involve the burden of incompetent family shareholders.

Co-operatives

You will probably associate the term 'co-operative' with the retail shops in your local town or city. However, this is just one example of the co-operative movement, albeit a prominent one. Co-operatives are found in production, marketing and banking as well as retailing.

The co-operative movement originated in Rochdale in 1844 with the so-called 'Rochdale Pioneers'. Twenty-eight weavers combined to purchase foodstuffs and then resold to themselves the goods ordinarily bought in the shops. In this way the retailer's profit was cut out, and prices were lowered.

Co-operative societies are based on the principle of 'self-help'. As with companies, people buy shares in co-operatives. But, unlike companies, members of co-operatives only have a single vote irrespective of the number of shares owned. This fact reflects the socialist origins of the co-operative movement. The shares of co-operatives cannot be sold on the Stock Exchange: if members wish to redeem their investment they simply sell them back to the movement.

The Co-operative Development Agency (CDA) was established in 1978 with the objective of encouraging and supporting co-operatives. It receives support from the UK government and the EC to help it attain this objective and increase the number of co-operatives.

Workers's Co-operatives

A workers's co-operative exists when the workers themselves own the shares of, and manage, the business in which they work. This has the benefit of motivating the workforce since in most workers's co-operatives they benefit in terms of profits from their efforts and industrial disputes are less likely. Workers tend to receive the same wages irrespective of their role, except on occasions when hired managers have to be paid more. A guiding principle is that workers have an equal vote when decisions are made.

The disadvantages of this structure are that workers can often only raise limited amounts of capital and frequently cannot afford to provide expert management.

Socialist organizations are in favour of workers's co-operatives since they believe that it will improve productivity and give workers a real say in their working life. For some time Triumph motorcycles were produced by a workers's co-operative at Meriden near Birmingham.

Retail Co-operatives

These are the most familiar example of the co-operative movement. The 'Co-op' is organized regionally and so is found throughout the country, selling groceries as well as home furnishings and other domestic items. People are invited to become members of their local co-operative society. They are then entitled to a share in the co-op's profits. These are often distributed in proportion to the value of purchases made at the co-operative. This is the famous 'dividend'. A few co-operatives give stamps to members which can be redeemed for a cash payment or exchanged for goods. Other regional co-ops make cash payments, such as 5 per cent of the value of purchases over a given time period.

Many people who use co-operatives are not members and so do not receive a share of the profits. Those who are members rarely attend the meetings of the co-operative at which decisions are made. As a result, societies are dominated by a minority.

As with workers's co-operatives, retail co-operatives tend to be short of capital which accounts for the old-fashioned appearance of many of their stores. Partly because of this and partly because of increasing competition from multiples such as Asda and Tesco, co-operatives have seen their share of sales decline over recent years.

Marketing Co-operatives

It is not surprising that small producers feel the need to club together to sell their products or services. As you will see in the book on marketing in this series (*People, Marketing and Business*), marketing can be very expensive and any sharing of the burden is welcomed. The marketing co-operative is common where firms are small and produce similar or identical products. Such co-ops will advise firms on what to produce and in what quantities as well as advertising to sell the product. They will use their joint power to negotiate favourable prices when implementing marketing plans to the benefit of the firms. This allows the firms to concentrate on production.

Marketing co-operatives are common in agriculture throughout Europe. In France, for example, wine is often marketed through a co-operative.

Co-operatives do not have an entirely successful history. Many, particularly workers's co-operatives, have failed within a few years of being established. Some have been established on idealistic rather than practical grounds and with a minimum of planning. Workers have taken over unsuccessful businesses only to find that they, too, cannot make it profitable. Others have failed because of a lack of capital or of the management skills necessary to make the enterprise a success. Marketing can pose a particular problem as many buyers tend to view co-operatives as something of an oddity. Recently, however, there have been indications that the number of co-operatives in the UK is growing.

Friendly Societies

A friendly society exists when a group of people join together for their mutual benefit to assist members (in sickness, old age, unemployment, etc). The members make regular payments to a joint fund which is then used to pay claims.

The first friendly societies were probably established in the Middle Ages, though there is evidence that they have existed since Roman times. Members of different societies often have common links, frequently through their profession or trade. Their traditional role has been overtaken since 1945 by the welfare state and, as a result, the number of friendly society members has fallen from 8.7 million to 3 million and the number of societies from 2 740 to 467.

Friendly societies are registered by the state to allow the society limited liability. They are, however, restricted in their activities by law.

Multinationals

Multinationals are companies which have productive capacity in more than one country. Often they are conglomerates – that is, they produce a variety of products or services – and own subsidiary companies in overseas countries. An example of such a conglomerate multinational is Imperial Chemical Industries (ICI) which has interests in chemicals, gas, agriculture and oil throughout the world.

The Ford Motor Company and General Motors are examples of companies which produce cars in a number of European and other countries as well as the USA. These are examples of horizontal multinationals which produce broadly the same product or service worldwide. In this case it is motor vehicles.

Multinationals control in excess of 34 per cent of the world's production and are found particularly in the motor vehicle, oil and chemical industries. It is usual for them to be quoted on the Stock Exchanges of all the countries in which they operate. Some multinationals have sales revenue in excess of the value of output of some of the world's smaller nations (such as Belgium).

Multinationals are particularly affected by changes in exchange rates and by any moves towards protectionism which prevent the free international flow of goods and services.

Most multinationals aim to increase their profits by purchasing raw materials and components as cheaply as possible worldwide; and producing in low-cost nations and selling in the richest nations where the highest prices can be obtained. The aim is to make the highest possible profit for all the companies which make up the multinational. They often succeed because their products are technically superior to those of their rivals and this helps them to overcome the disadvantages of producing in an unfamiliar country. They are also characterized by high quality and innovative management. It is a generally held view that part of the reason for the success of Japanese multinationals in the UK is their commitment to high quality and imaginative management which has helped to improve the performance of the UK workforce.

This seems to present multinationals in a very positive fashion, but there are two sides to the impact of multinationals on a 'host' nation.

Are Multinationals a 'Good' Thing?

Multinationals have been criticized on a number of grounds. Profits are invariably siphoned back to the multinational's home country to the detriment of the host nation's balance of payments. These funds are not available for investment in the host nation's economy. Some of the factories established are simply 'screwdriver' plants in which products manufactured in the home nation are assembled and, at the first sign of a slump in sales, are vulnerable to closure.

Furthermore, multinationals may indulge in unfair transfer pricing, a technique involving the 'massaging' of production costs in order to reduce tax liability in a particular nation or to prove that a particular location is uneconomic. The latter can then be used to justify the closure of a national plant. For example, assume a company makes chemicals, where one stage of the process takes place in one country with a high tax on profits and the second, final stage takes place in another country with a low tax on profits. The company might be tempted to state that most of the costs of production were incurred in the first country, and give a low transfer price from the first country to the second country. Consequently, there would be little profit in the first country and hence little tax to pay. With a low buying-in price and a normal retail price, the multinational

CASE STUDY

Management: The Multinational Myth Explodes

Managers and politicians take note. The term 'multinational company' has become so embedded in our business language over the last 30 years that few people now question what it signifies. But they should, for it is either meaningless, misleading, or both. You can certainly forget everything you have read about the emergence of 'stateless' corporations with their activities spread in balanced fashion across a 'borderless world'. Contrary to the new conventional wisdom, such enterprises do not exist: with a handful of exceptions, so-called 'multinational', 'global' and 'transnational' companies are merely national entities with foreign operations. This is the controversial thesis of Yao-Su Hu, an ex-World Bank economist who combines his vice-presidency of a Hong Kong college with visiting professorships at Sussex University and Henley. In arguing his case, Hu may be stretching a point or two. He also makes a few factual errors. But, in direction if not in degree, his argument is closer to the truth than most 'multinational' companies would admit. Writing in the issue of the *California Management Review* which is about to be published, Hu argues that there are precious few real multinationals. At the very furthest stretch of his definition, they include ICI, Nestlé, ABB, Shell and Unilever – though he says the last three should be classed as 'binational'. Hu's argument has several strands.

Most so-called multinationals – such as General Motors, Du Pont, and US General Electric – have less than half their operations and employees abroad. The only ones which do are British companies such as ICI, plus some from smaller European nations. But, just as home country economics and politics are of overwhelming importance to GM and Co, so they are to ICI: the company 'owes more loyalty' to the UK than to any other country. ICI's case is typical of most 'multinationals', claims Hu.

Ownership and control

At the level of the parent company, these remain heavily national (or binational), rather than multinational – however much the company may strive to attract foreign shareholders and stress 'good citizenship' within its various host nations.

Foreigners usually occupy a 'minuscule' fraction of the most senior positions in top management – much lower than the percentage of foreigners in the total number of employees. The national character of top management is especially pronounced in Japanese companies.

Legal nationality and taxation

In law, there is no such thing as a multinational or global company. So the multinational is exposed to many jurisdictions around the world. But it usually has a home government and a home tax authority – that is, a legal and fiscal nationality that matters to it more than others. In many cases, the home government can choose to tax it on its worldwide earnings. Hu then assesses the various implications of all this. First, the primary source of a company's international competitive advantage lies in its home nation, he argues. Foreign sources can supplement national ones but not replace them. Even Nestlé, with 95 per cent or more of its assets and employees outside Switzerland, gains considerable advantage from being perceived as Swiss.

Source: Financial Times, 4 March 1992

QUESTIONS

1 Do you agree with Yao-Su Hu that if a business has the majority of its employees based in the home country, it can hardly be called a 'multinational'?
2 Should foreign companies operating in host countries have all senior staff from the host countries?
3 Do you agree with Hu that the home country of a multinational is its most competitive advantage?

company would make most of the profit in the second country where taxes on profits are low.

Many governments offer substantial grants to encourage multinationals to locate in their countries because, at least in the short term, they bring prosperity and employment. This money can, however, be wasted if the multinational moves on within a few years. Multinationals often import large quantities of capital equipment from their home nation when establishing an overseas plant. These transactions can harm the host's balance of payments by increasing imports at a time when there is no corresponding rise in exports. Critics of multinationals suggest that the number of jobs that multinationals claim to create should be treated with caution. They note that the establishment of a multinational's new factory may lead to the failure of a number of domestic producers and raise unemployment.

Closure of a factory or office in an overseas country often causes bitter recriminations. Locals feel that multinationals have no loyalty to them and ignore the social and economic implications of their decision in a way that they would not do in their home country. Multinationals are frequently accused of ignoring national laws and being primarily concerned with minimizing costs. The Union Carbide Company (an American multinational) was heavily criticized for the appalling disaster in December 1984 at its pesticide plant in Bhopal, India. This disaster, in which contamination of an underground tank led to a chemical mist shrouding the city, caused 3 000 deaths and 26 000 serious injuries. The company has been blamed for flouting environmental and safety laws and also for delaying payment of compensation. The Indian government has been pilloried for not seeking rapid and substantial compensation. Critics use this case as evidence for the fact that multinationals are unaccountable to national, and particularly Third World, governments.

Holding Companies and Conglomerates

There is nothing to stop a company purchasing shares in another company. It is a legal and common practice. When a company owns more than 50 per cent of the 'voting' ordinary shares of another company, it can control the business completely and is called a holding company. Both companies still exist as legal entities and still produce separate financial accounts. The holding company may wish to do this in order to control a supplier or to diversify into related business activities. If a company owns less than 50 per cent of the shares of another company it is called a minority holding. Because it is rare for more than 50 per cent of all shareholders to meet at any one time to vote at the Annual General Meeting, a minority holding of almost 25 per cent is often large enough for complete control.

Companies which exist purely to invest in profitable companies are called conglomerates. As the word suggests, such organizations contain a large number of unrelated companies which have little to do with each other. The holding company at the centre of a conglomerate may hold from a small percentage up to all of the shares of the companies in the group, and is constantly trading shares to maximize the profitable activities. For example, a conglomerate may sell a major part of its shareholding in Company X and reinvest in Company Y because of short-term profit advantages rather than long-term considerations of growth. Figure 2.6 notes that a major Mexican conglomerate is extending its empire from brewing into banking!

KEY POINTS 2.4

- **Co-operatives involve groups or individuals working together for the common good**
- **Co-operatives can be found in producing, retailing and marketing**
- **Friendly Societies are non-profit making organizations mainly providing services**
- **Multinational companies operate in several countries and are becoming increasingly important in many developed economies**
- **Multinational companies can bring benefits to host nations, but also have disadvantages which are frequently ignored**

Figure 2.6 – ***Conglomerates***

Cadbury to buy Mexican mineral water company

CADBURY SCHWEPPES is spending £188 million to buy Mexico's largest mineral water company: Mexico is the second largest soft drinks market in the world after the US. Most of the purchase price is being met by Cadbury issuing new shares, which will raise £45 million. The business changing hands is called Aguas Minerales. It is being sold by Fomento Economico Mexicano SA (Femsa), one of the country's largest conglomerates, which is trying to raise money to fund a move into banking. The group also owns a large brewing group, which is said to be up for sale, and it bottles Coca-Cola.

Source: Guardian, 19 March 1992

Public Sector

All of the forms of business which we have discussed so far are classified as private sector businesses. This simply means that the owners of the businesses are either individuals or groups of individuals acting together as partnerships or companies.

The other types of business belong in the public sector of the economy. In the public sector businesses are owned by the state either at a national or local level. Your local council or local authority will provide a range of services such as education and social services. At the same time, the central government provides important services such as defence and policing. Furthermore, the state has established a number of organizations to supply goods and services which we all need (such as the Post Office and British Rail). These are public corporations which are usually created through Acts of Parliament. Finally, the state may own shares in companies (for example, BP). We shall look at each of these in more detail.

Local Authorities

Everyone in the UK has a democratically elected local council which looks after a number of services in their area. This category includes district councils, shire county councils and metropolitan borough councils.

Traditionally, they have provided services like education, swimming pools, bus services, housing and so on. In recent years the government has privatized a number of these services, which means that private businesses have taken over the local council's role.

Public Corporations

In the period following the end of the Second World War the government took control of a number of key industries. The government set up public corporations to run these nationalized industries. In the period between 1946 and 1951, coal mining, railways, airlines and a number of other industries were brought into the public sector. Some of these nationalized industries remain, but others created at that time have been privatized and returned to the private sector. A prime example of such an industry is British Gas which was returned to the private sector in 1986 amid much publicity.

Public corporations have been established to control nationalized industries and these operate differently to public limited companies. However, public corporations do have a legal identity. They can sue and be sued and own property. The question of unlimited liability is irrelevant in this context because the state will accept unlimited liability. Parliament has ultimate control over the UK's nationalized industries, though MPs are not allowed to ask questions about the day-to-day running of an industry.

Parliament exercises control over the public corporations it creates to run nationalized industries by:

- Establishing a committee on nationalized industries to examine the activities and accounts of the industries
- Discussing and debating the annual report of each industry
- Granting loan finance

Public corporations are also under the direction of the appropriate cabinet minister. For example, the Minister of Transport is responsible for British Rail. He or she appoints a board of directors who are responsible for the day-to-day running of the industry. A chairperson of the board is also appointed who takes responsibility for the industry. The chairperson sets up the internal organization of the industry and reports regularly to the minister who has ultimate responsibility for the industry.

The cabinet minister oversees important decisions and advises the board on important matters. The minister controls research and development and has the power to dismiss the board if it is considered necessary.

At the same time, as public corporations are created, so independent organizations are established to look after the interests of the consumers. An example of this is the Post Office Users's Council. Such councils do not usually have any legal powers to force changes, but they are important providers of information to the news media. It is often in the interests of the public corporations to keep on the 'right side' of their users's council to forestall bad publicity.

Figure 2.7 – ***How Nationalized Industries Are Controlled***

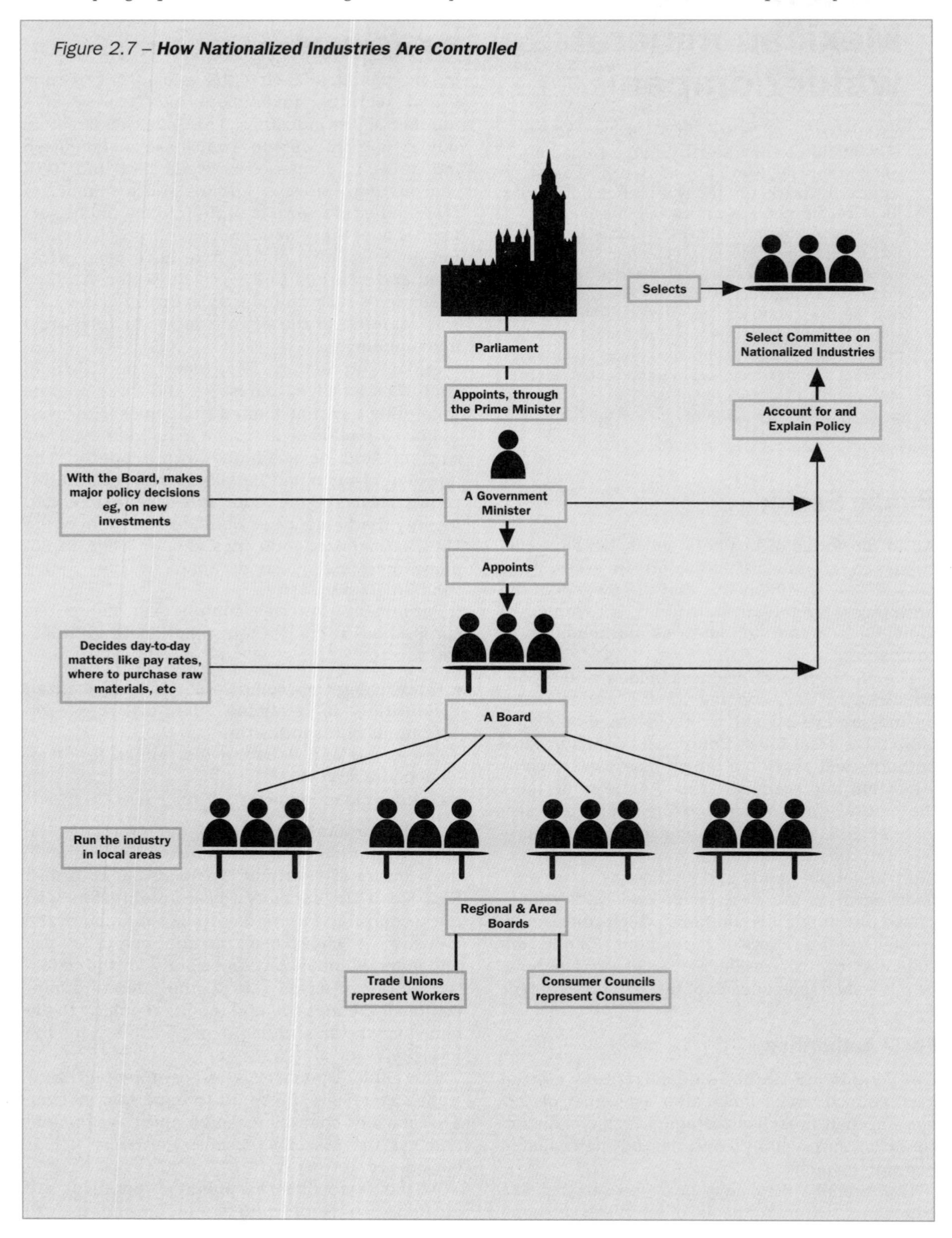

Central Government Departments

Central government provides a range of services, including defence, social services, trade and employment. The government has established departments to control and administer the provision of such services. These departments change as the situation changes. For example, during recent years, when matters relating to health and employment became increasingly important, the old Department of Health and Social Security (DHSS) became too large and slow to respond. The government's solution was to create two new departments: the Department of Health and the Department of Social Security. Within each department a minister was appointed to take charge and report to Parliament on the department's activities.

The departments's funds are raised through general taxation and each is allocated a budget by the Treasury at the beginning of the financial year. Departments cannot make a loss: they simply exceed their stated budget. The departments are staffed by civil servants who continue to work in the department even following an election which has resulted in a change in their political masters. Government departments have been heavily criticized for their inefficiency which has resulted from a lack of competition and absence of any mechanism to protect the interests of the general public. As with public corporations, the question of limited liability does not arise since the government will meet any excess expenditure. Excessive expenditure and poor management of the department's affairs may well result in political defeat at the next election, however.

Government Shareholdings in Companies

Previous governments have sought to encourage the growth of industry and prosperity by purchasing shares in companies as a way of providing capital and having a say in company policy. In 1975, the then Labour government set up the National Enterprise Board (NEB) to stimulate economic development by investing government funds in a variety of companies. More recently, Conservative governments have reduced such shareholdings as part of a drive to reduce the size of the public sector.

In 1981, the NEB's role of state holding company was altered to reflect the then new government's business philosophy. It was merged with the National Research and Development Corporation to form the new British Technology Group.

KEY POINTS 2.5

- **The state plays a role in the production of a range of goods and services, though in the UK this role has been reduced in recent years**
- **The government has established public corporations to run some major industries**
- **Local authorities and government departments provide a range of goods and services**

EXAM PREPARATION

SHORT QUESTIONS

1. Distinguish between an 'aim' and an 'objective'.
2. Give two examples of businesses which operate in each of the following sectors of the economy – primary, secondary and tertiary.
3. Define the term 'multinational company'.
4. Distinguish between a 'public company' and a 'public corporation'.
5. What is the liability of shareholders in an organization which benefits from the protection of limited liability?
6. Give two reasons why the actual power of a shareholder is likely to be less than the theoretical power.

7 Name the two documents a company must complete before it receives a Certificate of Incorporation.

8 Distinguish between 'ordinary shares' and 'debentures'.

9 What is the role of the appropriate Minister of State in controlling a nationalized industry?

10 If no deed of partnership exists, how should any profits made by the business be divided up between the partners?

DATA RESPONSE QUESTIONS

1 The following extract is part of a document sent to Trafalgar House shareholders informing them, among other things, of a proposed acquisition. Read the article and answer the questions that follow.

Trafalgar House and its activities

Trafalgar House was incorporated in England on 22nd December, 1965 as a private limited company under the Companies Act 1948 with registered number 867281 and was reregistered on the 20th January, 1982 as a public limited company pursuant to the Companies Act 1980. The company now operates under the Companies Act 1985. The registered office of the Company which is also its principal place of business is at 1 Berkeley Street, London W1A 1BY. The principal objects of Trafalgar House, as set out in clause 4 of its Memorandum of Association, are to act as a holding company and to invest in and develop property and to enter into financial and commercial transactions of all kinds.

Trafalgar House is the holding company of a group whose principal activities include property and investment, construction and engineering, shipping, aviation and hotels, and oil and gas.

Questions

(a) What distinguishes a public limited company from a private limited company? *(6 marks)*

(b) Explain the main purpose of the Memorandum of Association. *(4 marks)*

(c) List two pieces of information, other than the Memorandum of Association, required by the Registrar of Companies when forming a public limited company. *(2 marks)*

(d) Explain the term 'holding company'. *(2 marks)*

(e) Suggest and explain three factors that might be considered by Trafalgar House when assessing whether to go ahead with any acquisition. *(6 marks)*

2 The following article has been adapted from the *Independent* on 13 August 1990. Read it and answer the questions.

Tunbridge Wells Equitable is the best known member of a family of financial institutions that have been all but forgotten; it is a friendly society. It is also acutely aware that unless the government soon makes proposals to broaden the market it is allowed to serve, it along with 500 other similar institutions could disappear. With the total assets of all friendly societies standing at £4 billion, that means headaches for regulators who want to ensure that investors do not find themselves losing savings.

Last week Tunbridge Wells Equitable Friendly Society, TWEFS, took advantage of a change in legislation which allows it to merge with Boots Life Assurance Society, an insurance company associated with the chemist's chain. Despite the 40 per cent increase in assets that will result from the merger with Boots Life, survival will be 'tough, very tough' says TWEFS general manager Peter Gray.

TWEFS would like to sell Personal Equity Plans, sell unit trusts, provide loans, act for other insurers and advise clients. It needs a change in the law if it is to be able to do so. If these changes in the law do not come about one spark of hope is that as the welfare state is further eroded, friendly societies may come back into their own.

Questions

(a) What are the differences between a friendly society and a public limited company? *(6 marks)*

(b) Find out the meaning of the following terms used in the text: 'personal equity plans', 'unit trusts', 'mutual insurance company', 'welfare state'. *(8 marks)*

(c) Why do you think the erosion of the welfare state might help friendly societies to survive? *(6 marks)*

3 Read the following case study and answer the questions.

Simon Hewitt is a successful and ambitious businessman. He enjoys being his own boss and has the objective of becoming a rich man. For the past three years he has run a petrol station in his home village near Worcester. As a sole trader he took out a loan to buy the lease on the site and to purchase stocks of petrol and other motoring items. Due to the growth of the village he has attracted a greater number of customers than expected. In spite of heavy interest payments he has earned a reasonable profit and this has allowed him a small sum to invest back into his business.

A month ago a nearby garage came up for sale and Simon was very keen to purchase it. Ultimately his ambition is to develop a chain of these garages and then to diversify his business interests.

The second garage was expensive and Simon made an appointment with his accountant to discuss how he might finance his expansion. His accountant was cautious. 'If you can get a loan to purchase this garage,' she advised, 'the interest payments could be too great for you to survive. You must remember that the general level of interest rates could rise. Another option could be to look for a partner. You should think carefully about this if you want your business to grow quickly.'

Questions

(a) Draw up a table for Simon setting out the advantages and disadvantages of taking a partner. *(5 marks)*

(b) If Simon decides to take on a partner he should draw up a Deed of Partnership. What should he include in his Deed? *(8 marks)*

(c) If Simon and his partner failed to draw up a Deed of Partnership, what would happen to any profits they made? *(3 marks)*

(d) Why do you think that a 'sleeping partner' might be suitable for someone like Simon? *(4 marks)*

ESSAYS

1 In 1988 a number of firms decided to revert to private limited company status, after being quoted on the Stock Exchange for some time. Discuss the factors which might influence them to make such a move. (AEB June 1990)

2 Examine the particular problems posed for a country by the existence of a multinational firm. (AEB November 1987)

CHAPTER 3

Finance for Business

▷ ▷ QUESTIONS FOR PREVIEW ▷ ▷

1 *Where does the cash come from to start or expand a business?*

2 *What information do investors in a business need to know?*

3 *What information do the financial accounts of the business supply?*

Financial Information

BEFORE A business can start its operations, it has to calculate how much cash it will need to pay for all the equipment, machines and buildings it requires. These resources, called capital assets, will be used by the business to make a product or to give a service. A fork-lift truck for moving heavy objects is an example of a capital asset.

Some assets are rented or leased. When an asset is leased, ownership of the asset often passes to the user after a time period during which regular payments are made to the leasor, the initial owner of the asset.

In addition, the business will also have to pay wages to its employees and purchase goods for resale or materials, usually before any money is received from its customers. Most probably, the business will also have to pay other bills such as local taxes, power and telephone 'connection' costs and professional fees to its solicitor and accountant. The money required to pay for these costs is called working capital. People who are starting a new business not only have to find money to pay for the new equipment, such as a fork-lift truck, but also have to cover the many bills for services and materials.

In most organizations, the product or service is sold and a profit is generated by subtracting the costs from the selling price. This profit is used to pay interest charges, to pay back loans, to reward investors by paying them a dividend, to purchase new resources which are needed for new activities and to replace those which have been used up. As we saw in Chapter Two, a dividend is similar to an interest payment on the money invested, but in most businesses the dividend is variable and depends on the profits generated. Obviously, the profit generated in one year will not do all these things at once, but over a reasonable time span of, say, ten years most of the assets will have been replaced except for land and buildings.

Some businesses do not sell their service to the users. For example, local governments support public libraries which are mostly free to users. But these organizations need money to pay for resources like any other business. The money is given to them by local and national government from money collected as taxes or by loans. Although there is no profit to generate, action has been taken to make more and more services 'cost conscious'.

Even Royal Air Force station commanding officers now have to run their organizations on a very 'business-like' basis. Many services which were once non-profit making, such as hospital cleaning, are now operated as profit-generating businesses by independent agencies. It has been argued that profit-making businesses are more efficient than non-profit making businesses. This trend towards a greater reliance on the market is discussed fully in *The Business Environment* book within this series.

Do not think, therefore, that business finance is restricted to profit-making organizations. All organizations have costs. All organizations need to control their cash requirements, and to be efficient users of their many and varied resources. When a business starts, or changes from one level of activity to a higher level, extra funds are required to pay for extra assets and extra working capital.

In this chapter we will consider profit-making organizations and their need to obtain and control cash. However, the basic financial reporting and cash control methods are similar whether the business is designed to generate a profit or not.

Sources of Finance

Funds for a business fall into two categories:

a Expansion of the equity of the business
This means that the lender gets involved with the risks of the business by becoming a shareholder. If the business makes a profit, the interest on the shares, and the value of the shares themselves, may be quite high. On the other hand, the investor could lose all his or her money, but as we saw earlier, limited liability restricts the shareholder's risk to the money invested.

b A loan of fixed or variable interest rate (with an agreed repayment rate)
In most cases, such loans are provided only if a guarantee is supplied to minimize the lender's risk in losing his or her money. Such guarantees could be on the personal wealth of one of the directors of the business, or on a fixed asset belonging to the business which has a present value and life expectancy greater than that of the loan. The lender would have a legal right to repossess the asset if payments of interest on the loan stopped. This is similar to the rights of a house mortgage company which has advanced funds to an individual for purchasing property. These loans can be short, medium or long term and are briefly described below.

Example
Investing in a business by either buying shares or by lending money at agreed interest charges is very similar to the way some film stars are paid. Actors are sometimes offered the choice of being paid a fixed sum for their film appearance or by receiving a percentage of the profits. Some actors have regretted opting for a fixed sum when the film becomes a surprise smash hit. Others no doubt have been pleased to have received a fixed sum for a film which was later found to be a big flop. Investors in business either play safe and give a loan, whereas others are tempted to invest in shares and take a share of the expected big profits. Like actors, some investors realize afterwards that they have probably done the wrong thing!

As in many business situations, a professional adviser is usually required to help those seeking initial or extra funds. This is especially important when taxation allowances or government grants are possible. In many cases, allowances and grants have to be examined before the event since they are often not retrospective. This means that sometimes you cannot apply for a grant after the business has started. Many professional accountants can provide this type of help, although the bank will often be the place where borrowing discussions first take place.

Short-Term Finance

Short-term finance can be defined as finance made available for periods up to three years.

Such funds would be used to overcome seasonal troughs and peaks, such as the level of the tourist business over a twelve-month period; for fluctuations in working capital during which there will be a need to build up stocks; and to support all those other activities which happen in expanding firms where costs are incurred before cash from increased sales is available. For example, if you owned a number of hire cars as a business activity, and wished to increase the size of your fleet, you would need significant short-term funds to pay for the new cars.

The cheapest form of short-term finance is a bank overdraft. It is also easy to arrange, with the minimum amount of form-filling. The disadvantage is that an overdraft is repayable on demand. An overdraft works by allowing the business to pay bills without having sufficient money in the bank to cover them. The bank gives you permission to overspend up to an agreed amount. For example, if you had £50 in your bank account and the bank had given you an overdraft of £500, the bank will allow you to draw up to £550. The bank will in fact be giving you a variable loan up to an agreed maximum; the amount of the loan is calculated each day and the interest charged to your account accordingly.

A short-term loan is given for a specific purpose rather than for general working capital. Repayments and interest charges are formally agreed and, in general, the cost of supplying the loan and the interest charges are higher than for an overdraft.

Trade credit is equivalent to a loan, whereby a

*Figure 3.1 – **Time to Pay***

Buy now, pay later . . . and later

ONLY 3 per cent of firms receive payments on time and the position is getting worse, according to Trade Indemnity, the independent insurance group.

On average, payments are received 27 days late. About a quarter of all bills are settled more than 30 days after the stipulated date.

The figures are contained in a survey of financial trends conducted in March. Trade Indemnity intends to conduct similar surveys every quarter.

The results are supported by a survey of 1,900 managing directors by Dun & Bradstreet, the business information company. The company's director for risk management sales says: "Nine out of ten managing directors have seen no improvement in payment habits over the past year despite government attempts to encourage prompt payment."

Clive Brand, senior economist at Trade Indemnity, says: "A knock-on effect of this problem is that these companies kept waiting for payment by their customers are passing the burden on to their open suppliers. The resulting vicious circle of delays has a major impact on cash flow for all companies but it is the smaller businesses that are suffering most."

The plight of small businesses, which are often at the mercy of slow-paying larger companies, has already led the Confederation of British Industry to launch a code of practice on prompt payments. To date, about 400 CBI members have signed the code.

The Trade Indemnity survey covered nearly 1,000 companies with turnover ranging from less than £1 million to more than £50 million. Nearly half the companies had more than £50,000 outstanding for at least a month while some companies with turnover of less than £1 million had long outstanding debts of more than £100,000.

The construction and engineering industries were hit particularly badly with the average bill paid 31 days late.

Trade Indemnity says most companies are tightening up on credit management, mainly by making increased use of credit information from banks and reference agencies. They are also resorting more frequently to debt collection agencies.

Dun & Bradstreet says seven out of ten managing directors of British companies want legislation to enforce a statutory right to interest on late payments.

Source: Times, 6 June 1992, Rodney Hobson. © Times Newspapers Ltd. 1992

supplier allows its customer a certain period of time in which to pay for goods or services after receiving them. Instead of paying the bill, the customer can use the cash for other purposes during the short term. Obviously the bill has to be paid eventually, but the same delay applies to all creditors. For example, say I purchased materials regularly at the rate of £1 000 each month and took the agreed credit period of one month before payment was made. This is equivalent to an interest free loan of £1 000 for as long as I want. The problems are that you can upset the supplier who may withhold future supplies of essential goods, or a discount for prompt payment of the bill could be lost. Sometimes even false rumours start, that your business is in trading difficulties. Some small suppliers are put under great financial pressure by larger firms who are slow to pay (see Figure 3.1).

Medium-Term Finance

Finance which has a three to ten-year repayment period is called medium-term finance.

Usually it is used by businesses to help purchase equipment which has a corresponding life – the 'golden rule' in finance being to match the life of the loan to the life of the asset being purchased.

Medium-term loans are provided not only by the high street banks but also less-known institutions, such as 3i (Investors in Industry), which are supported by these banks and specialize in providing medium-term loans. Repayments of these loans can be by one sum at an agreed date, but more often they are by instalments over a period which can be tailored to fit the earning capacity of the asset being purchased. The interest charged can be at a fixed or variable rate, depending on current charges. In addition to some form of security, the lenders will also want to satisfy themselves on the quality of the management and the level of projected cash flow to establish that repayments can be met.

Leasing is a distinctive form of finance whereby the asset is purchased by another organization which then leases it to the user at an agreed rental. The leasor (the person or organization leasing out the asset) still retains ownership and can claim allowances from the Inland Revenue against tax paid on profit. The allowances, if approved, will lower the tax payments and give higher net profits. The leasor can decide to pass some of these extra profits to the user in the form of lower rental charges. Often, these rental charges can be much lower than any equivalent costs incurred by the user if a decision was made to buy rather than to rent. There are many forms of leasing, and most result in the user acquiring ownership, sometimes for a very low sum.

Leaseback is a procedure whereby the owner of an asset sells it to another party, and then leases it back for a 'rent'. Figure 3.2 reports on an example of leaseback in the leisure business.

*Figure 3.2 – **Leaseback***

French property

TRAVELLING around the coasts and ski resorts of France, you might have noticed the name Pierre & Vacances. You might even have thought it rather odd in translation: Peter and Holidays. In fact, it is not really translatable. 'Investment in leisure' is probably the closest you get, for the group is a leading French leisure/property developer and tour operator. On the one hand, it builds and sells holidays properties; on the other, it rents them out. It is expanding into Spain and Portugal and has just opened an office in London.

The group's interest in leisure began in the 1960s when, during a period of tremendous expansion in the industry, it created the traffic-free resort of Avoriaz in the French Alps, offering apartments and facilities for holidaymakers. It then undertook their management for private owners and institutional investors. As it increased the number of its developments, it provided a growing range of services for owners and now has 100 complexes in 50 locations in France, representing 20,000/25,000 apartments and 72,000 beds available for letting. Overall, the average price of its apartments is £60,000 although it has villas on the Cote d'Azur at up to £1m. Surveys by the group showed that people who bought holiday apartments used them for only four to eight weeks a year. So, leaseback was born. If a buyer wishes, he can pay 30 per cent less for an apartment, furnish it, and lease it to the group for 11 years. During that time, he can use it himself for six weeks annually. He has no maintenance or management charges to pay and P&V guarantees to hand the property back at French government 'three-star' standard. The group has sold 15,000 of its apartments under leaseback (of which there are variations), although many buyers still prefer outright ownership and the freedom to use their property when they choose.

Source: Financial Times, 7 March 1992

The high street banks are also known as clearing banks – that is, banks which offer cheque facilities for the public – and they are major providers of medium-term finance for loans over £5 000 for periods of up to seven to ten years. Merchant banks, which are often subsidiaries of clearing banks, provide loans in excess of £50 000.

Long-Term Finance

Long-term finance is used to describe finance made available for ten years or more.

*Figure 3.3 – **Funds for Small Firms***

Recession may restore equity gap stunting small firms' growth

THE considerable extension of lending to small firms by the clearing banks and the development of more term lending have been crucial. These developments helped many small firms to start up and grow and widened the availability of crossing the threshold at which venture capital has been a realistic option.

National Westminster Bank has a total of £3 billion term loans outstanding to 225,000 small businesses at May, 1991. The average loan was £14,000 and 30 per cent of the bank's total lending to small firms was accounted for in this way. "Having been criticised for many years for failing to lend to small firms, the banks are, in the current recession, being criticised in some quarters for having lent too much in the past and not enough now. All this shows how important it is that an appropriate mix of financial instruments is available to, and employed by, small firms," say Bannock and Doran. Their calculations indicate that the amount of formal investment in seed and start-up capital by the venture capital industry here compares favourably with that in the US if differences in gross domestic product are allowed for.

Source: Guardian, 13 January 1992

It is used to purchase capital assets which have a long life, to purchase or construct buildings or to purchase other businesses. Long-term loans are usually at a fixed rate of interest and only given after an independent valuation of assets used as collateral has been done, together with a comprehensive report of the firm's past performance and future prospects.

A mortgage loan is one which is secured by land or buildings and is usually for periods of twenty years or more. The lower limit for such loans is about £50 000 and the cost of organizing such a loan is about 2 per cent of the amount borrowed.

An alternative method for raising long-term finance is by sale and leaseback. A business sells a specific major asset to a buyer (usually a financial institution) who then leases it back to the original owner on a rental of up to twenty-five years. Naturally the lender will want to make sure that the asset can be resold elsewhere if the borrower defaults on payments. Therefore, extensive valuations are made in addition to company reports.

Figure 3.3 (previous page) shows the extent to which a well-known high street bank lends 'term' money to small businesses. 'Term' lending generally means medium and long-term lending as opposed to short-term overdrafts.

ACTIVITY 3.1

Visit a few high street banks or building societies and ask at the reception desk for a brochure on the different types of loan that can be obtained. Read the brochures carefully and write a short report summarizing the information they contain. If you have been able to obtain the interest rates for these loans can you find any connection between this rate and the time for repayment of the loan?

Debentures

A debenture is a secured, transferable loan that enables the lender to sell the loan, or part of it, to others to minimize any risk.

An example of a debenture is a loan for £5 million repayable in full in ten years's time with a fixed annual interest to be paid of 10 per cent. The debenture is secured on specified or unspecified assets of the business. Only large or well established companies issue debentures to raise money from merchant banks, insurance companies, pension funds and others who wish to invest money in a reasonably secure situation. Companies which are listed on the Stock Exchange can issue debentures to the public.

Equity Capital and Start-Up Finance

Equity capital is the owners's interest in the business and is permanently invested by them together with any undistributed profits. It is often described as 'risk capital', because investors have no guarantee of any return on their investment or its repayment.

Most businesses begin with the founders providing the initial equity with help from the bank in providing short-term working capital as described above. If the founders cannot raise sufficient funds, specialist organizations may be able to help by buying some of the shares and even by participating quite actively in the running of the business. However, most of these organizations prefer businesses in which they are able to sell their stake at a later date, and to recover their investment at a profit.

Venture capital is the name given for start-up capital used to support particularly innovative businesses. These are usually high-risk activities and the returns required by such investors can be extremely high. The services of a professional adviser are essential in order to obtain the best deal.

An established business may be able to issue further shares to its existing shareholders at a favourable rate in order to obtain more funds. For example, a company may offer one new share at a discount of 25 per cent for every two shares now held. This is known as a rights issue. Alternatively, new shares can be issued or 'placed' with a financial institution. If the company is listed on the Stock Exchange, these new shares can be traded with the public, often at a quick profit for the shareholder.

Government Support

The degree of involvement of national and local government in supporting individuals to develop their own businesses varies significantly with time and the political leanings of the government. In the UK, businesses can obtain up-to-date information on all current assistance by writing to or visiting its local Chamber of Commerce.

The debate about support centres around whether government should direct cash to entrepreneurs, or whether it would be more beneficial for this money to be spent on improving the social environment. Supporters of the latter argument suggest that better environments, such as improved schools and social services, will encourage more business. Figure 3.4 contains a report on the World Bank's attitude towards this debate.

*Figure 3.4 – **Investing in People or Business?***

Mother of investment

INDIRA GHANDI once said that "poverty is the worst form of pollution". What she failed to add is that, increasingly, its face is female; and that females caught up in the vicious circle of poverty can at once be unwitting causes of pollution and a key source of its future cure.

This is the latest conclusion of the World Bank, which is again focusing its efforts on educating women in its search for a solution to the linked problems of poverty and pollution. In a related development, the US administration is also focusing attention on women living in poverty as it sifts through the ashes of the Los Angeles riots for answers to the renewed violence in America's cities.

Lawrence Summers, chief economist of the World Bank, was one of the first to proclaim officially the new economic doctrine that educating females was one of the best investments a country could make.

He pressed for more social justice on economic grounds in a controversial speech delivered in Pakistan, where women are treated as second-class citizens. Only one-third of primary school students are females and women comprise less than 10 per cent of Pakistan's labour force, among the lowest ratios in the world.

Mr Summers' main message – that investment in women would promote growth by lowering birth rates, raising nutrition levels, improving resource allocations and increasing opportunities for all – drew a mixed response in Pakistan.

A similar ambivalence exists in the Bush administration.

Although it is generally acknowledged that US inner cities are becoming walled-off pockets of poverty, violence and drugs in which female headed families dominate, there is no agreement on solutions.

Should the emphasis be on creating more business investment and employment through enterprise zones and other devices, or should it be on the people, on the "human capital" of cities and regions? This is the question that divides Republicans and Democrats as they wrestle with a political response to the burning and looting in Los Angeles.

Reform does not mean a simple choice between promoting more business investment and investing more in human capital. As the World Bank has rediscovered from its own experience, and as the US should have discovered from the successes and failures of the 1960s and 1970s, it is a two-pronged process. Sustained economic progress is impossible without social progress.

Source: Independent on Sunday, 17 May 1992

CASE STUDY

Tulips for Orchards

A firm which had been an established horticultural family business for over twenty-five years decided that expansion and diversification was essential.

The current owners of the business were all members of the same family and they all worked in the business.

Currently, the business had a turnover, which was highly seasonal, of approximately £1 million per year mainly in selling potted plants and cut flowers to a variety of outlets, including several local supermarket stores. The plans for expansion were to build a large greenhouse to replace a very old one and to develop a range of exotic plants to meet the needs of the increasing number of householders who have a conservatory. Local supermarket organizations have expressed an interest in marketing these plants.

The cost of a new greenhouse with all the heating and cooling facilities would be £250 000 and extra money was needed to purchase other equipment, pay for training courses and also to support the business during the construction process, when normal activities would be severely disrupted. In total an estimated £500 000 was required.

The land owned by the business had been valued at £300 000 and the owners of the business were prepared to offer their private homes (total valuation £400 000) as guarantees for a loan if necessary. Last year the business made a profit of £150 000.

QUESTION

1 If you were asked by the owners to suggest how the money for development could be raised, what suggestions would you make?

Gearing

Gearing can be defined in different ways, but the definition which is most common and which will be used here is:

gearing is the amount of money borrowed as a percentage of the amount of money invested by the owner.

For example, if you started a business with £1 000 of your own money and managed to borrow another £500 which was lent to you for a period of more than one year, the gearing is:

$$\text{Gearing} = (£500/£1000 \times 100)\% = 50\%$$

In normal business activities it is not considered prudent by a lender (such as a bank) to lend to an owner more than that amount which will bring the gearing up to 50 per cent.

For example, take the case of a business owner who has £500 000 invested in a company which currently owes £150 000 to creditors who will be repaid in five years's time. The normal maximum amount that the owner could ask of a new lender is £100 000 which will bring the gearing up to 50 per cent.

The maximum of 50 per cent gearing is only an indication. Owners of businesses which are highly profitable and with a long 'track record' of continuous profits over many years could well borrow extra money to take the gearing up to or beyond 100 per cent. On the other hand, a business with a history of low profitability may not even reach a gearing of 25 per cent.

This limitation of gearing can sometimes be a severe handicap to a young business, where the owner has limited funds and yet the capital requirements are high. This is an example of where suppliers of venture capital can operate. But the costs of borrowing by a small business are often very high. Alternatively, in many cases, the government can help by either guaranteeing risk capital lent by a bank in excess of 50 per cent gearing, or by offering favourable tax advantages to other private investors who lend money for a time period. In the former case, the business pays a higher interest rate on the guaranteed funds, but the government takes the risk that the extra money may not be paid back if the business collapses. In the latter case, the business owners have 'non active' partners who take no role in the business activities and hopefully withdraw their money with significant accrued profits after five years or more.

Risks in Business

Whether or not an investor, or an investing organization such as a bank, will in fact provide any funds for short, medium or long-term financing depends on the perceived risks in the proposition.

In most cases, investors put money into businesses which match the investors's own risk-taking attitude. You may know people who regularly bet on a wide variety of activities from football pools to horse racing, because they are certain that a big win is imminent. You may also know people who never bet and put all their savings into a building society or National Savings. The first category are risk-takers and the second are risk-avoiders.

People who are risk-takers tend to invest in businesses where, although there is a chance that

KEY POINTS 3.1

- **Businesses can apply for funds from a number of different sources apart from the funds put in by the owners**
- **Sources of funds are categorized into short, medium and long-term finance**
- **The 'golden rule' in borrowing money is to try to match the loan repayment period to the useful life of the asset purchased**
- **Special schemes exist to help new businesses to raise funds – this is called 'start up' finance**
- **Normally, a business can borrow up to 50 per cent of the value of the owner's investment**

they could lose their investment, there is also a chance that they could make a lot of money. An example of a high-risk business is a new play or show in a London theatre. Will it be well received by the critics and the public? Will it 'fizzle out' after two weeks? Or will it, like Agatha Christie's *The Mousetrap,* continue successfully for decades?

People who are risk-avoiders tend to invest in businesses where there is little or no chance of them losing their money. There are few examples of businesses which are truly risk-free and, therefore, risk avoiders would never put their money into a business if the investment was not protected. However, there are a number of well-known businesses, such as ICI and Marks & Spencer, which are regarded as blue chip – that is, the business is usually able to pay a regular dividend to its investors with only a very low chance that the investment would be lost.

ACTIVITY 3.2

If you want to have some indication of your own risk-taking attitude, consider the following proposition:

You are invited to take part in a game of chance using playing cards, containing thirteen cards of each suit of spades, hearts, diamonds and clubs. There are fifty-two cards in total. It will cost you a sum of money to participate (your stake) before a card is given to you. You are dealt a card from the top of a well-shuffled pack. If the card is a club you will lose you entrance stake. If the card is not a club, you will be given £10. You will only be allowed to play this game once.

How much would you be prepared to pay for your stake? There are a number of people wanting to play and only the person offering the highest stake will be invited to take part.

If you offer more than £5, you are quite a risk-taker. If you offer less than 50p you are a risk-avoider. £2 would possibly be about average, but this depends on how much 'ready money' you have available. If you are broke, the proposition is pointless. If you are a millionaire, you probably would not even bother to participate!

Ask some of your friends this question. What are the highest and lowest answers? What is the average? Are there any surprises?

A Business Proposition

Read the Case Study on the next page. It asks you to become a big investor in a new business.

What Investors Need to Know

FINANCIAL QUESTIONS

Typical questions which investors would be expected to ask include:

- What has happened to my investment? Can I see what you have used it for or has it been spent on paying wages? Can I get it back?
- How successful is the company in making and selling its products and what reward (dividend) will I get as my share of the profits? Does this return meet my expectations considering the risks I am taking?
- Is the company generating enough cash to pay for future activities or is it likely to ask me to put in more money?

The answers to most of these questions can be answered by the company's financial statements, which is a set of financial accounts which we will cover in some detail later in this chapter. Whether or not investors are able to get their money back depends on the conditions they agreed to when they put their money in.

NON-FINANCIAL QUESTIONS

There are a number of other questions which a major investor in a business would ask. These are questions which are not financial, but obviously have relevance to the investor's expectations of future financial profits. Typical questions include:

- Is the management any good?
- Do the customers really like the products?
- Are the risks increasing or decreasing?
- Are the market and competition changing?
- Are the suppliers of materials and services reliable?

The answers to these types of question are crucial to determining the success of the business. However, the answers will not be found in the financial statements.

Obtain a copy of the published annual report of a business. You can do this by contacting your public, school or college library. A copy of the annual report for the year ending 1991 of a UK subsidiary of a European business is contained in Appendix A in this book. This report will contain the financial accounts of the business together with a report from the chairman of the business on performance over the past year and expectations over the next year.

Companies do not wish to give useful information to competitiors, such as material costs, wage costs, prices charged on contracts and so on, and therefore most published accounts do not contain any more information than the minimum required

CASE STUDY

A Business Opportunity

You have been approached by a small group to help them finance a business which they wish to start. You have recently inherited £200 000 from an aunt and although you have several 'short-term' uses for £100 000, you are wise enough to realize that a significant proportion should be invested. You have in mind a small manufacturing business because the process of creating something appeals to you. You are hoping that later on you will actually join the business on a full-time basis when you have completed your studies.

The group has produced a plan giving details of a toy-making business. It has researched the market opportunity for a range of highly original products which it has already taken steps to patent. The business has also produced a detailed plan of production operations, the equipment needed and premises required. The plan shows operations over the next two years and it would appear that there is the basis for a very successful company. The group had spent most of their own money in preparing the plan and paying themselves small salaries over the last few months. Although they can raise another £150 000 between themselves, they still need an additional £100 000 to get going. The cash requirements were carefully laid out in the plan.

You showed the plan, called a business plan, to your bank manager who had a long talk with you on the potential risks involved with the toy business. But you considered that the risks were worth taking, providing you limited yourself to an investment of £100 000. Your remaining funds were invested in a range of activities suggested by your bank manager. Most of these were very well-known, such as building societies, large international companies and other reasonably 'safe' investments.

The group was naturally overjoyed to know that you would invest your money, and suggested that you would like to be a non-executive director of the private limited liability company formed to produce and sell the toys. That means that you would not have a full-time job in the company, but you would spend about one day each month visiting and attending a meeting of the directors (the board meeting).

The company was duly formed and you were told that you now owned 100 000 shares of £1 in exchange for your investment which you paid into the company's bank account. The other five members of the group each received 30 000 £1 shares for which they each paid £30 000.

Although you do not have a majority shareholding, your 40 per cent holding of the company shares is very significant. You only need the support of one of the other founders, who each hold 12 per cent of the shares, to give you 52 per cent and therefore an automatic majority at any meeting of shareholders. There is no limit to what you could do to change the business. You will not be involved in the day-to-day business of the company, but there is no doubt that you would want to know what is happening to the firm on a regular basis.

QUESTION

1 What information would you need to receive about the business in order for you to know that your investment is as safe as you think it should be?

KEY POINTS 3.2

- **All businesses are operating under some degree of risk – the business could fail and investors could lose some or all of their investment**
- **The attitude towards risk by the investor should be matched to the risks inherent in the business activity**
- **In order to obtain information about business risks, investors need answers to both financial and non-financial questions**

by law. To obtain further information, you would probably have to be one of the company's directors or employees at least. Otherwise, it could be extremely difficult to get the additional information you want.

Accounting Concepts and Principles

Before we go on to examine the financial accounts for an organization, we must first consider the rules governing the preparation of these accounts so that information can be interpreted accurately.

The rules for the preparation of accounts fall into three classifications:

- Legal rules passed by Act of Parliament and which are enforceable by law
- Statements of Standard Accounting Practice (SSAP) produced by the accountancy profession. The Standards define procedures which must be followed unless a valid reason is supplied. For example, SSAP 20 defines how foreign currency should be translated and used within UK accounts
- Statements of Recommended Practice (SORP) produced by the accountancy profession. These give guidance on specific issues and, although not compulsory, there should be a good reason why they are not being followed. The Highway Code for using roads in the UK is a similar set of statements of recommended practice

All accountancy rules are themselves based on a number of concepts, which are in turn based on the over-riding principles of fairness and accuracy.

The main concepts are:

- The Cost Concept
- The Going Concern Concept
- The Accruals Concept
- The Consistency Concept
- The Prudency Concept

The Cost Concept

The Cost Concept means that capital assets are normally valued at the cost price.

Example
A company buyer purchases a large quantity of copper wire for £100 000 since part of the company's business is the manufacture and sale of electrical wiring. Shortly afterwards, there is a strike at the world's largest producers of copper and the price of copper wire soars. The same quantity of wire would now cost £300 000. Although the buyer may well be congratulated on the wise purchase, the value of the wire is recorded at £100 000 in the company stores.

The Going Concern Concept

The Going Concern concept assumes that the accounts are prepared on the understanding that the business will continue to operate indefinitely.

Example
Consider the valuation of a special machine which has been purchased by an organization to do a unique job. Machines which are designed to wrap products fall into this category. Such a machine would be of very little value to anyone else except the user, and frankly if the machine was part of a batch of bankrupt stock it would fetch a very low price at an auction. However, the current owner does not take this pessimistic view of its value; the machine is valued on the basis that it will be continuously used. It may not be worth much to someone else, but it is worth a great deal to the current owner. This concept is obviously linked with the Cost Concept.

The Accruals Concept

The Accruals Concept states that when the profit for a period is calculated, all expenses and revenues must be matched to the period when the service or goods were actually used by the business or supplied to the customer, and not to the period when payment was made or received.

Example
It is now 8 January 1994, and a business is trying to calculate the profit for the trading year ending 31 December 1993. During the year, sales amounted to £5 million.

Situation 1
Wages for the year amounted to £2.5 million including £100 000 earned in December but not yet paid.
Treatment
The wages must be matched to the period they were earned, and therefore all wages are recorded in the 1993 accounts.

Situation 2
A large consignment of materials was delivered just before the Christmas holiday, but still remains unopened. The bill of £100 000 has been received from the supplier and it has been paid. Total material costs for the year, including this bill, amounted to £1.5 million.
Treatment
Since the materials have not been used, the cost is not included in the 1993 costs. The value of the material is carried forward to the next period.

Situation 3
During the year, power costs have amounted to £250 000. The electricity bill is usually paid monthly, but the December bill (estimated at £1 500) has not yet been received due to industrial relations problems at the electricity office.
Treatment
If electricity was used, then it must be included in the 1993 accounts. The fact that a bill has not been received means that we must estimate it. Any errors can be corrected when the bill finally turns up.

Situation 4
All December's output was sold to one customer on normal trade credit terms, which means that payment will not be received until 31 January. Most businesses allow approved customers thirty days to pay bills. The invoice (the bill sent to the customer), amounting to £100 000 and included in the total year's sales, was issued on 30 December 1993.
Treatment
It is usual in business to date the sale of services or products as the date given when the invoice was prepared (not necessarily posted). The sale of the product is therefore to be included in the 1993 accounts. However, it is easy to see how 'window dressing' can be carried out by deliberately delaying or advancing the invoice date for services or goods supplied near to the end of an accounting period! 'Window dressing' means showing the accounts in the best, most favourable way from the managers's or business owner's point of view.

If the gross profit is defined as sales less material, wages and electricity costs, what is the gross profit for the year ending 31 December 1993?

The Consistency Concept

Constantly changing the methods by which assets are valued or making different allowances for wear and tear or any other change in procedure will not help a comparison of accounts between one period and another. A consistent approach is recommended until perhaps a situation is reached when change is urgently required.

At this stage, a full explanation for the change in method must be clearly given in the accounts.

Example
In 1987 a timber company, which initially only supplied wood from trees which it cut down in its own forest, started to import sawn wood for resale to existing customers. Because it is very difficult to work out the value of sawn timber cut from woodland which had been planted forty years previously, an acceptable method for valuing sawn wood in stock was to value it at 70 per cent of the expected selling price. This method had worked well for many years.

Gradually, over the next few years, the sawn wood in stock increasingly consisted of 'bought in' material at a known cost. This cost was significantly different from 70 per cent of the selling price, which was still the method used for valuing stock. Eventually, in 1993, the distortion in the financial system of the old stock valuation method became so great that the method was changed to one of valuing stock at cost.

The Prudency Concept

In general, it is always considered prudent in accountancy systems to over-estimate expected costs and to underestimate expected sales. Assets tend to be valued at the lower end of a range of possible values, and allowances for future taxation charges tend to be pessimistic. These examples and others like them have given the accountant a very dour and conservative image. Over recent years, however, this image has gradually changed as a more optimistic viewpoint has been established. There is a danger that the reduction of the prudency concept could lead to inaccurate, if not misleading accounting. Throwing caution to the wind is possibly not in the best interests of the average investor.

The problems arising in 1990 with the British & Commonwealth organization were caused by significant over-estimates of profits reported by a subsidiary company involved with computer leasing on the basis of expected revenues, which did not materialize.

Financial Statements

Your toy-making business eventually started to manufacture and sell products. The marketing director won a good long-term contract to supply a national multiple store whose quality standards are held in high esteem. Obtaining this contract was a tremendous morale booster for both employees and investors in the company.

At the end of the first year of operations you were given the set of financial statements shown in Figures 3.5, 3.6 and 3.7, with an invitation for you to attend a shareholders's meeting to agree to accept the dividend proposed by the directors.

The Companies Act 1985 specifies in detail how companies *must* construct their profit and loss accounts and their balance sheet if these accounts are intended for assessment by the public rather than for purely 'in company' purposes. If the accounts are for internal purposes only, they may be constructed in any way the company thinks fit.

Figure 3.5 – ***Balance Sheet***

THE TOY COMPANY
BALANCE SHEET
for 31 December 1993

FIXED ASSETS	£	£
Land and building at cost	125 000	
Plant and machinery at cost	130 000	
less depreciation to date	(13 000)	
Fixtures, fittings and equipment at cost	82 500	
less depreciation to date	(7 000)	
		317 500
CURRENT ASSETS		
Stocks	38 500	
Debtors	32 000	
Cash	20 000	
	90 500	
CREDITORS		
less Amount falling due within 1 year	24 000	
NET CURRENT ASSETS		66 500
TOTAL ASSETS *less* CURRENT LIABILITIES		384 000
CREDITORS		
less Amount falling due after more than 1 year		(52 000)
NET ASSETS		322 000
Financed by:		
CAPITAL and RESERVES		
Share capital	250 000	
General reserve	15 500	
Profit and loss account	56 500	
SHAREHOLDERS'S FUNDS		322 000

Figure 3.6 – ***Profit and Loss Account***

THE TOY COMPANY
THE PROFIT AND LOSS ACCOUNT
Period 1 January to 31 December 1993

	£	£
Turnover		285 000
Cost of sales		95 000
Gross profit		190 000
Sales and distribution costs	45 000	
Admin. expenses	60 000	105 000
Profit before interest and tax		85 000
less Interest payable		1 000
Net profit before tax		84 000
Tax on profits		12 000
Profit after tax		72 000
less		
Transfer to general reserve	15 500	
Dividend to shareholders	0	15 500
Transfer to profit and loss account		56 500

Figure 3.7 – ***Cash Flow Statement***

THE TOY COMPANY
THE CASH FLOW STATEMENT
Period 1 January to 31 December 1993

SOURCES	£	£
Operating profit	72 000	
Depreciation provision	20 000	
Loan	62 000	
Shareholders	250 000	
Total source of funds		404 000
APPLICATIONS		
Purchase of fixed assets	337 000	
Increase in stocks	38 500	
Increase in debtors	32 000	
less Increase in creditors (due to be paid within 1 year)	(24 000)	
Total application of funds		384 000
NET CASH FLOW		20 000

Notes:
It is assumed that tax on the year's profits have not been paid, and are part of the current liabilities.

Since this represents the first year of trading, the net cash flow, or increase in cash within the business, is also the value of the cash account at the end of the year.

The Profit and Loss Account

The profit and loss account shows how efficiently the company carried out its operations over the year.

This account deducts from the sales for the year all the costs attributed to the sales. It also shows what happens to the eventual profit. The entries in the profit and loss account are examined in sequence below.

TURNOVER

Turnover represents the value of sales during the period less any returns by customers for which refunds were given, and also less any sales taxes (such as Value Added Tax).

COST OF SALES

The cost of sales includes all manufacturing costs (such as material costs, wages, factory rent, electricity costs) and all other manufacturing costs which could have been avoided if the business had decided not to make toys but simply to sell toys purchased from elsewhere.

GROSS PROFIT

Gross profit is a very common measurement and is the difference between the total sales revenue and the total manufacturing costs of products, or the difference between total sales revenue and total purchase costs of trading organizations.

If the gross profit made by a business which manufactures a product is less than the gross profit of a similar business which buys in the product from elsewhere for resale, then the manufacturer must surely reconsider the continuation of the manufacturing process. Cotton shirt manufacturers in the UK found out in the 1960s that it was more profitable to import shirts for sale rather than make their own.

SALES AND DISTRIBUTION COSTS

Sales and distribution costs include all the costs of getting the product from the manufacturing department to the customer. Advertising, packaging, promotional activities, cost of running cars for sales staff and so on should be included.

ADMINISTRATIVE EXPENSES

The administrative expenses are all the costs for supporting the business. It includes clerical costs for invoicing, wages, debt collection, computer services, directors's fees and most centralized costs which cannot be easily defined as sales or distribution costs (for example, telephone costs, the cost of preparing the accounts).

PROFIT BEFORE INTEREST AND TAX

The profit made before deducting interest charges on borrowed money and before tax is deducted is often called the operating profit. This is the profit made from the business operations and is rightly the responsibility of the director of operations who usually has no control over how loans have been raised and how much tax is to be paid.

INTEREST PAYABLE

This covers the interest charges on a bank overdraft and other loans which incur a known fixed or variable interest charge.

TAX ON PROFITS

The amount of tax payable on company profits depends on the size of profits generated. Each year, on Budget Day, the Chancellor will announce any changes in the Corporation Tax payable by companies and any concessions on business profits, although announcements can be made at any time dependent on political pressures. Tax on profits on the profit and loss account will be amended by tax reliefs, grants, allowances or extra taxes and, therefore, the tax stated in our example is a *provision* rather than a specific *liability*. That is, the company is saying 'We think this will cover it'!

PROFIT AND RESERVES

After deducting tax, the balance of profits made by the company belongs to the shareholders, and theoretically it could all be distributed in the form of dividends per share.

For example, if 250 000 shares of £1 are issued in return for the initial investments by the shareholders, it would be possible to give the owner of each £1 share certificate a dividend of 28.8 pence. This also represents the earnings per share (EPS).

Total distribution of profits = £72 000
Total number of shares issued = £250 000
Earnings per share = £72 000/£250 000
= £0.288 or 28.8 pence per share

However, it is not often considered prudent to distribute all profits after taxation. Some profit needs to be 'earmarked' for possible expenses which could arise, such as a higher than expected tax liability. Other profits should be retained to 'make up' possible lower profits in the future and maintain a steady dividend policy. In addition, it might be prudent to retain profits for future investment in new assets, such as new plant and equipment, to replace old assets or to increase manufacturing capacity. In the UK, such retained or undistributed profits (called reserves) are the most important source of investment funds.

In our example in Figure 3.6, a decision has been made not to pay any dividend during the first year of operations and to make a reserve of £15 500. The reserve is called a general reserve in the absence of a specific reason.

TRANSFER TO PROFIT AND LOSS ACCOUNT

We have been looking at the profit and loss account for the year ending 31 December 1993. The final profit after distributions is added to (or 'credited to', in accountancy terms) the running profit and loss account. We are not told what is the new balance in this account. However, do not think that the reserves and the profit and loss account monies are put into a 'jam jar' to await the time that need arises! Cash is always in demand in any business, and profit which is retained is usually put to use in all those activities which will strengthen the business and increase profitability, such as buying materials and paying wages. However, the shareholders know that what they have done is to increase their stake in the business, and to increase the value of their shareholding, as we shall see in the balance sheet.

The Balance Sheet

The balance sheet shows the assets and liabilities of the company at the end of the year. It is a 'snapshot' of the company's wealth at a specified time, which in our example (in Figure 3.5, page 39) is midnight on 31 December 1993. An asset is something which has a monetary value to the company and which is owned by the company. A liability is a monetary debt owed by the company.

The balance sheet lists all the assets of the company and from this list is subtracted the money owed. The net value *must* equal the amount of money invested by the shareholders. The latter consists of the initial investment by shareholders together with retained profits (represented by the reserves and the profit and loss account).

The balance sheet of the Toy Company at the end of its first year of trading is shown in Figure 3.5.

Fixed Asssets and Depreciation

The fixed assets comprise all the 'hardware' of the company which have a life expectancy of more than one year (for example, land, buildings, machinery). Apart from land, fixed assets will eventually crumble into dust, some more quickly than others. Therefore, each year of ownership of a fixed asset must mean that some value has been consumed and the asset is worth less at the end of the year than at the beginning. This loss in value is called the depreciation cost for the year. Eventually over the life of the asset, the cumulative depreciation charged will equal the total loss in value of the asset.

For example, a motor car which is a fixed asset is purchased for £6 000. Each year, a depreciation charge (or a 'provision for depreciation' in accountancy terms) is agreed at £1 200 which represents a fair estimate in the loss in value of the car over the year. At the end of three years of ownership, the 'written down' value of the car is £6 000 less the accumulated depreciation charge of £3 600, which equals £2 400. Theoretically, if the car is sold at this time, the owners would expect to receive £2 400 for it. A fuller description of how depreciation is calculated is given in Chapter Six.

All fixed assets are shown at their historic cost in the financial report, thus conforming to the Cost Concept, but in the balance sheet the accumulated depreciation to date is subtracted to show the net value.

It is sometimes important to tell the owners of a business if any fixed asset has increased in value due to a scarcity premium or, more likely, due to inflation. A scarcity premium is simply the extra value of an item because it is in demand and has a rarity value. The old Rolls-Royce may now be a collector's item and worth many times more than the original purchase price. In these cases, the fixed asset is revalued, detailed notes are made in the financial report, and the provision for depreciation is usually increased to reflect the higher loss in value each year. As can be expected, inflation, which simply changes the value of money, complicates how depreciation can be properly estimated.

In the balance sheet, the fixed assets of a business are listed in order of decreasing life expectancy. Land would be at the top of the list and office equipment would be at the bottom end.

Depreciation is an expense just like any other expense for the period (for example, wages or material costs). However, the big difference is that depreciation is a 'non-cash expense'. For example, consider the case of a farmer who purchased a large tractor for £30 000 and at the end of the year the estimated value of the tractor was £24 000. The difference, £6 000, is the depreciation for that year and would be added to the expenses in the profit and loss account. However, there was no cash flow associated with the depreciation. The farmer did not have to pay anyone £6 000. The 'flow' of cash took place when the tractor was initially purchased.

In Figure 3.5, no provision for depreciation has been taken on the land and building, and relatively high charges have been taken against the plant, machinery and fixtures, etc. Since this is the first year of operations of the Toy Company, the total provision for depreciation of £20 000 is the same as the depreciation charged in the profit and loss account.

In the profit and loss account in Figure 3.6, depreciation was not mentioned specifically, but would be included in the cost of sales (depreciation in the manufacturing department) and the balance within the administrative expenses.

Current Assets

Current assets are a list of all the assets owned by the business and which have a life expectancy of less than one year.

STOCKS

Stocks are all the materials owned by the business which are to be used in the production and sale of goods. In a manufacturing business, materials are purchased for conversion to finished goods. At any instant in time, the manufacturing process contains materials at various stages of completion and also perhaps significant stocks of part-finished components. Thus, a manufacturing business can have purchased material stocks, work in progress stocks and finished goods stocks.

A business which simply buys and sells (a trading business) will only have stocks of goods for resale. However, as is also the case for manufacturing businesses, there is probably quite a large amount of stock of stationery, heating fuel, spare parts for machines, computer disks and other consumables which are also added to the stock if the valuation is significant.

Stock is valued at the lower of cost or net realizable value (NRV). NRV is the price that could be expected if the item were sold within a reasonable time period. Assume that a fashion shop has purchased a red leather jacket for £100 for resale at £150. The jacket would be valued at £100 in stock. However, if the colour red became unfashionable it might be prudent for the shop to value the jacket at £60, which might be the price it could expect to sell the jacket in a Sale.

Valuing stock is quite difficult if it is not possible to trace the buying or making price of the item. For example, how do you value a pile of coal which contains the remnants of three deliveries which were all at different prices? When was a particular lump of coal delivered? This problem is examined in Chapter Six.

DEBTORS

Debtors are people who owe money for goods and services they have purchased for which they have not yet paid. They have bought the items 'on credit'. It seems strange to think that people who owe money to a business are 'assets'! More of a liability you may think!

However, most businesses carry out sales transactions with other businesses or private people who have accounts, on credit, which generally give the customer thirty days to pay. Therefore, at any one time, there would be at least thirty days of sales as debtors.

As proof that a debtor is an asset, you can usually sell the debt to another business – a debt collecting business. These organizations are professional and should certainly not to be confused with 'minders and musclemen'. Using threatening behaviour in order to recover a debt is illegal.

Debt collecting businesses are called debt factors, or cash management organizations. They will operate in a number of different ways: from undertaking all the invoicing system – that is, the sending out of bills and monthly statements – through to collecting those debts which a client company may have trouble in recovering. The difference is that they are good at debt collecting because that is their business and you, hopefully, are good at making toys which is your business. Debt factors either charge a percentage of the sum collected or buy the debt from you for a percentage of its face value.

Possibly the most important role of a debt factor is to improve the 'cash flow' of a business since they buy debts for cash. For a business which is trying hard to expand, slightly less cash 'up front' is preferable to full payment in possibly six to eight weeks's time. Figure 3.8 contains a report on the growth of debt factoring.

For example, if you owed me £100, I could sell the debt for, say, £80 to someone else who might have a better chance of recovering the debt. You would still have to pay the same £100 to the new 'owner'. I am happy to receive £80 rather than the risk of getting nothing! I would also put the loss of £20 into the profit and loss account as a legitimate cost for the year, which could reduce my tax bill.

Many businesses do not sell debts outside the company but use a credit controller whose job it is to check the credit worthiness of any customer and to follow agreed procedures for payment of invoices. One of the duties of a credit controller would be to prepare an 'aged' debtors list for management, showing how much was due from who for how long. Persistent bad payers may well be told that no more business can be transacted until debts are settled.

It is one of the problems of the terminology of accounting that, when a business supplies goods on credit to customers, we talk about 'debtors',

Figure 3.8 – ***Debt Factoring***

Boldly going where banks dare not go

THE FACTORING and invoice discounting industry is seen as a leading indicator of the state of the economy. Its clients supply basic products to industry and commerce and it lends against the unpaid invoices of its clients. It should therefore be the first to detect a general trend towards reviving business confidence and demand.

Although no one is getting wildly excited, factors see signs that their clients are beginning to pull out of recession. And when those signs become a strong trend, the factoring industry believes it is ideally placed to fund the growth.

Ben Allen, the deputy chairman of the Association of British Factors and Discounters (ABFD) and managing director of Kellock, the Bank of Scotland-owned factoring company, says: "We're on the edge of a bonanza as we come out of recession. We have a strong product, which can help companies with weak balance sheets."

Factors believe they can boldly go where no clearing bank would dare. Clearing banks lend on historic balance sheet information, whereas factors lend against current invoices and increase their lending as sales rise, ensuring a flow of working capital for expanding companies. Clearing banks have reduced the amount they will lend against last year's debtors to as low as 30 per cent in some cases; factors lend about 80 per cent of the value of invoices as soon as they are issued.

The expected inability or unwillingness of the clearing banks to fund recovery presents an opportunity to the factoring industry. Leslie Bland, the managing director of Century, says: "Companies will run out of money to expand and the banks won't provide it. We can."

The recovery still appears to be patchy. Mr Bland says that from the end of March there were signs that clients were selling "a bit more".

Stuart Parker, chief executive of Trade Indemnity-Heller Commercial Finance (TIH), saw the beginnings of an upturn as early as last September. October was a record month and the improvement has been sustained since. Despite the upturn in sales, Mr Parker believes clients still do not have the confidence to invest and are borrowing 25 per cent less than usual. On average, clients have a little more than 50 per cent borrowed against receivables; at present it is just over 40 per cent.

Factoring does not prosper in a recession. If clients go out of business, suffer bad debts or a decline in turnover, factors also fail to grow. Although demand for factoring services increases, it is often from companies about to go bust and desperate for money.

Bad debts arose both through clients customers going bust, in which case factors providing 100 per cent bad debt cover picked up the tab, and through fraud. The raising incidence of fraud, including "fresh-air invoices", where clients have drawn down finance against non-existent sales, and money received being paid into the wrong bank account, has been more marked in invoice discounting than factoring.

Confidential discounting, where the discounter pays out money against invoices but has no control over collecting debts and no contact with the clients' customers, makes it a higher risk activity than factoring.

Source: Independent, 5 May 1992

people who owe the business money. Similarly, when a small business is 'in debt' to others – that is, it owes them money – they are the business's creditors! This confusion stems from the relationship between a person and the accounts of a business. Being 'in credit' means that the person is a creditor as far as the business is concerned. Being 'in debt' means that the person is a debtor as far as the business is concerned.

CASH (AND OVERDRAFTS)

Cash is the name for money available on short notice. This is usually cash in a current account at a bank which can be withdrawn immediately. However, the definition also covers short-term deposits which may need seven days notice of withdrawal. If the current account at the bank is minus – that is, the business owes the bank money because it has written out cheques for more than it has – the account is called overdrawn.

Creditors and Current Liabilities

Creditors are people who are owed money by the business, and are separated into two types:

- Creditors who have to be paid within the next year (the current period)
- Creditors who have to be repaid after the next year

Creditors who have to be paid within the next year are often called current liabilities and include:

- People who have supplied goods on credit
- Wages which have been earned but not paid
- Tax due but not yet paid

- Dividends to the owners which have been agreed but not yet paid

Current liabilities often include an overdraft, which is a short-term loan given to a customer by the bank. Overdrafts are normally taken by a business to cover a short-term cash problem and originated in the UK when banks lent farmers money to buy seed before the farmer had received money from the sale of the harvest.

Overdrafts can be cancelled within a day or so by a bank so that the customer has to obtain cash from elsewhere very quickly. However, it is normal for many businesses to have quite long-term overdrafts because the interest charged is relatively low, and is calculated daily on the end-of-day overdraft value. This means that a very short-term lapse into an agreed overdraft for a few days will only invoke insignificant interest charges based on a rate per day equivalent to, say, 15 per cent per year. This state of affairs will possibly not last for too long in the UK since it is not a common practice in Europe where overdraft facilities are very rare and fixed-term loans for short periods are preferred.

Most banks will agree to provide businesses with an overdraft which will allow them to cover short-term cash requirements. If this overdraft is exceeded, the bank may not 'honour' a cheque – that is, the bank will refuse to pay the recipient of the cheque. In business, this could be fatal since word might get around that the business is unable to support any cheques, and suppliers of essential materials may insist on cash 'up front'. An alternative is to ask the bank for a longer-term loan.

Creditors falling due after one year are people who have lent money to the business over a long period, and who expect to receive a regular interest payment. These used to be called 'long-term loans' and they form part of the capital structure of the business. The gearing of a business is the ratio of the long-term loan capital to the risk capital invested by the owner.

Net Current Assets or Working Capital

Current assets – Current liabilities

In the Toy Company balance sheet, the net current assets are listed at £66 500. This is the difference between the current assets and the current liabilities.

It represents the amount of cash the company can expect to receive if it paid all its bills, received all the money owing to it, and sold all its stock at valuation. This is also called working capital.

In well managed businesses, every effort is made to plan and control the working capital so that sufficient cash is available to pay wages, salaries, suppliers, essential expenses and specific obligations such as tax at known times during a year.

Net Assets

(Fixed Assets + Net Current Assets) – Creditors falling due after one year

Net assets are the fixed assets plus the net current assets (or working capital) less the creditors who have to be repaid after the next year. The net assets measure the total assets owned by the business less the money which has to be paid in the short and long term to the creditors of the business. The following definitions need to be remembered:

Net current assets = current assets − creditors of less than one year

Total assets = fixed assets + current assets

Net assets = total assets − all creditors

Shareholders's Funds and Owner's Equity

Shareholders's initial investment + Undistributed profits

The shareholders or owners of the business are credited with their initial investment (the share capital) plus all the undistributed profits generated by the business since the start of operations. These undistributed profits are either 'earmarked' for a possible expense or charge and called a reserve or recorded in the profit and loss account. The general reserve in Figure 3.5 indicates that a sum has been reserved for a possible expense in the future and is not part of the profit and loss account. The profit and loss account can be used to pay future dividends. For example, perhaps next year there is no profit and yet the owners require a dividend of £30 000. Providing cash exists in the cash account, this dividend will be paid to the owners and the profit and loss account will be reduced to £26 500.

The shareholders's funds in the Toy Company amount to £322 000, which is exactly the same as the net assets. This should come as no surprise: all transactions must be reported in the accounts; money cannot appear or disappear without being recorded. Therefore, all the liabilities must equal all the assets.

Cash Flow Statement

Figure 3.7 (page 39) shows the cash flow statement of the Toy Company for the year ending 31 December 1993. This statement is also called the 'source and application of funds'.

The cash flow statement lists all the sources of cash available to the business during the year, and also lists all the areas where cash is 'consumed' during the year. The difference between sources and application is the final cash account increase or decrease. One of the principal aims of all profit-making businesses is to get as much cash coming in as possible and to stop cash going out!

Since the Toy Company has only been in existence for one year, the sources of cash include the owner's investment and any long-term loans which have been negotiated at the start of the business.

Generally, for a healthy business which has been operating for a few years, the main source of cash is from the business operations. That is, from the operating profit which is shown in the profit and loss account. The operating profit is calculated by subtracting costs from revenue, and these costs normally include a depreciation provision. But depreciation is not a 'cash flow' as has been explained above, and therefore, the profit underestimates the actual cash available to the business by an amount equal to the depreciation provision. For example, if I lent my car for a week for £50 and calculated my costs as £25 and also £20 for depreciation, my profit would be £5. However, I would find I had £25 in my pocket!

The cash available to the Toy Company during the first year of operations is the sum of the operating profit plus the depreciation provision plus the shareholders's investment plus the long-term loan (or creditors falling due after more than one year).

The application of funds in the Toy Company are to the purchasing of fixed assets and the increase in working capital. The concept of increasing working capital is not often clearly expressed in many published accounts. Basically, what it shows is that some funds have been used to increase stock levels, some funds have not materialized because of an increase in debtors, and some funds have been saved because of an increase in creditors due to be paid within the next year. If debts are not paid, there is more cash left 'in the till'.

ACTIVITY 3.3

Turn to *Appendix A* and examine the financial statements of the UK subsidiary company. Compare the entries in the consolidated profit and loss account, the consolidated balance sheet, and the cash flow statement with the similar entries examined in this chapter. (Note: the word 'consolidated' includes all the companies within a group of companies.) Many entries in the financial statements are given a 'notes' reference number. Read these notes.

It is conventional to put sums in brackets if the value is negative.

Prepare a short report on the main differences between the 1991 financial accounts for the company and the 1990 accounts. What information about the company do the financial statements fail to give you?

KEY POINTS 3.3

- **There are a number of accounting concepts and principles which enable fair and accurate analysis of financial reports**
- **The profit and loss account subtracts the expenses for a period from the revenue for the same period. The resultant net profit is used both to reward investors and to develop the business assets**
- **The balance sheet shows the balance between the assets of a business and the capital employed in the business**
- **The source and application of funds shows the flow of cash – where it comes from and where it goes to**

EXAM PREPARATION

SHORT QUESTIONS

1 What is the importance of gearing?

2 List three sources of finance available to a small business enterprise.

3 What are the advantages to a firm of using debt factors?

4 Give three examples of how a firm might raise finance by liquidating its assets.

5 State two advantages of leasing equipment rather than purchasing it outright.

6 What is the Prudency Concept of accountancy?

7 Explain the purpose of a funds flow statement (source and application of funds).

8 Define the term 'working capital'.

9 What is the shareholders's equity?

10 What is the Accruals Concept in accountancy?

DATA RESPONSE QUESTIONS

1 Smallbrook Ltd was a trading company formed on 1 January 1993 with a total capital invested of £100 000, which comprised £60 000 supplied by the owner and sole shareholder, Fred Brotherton, and £40 000 supplied by the Workshire Bank as a fixed interest loan of 15 per cent per annum paid every six months on 1 July and 1 January, starting 1 July 1993, repayable in ten years's time. The loan was secured on Fred's private house which had been valued at £120 000.

During the first month of operations, fixed assets valued at £40 000 were purchased and depreciated at a constant rate of £5 000 per year.

Sales in the first month of operations amounted to £10 000 and these increased by £1 000 per month over the first twelve months. Sales were all on credit and were paid by the end of the following month.

Stock for resale was purchased at the start of each month for cash. A gross profit of 40 per cent was made on all sales. At the end of the first year of operations, £5 000 of materials were held in stock.

Office expenses, paid in cash, amounted to £1 000 per month, and Fred paid himself a salary of £1 500 per month.

Questions:

(a) Calculate the profit and loss account for the year.

(b) Produce a source and application of funds statement for the year.

(c) Produce a balance sheet for the business at the end of the first year.

(d) Calculate the gearing.

2 A large insurance company acquired a new computer system which had an expected life of ten years. The system cost £1 000 000 and the company initially considered that the costs could be spread evenly over ten years. However, a consultant in computer technology advised the management after the first year of operations that a new design breakthrough would probably make their system obsolete in three years's time and in need of replacement. The company decided therefore that it would be prudent to 'write off' the computer over the next three years with the result that annual costs increased very significantly. As it turned out, the consultant was correct and a new computer system was installed. Even though assured by the manufacturers of the new system that it would be efficient for at least eight years, the company decided to plan for a four-year usage – just to be safe!

Questions:

(a) What is meant by 'writing off'?

(b) What is the difference between the annual cost of the computer system as suggested by the manufacturers and the insurance company?

3 Fisher's Furniture Ltd is a small furniture retailer whose accounts for the year ending 30 April 1986 are given below.

	£			£
Shareholders's Funds		*Fixed Assets*		
Share capital	100 000	Land & Buildings		120 000
Reserves	30 000	Van	12 500	
		Depreciation	(2 500)	10 000
Long-term liabilities				
Loans	60 000	*Current Assets*		
		Stock		85 000
Current Assets		Debtors		8 000
Creditors	24 000	Cash		3 500
Provision for tax	12 500			
	226 500			226 500

(a) Explain what you understand by the following terms which appear in the balance sheet above:

(i) Shareholders's funds
(ii) Long-term liabilities

(b) During the year ending 30 April 1987, the following transactions took place:
£240 000 of goods were bought.
£300 000 of goods were sold. These were originally bought by Fisher's for £195 000.
£220 000 was paid to suppliers.
£7 500 was paid on average each month to cover wages, the running expenses of the shop and van, and interest on the loan.
£12 500 was paid for last year's tax.
£2 500 allowance was made for depreciation on the van.

All profits are retained within the firm and tax is chargeable on them at the rate of 50 per cent. Debtors have risen by £2 000.

(i) Calculate the profit made for the year ending 30 April 1987 and the cash in hand at this date.
(ii) Draw up a balance sheet for the year ending 30 April 1987.

(c) Explain how the following assets which appear in the balance sheet have been valued and identify alternative methods that could have been used:

(i) The van (which was purchased on 1 May 1985 and was expected to have a five year life).
(ii) Stock.

(d) What else is legally required (other than the balance sheet and profit and loss account) to appear in all published accounts?

(Cambridge June 1987)

ESSAYS

1 A medium-size retail chain wishes to expand. To do so it needs to raise additional capital. Suggest possible internal sources of funds for this exercise and comment on the relative merits of financing the remainder by either equity or debt methods. (Cambridge June 1991)

2 A shareholder finds certain aspects of a company's activities recorded in the annual report and accounts. To what extent do the details supplied allow the shareholder to make an assessment of the state of his investment? (AEB 1988)

CHAPTER 4

Statistics for Business

▷ ▷ QUESTIONS FOR PREVIEW ▷ ▷

1 *How can a large amount of data be presented?*

2 *What is probability?*

3 *How accurate is sample information?*

4 *How can the future be predicted?*

Business and Numbers

NO BUSINESS can exist without the information given by numbers. Numbers are needed to give clear, unambiguous measurements of a very wide range of different variables. How much money is available? How many people do we need to employ? How long will it take to make one product? How many items have been scrapped this week? Numbers are also used to represent proportions, to measure risk, to plan activities, to formulate decisions and to control processes. Numbers are so important to a business that it is vital that information expressed in numbers is fully understood by all members of the business whether they are in selling, marketing, personnel management, administration or production.

This chapter will concentrate on methods of presenting numerate information and describing large sets of numbers, and on using numbers to measure risk, estimate performance and forecast the future.

One of the challenges that has to be tackled is the ability to communicate with numbers. Consider the following statement made by a manager employed in a pen manufacturing business:

> 'The market research people forecast quite a demand for our roller type pens, so we produced a lot at the beginning of the year. The pens are about the same size as a pencil, but they have to be made to a pretty exact specification with very accurate tolerances on the body diameter to make sure it fits the cap OK. Unfortunately, a large percentage of production had to be scrapped because it went out of tolerance. Consequently, the production cost went through the roof, and the profit disappeared.'

This is a conversational statement. There is no denying that the business manager is giving the listener information which is easily understood. It seems that there were some problems with the manufacture of the pen barrels, and it is quite interesting to hear about them.

Now consider the following statement about exactly the same problem, but this time given by a person with a passion for numbers:

> 'The market research department forecast a demand for 25 000 of our roller ball pens per week, and growing at 10 per cent per month. Consequently, we set production to 30 000 per week for the first six weeks of the year. The pens are 7.5mm in diameter and 15cm long, and the tolerance on the diameter is plus or minus 0.01mm. 8 per cent of production was scrapped because the barrel diameter was greater than the design limits, and the costs estimated at 2.67p increased to 3.5p per unit. This reduced the profit from a planned 0.5p to 0.1p per unit.'

This is a very precise statement of what happened to the pen production, but the trouble is that the statement is pretty boring, and it is likely that most of the numbers are soon forgotten.

The challenge in business is to present numerate information in such a way that interest is held by the listener. The precision of the second statement has to be communicated with the ease of the first statement.

Defining 'Information'

Information has to be useful. It needs to be applicable, timely, accurate and understood. Information also has to be new to the recipient. Much information can be obtained quite cheaply, such as the cost of obtaining the telephone number of a friend who lives in another part of the country. However, some information is extremely expensive since its collection requires many people and a large amount of time. Obtaining information about the merits of a new measles vaccine would involve thousands of experiments over many years, and the cost could be many hundreds of thousands of pounds.

Information does not have to be about numbers. For example, knowledge that a friend has a passion for over-ripe bananas could be very useful information at a certain time. However, in this chapter we will only consider information expressed in numbers. Such information is obtained by measuring, counting, processing and logical deduction. For example:

Measuring: How high can you jump?

Counting: How many people did you over take on the way to work?

Processing: What is the square root of 16?

Logic: What proportion of tosses of a fair coin will be 'heads'?

Much numerical information is termed 'statistical', in that it contains statistics about sets of numbers. A statistic is a number representing a property of a group or thing. Your height is one of your statistics: it is a measurement of one property of your body. In business, most statistics represent properties of sets of numbers. A common statistic for a business would be the average sales per week.

Information is also either primary or secondary. Primary information is obtained from data or measurements taken for a specific purpose of generating that information. Secondary information is generated from data obtained for another purpose.

An example of primary information might be the numbers a vehicle census observer would collect to calculate the average number of cars passing a specific point over a selected time period. Secondary information could be based on an analysis of car registrations published in a motoring journal.

Decision-Making

One of the most important applications of information in business is for decision-making. A 'decision' is rather like a balance, with a preplanned method of selection between alternatives. For example, if we want to know if an item weighs more than 1kg, we put it on one side of a set of scales, and put a 1kg weight on to the other side. We know the item weighs more than 1kg if the side of the balance holding our item drops. The test for finding the heavier item is called the 'criterion'. The movement of the scales is called the 'outcome'.

Decision-making in business follows the same principles as those for the balance scales. The first step is to predict the possible outcomes; the second step is to select the criterion to be applied to these outcomes in order to find which outcome 'wins'.

An example of a decision-making process is in the selection of a new product to manufacture from a large number of possibilities. The criterion most likely to be used would be 'greatest profitability'. Consequently, all the possible new products are examined to see what the likely profitability will be. Each product profit is an 'outcome'. The criterion of 'greatest profitability' is now applied and the product with the largest profit is selected.

Decision-making appears to be a reasonably easy process, if the outcomes are all known and the criterion is fully defined. Unfortunately in many businesses there are problems in agreeing the choice of criterion, or the applicability and priority order of a combination of criteria. There are also problems in measuring some types of outcome, since they are not all straightforward (like estimating profit). Moreover, the information necessary to make a correct decision might not be readily available.

For example, the decision on whether to move the location of a factory to a new site may be based on maximizing profits by the owners, but staff may use a criterion based on minimizing the cost of housing. If the new site is more profitable as opposed to staying, the owners will decide to move. However, if the staff find that houses cost more in the new area than where they are now, their decision will be to 'stay put'.

Information for Decision-Making

It is generally agreed that better decisions are made when people are better informed. Information is required both to understand all the possible outcomes that could arise and also to measure the values of these outcomes.

Let us assume that there is a problem with a

city centre street which is now turning into a conflict of space between vehicles on the road and the increasing number of shoppers who find it difficult to stay on the pavement. The city planners have to make a decision on how to solve the problem. Should they ban all traffic, or put in a large number of 'humps' in the road to slow down traffic, or make the street restricted access? There is no doubt that the planners will have to agree a criterion for the decision, and they will have to evaluate the outcomes in terms of this criterion.

It is at this initial stage in the planning activity that the planners will require information relating to the problem. What is happening at the moment? In order to find out this information, instructions are given for a traffic census to be made. The results of the census are to be presented to the next planning meeting. The following example processes typical raw data.

Example

An observer was posted at the side of the city street and told to measure the number of different types of vehicle passing in one direction over a one-hour period. The categories of vehicle were defined as: bus(B), car(C), lorry(L), motorbike(M), pedalcycle(P), any other not defined category(O).

The results over the first few minutes were as follows:

CCCCLMPPPCLLBCCMCCLLOBCCC CCCCCLLOCCMCCP....

This is indeed very boring stuff and, when presented in this way, conveys little or no information. We have here a quantity of data which needs to be processed and presented clearly before it can be defined as information. Making tables from data and depicting the tabulated data are processes for converting data to information.

Tabulating Numbers

It is possible to process the raw data in the example above in the form of a table, as shown in Figure 4.1. By tabulating it in this way, the data has taken on a new meaning, which is the start of the information process. The addition of a percentage column increases the reader's understanding of the information. Remember, the symbol '%' is a shorthand way of writing 'divided by 100'. There is no difference between, say, 0.2 and 20% – it is exactly the same.

Figure 4.1 – ***Results of Observations: Traffic Count Over a One-Hour Period***

Vehicle type	*No. observed*	*Percentage of total (%)*
Bus	10	5
Car	100	50
Lorry	40	20
Motorbike	30	15
Pedalcycle	15	7.5
Other	5	2.5
Total	200	100

Pictorial Displays

A way of depicting the information shown in Figure 4.1 is through a pie chart, which is a circle cut into sectors (parts of a pie) which are in proportion to the information blocks. In order to do this, you must convert the percentage column into an equivalent number of degrees (thus, 100% equals 360°, or a full circle).

Figure 4.2 – ***Results of Observations***

Vehicle type	*Percentage of total (%)*	*Number of degrees*
Bus	5	18
Car	50	180
Lorry	20	72
Motorbike	15	54
Pedalcycle	7.5	27
Other	2.5	9
Total	100	360

This can be easily done by multiplying the numbers in the percentage column by 3.6 to get the results shown in Figure 4.2. For example, the sector angle showing the percentage of lorries is obtained by multiplying 20 by 3.6 to get 72 degrees. The resulting pie chart is shown in Figure 4.3.

Figure 4.3 – ***Traffic Census***

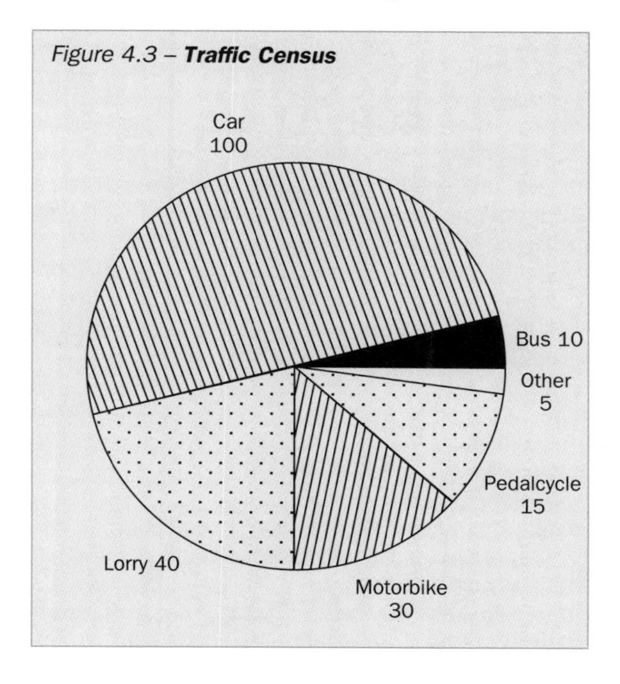

Alternatively, it is possible to present the observations of vehicles in the form of a bar chart, as shown in Figure 4.4. The horizontal axis means little apart from being a convenient base for sitting the bars on. Normally, all bars and columns would be the same width, although the actual width is not important. The height of each column is proportional to the percentage frequency of observations (alternatively, it could be proportional to the number of observations). Since all the vertical bars are of one-unit width, the area of each column is proportional to the value of the variable. Bar charts can also be drawn with the bars horizontal.

Figure 4.4 – ***Traffic Census***

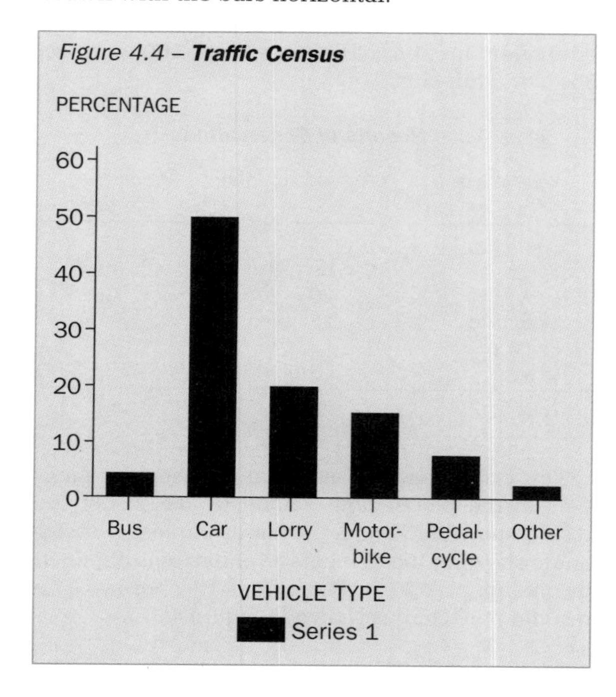

ACTIVITY 4.1

Conduct a survey by asking at least twenty males which daily newspaper they prefer to read first if they had a choice. Include in your list of allowed answers the possibilities of 'do not know' and 'none'. Construct a table like Figure 4.2, showing the answer with the percentage response for each newspaper named.

Construct a percentage frequency pie chart as shown in Figure 4.3 and a vertical bar chart as shown in Figure 4.4.

Repeat the survey, but this time ask at least twenty females. Construct a percentage frequency bar chart and pie chart as before.

Can you spot any significant differences between the two bar charts and the two pie charts? What conclusions can you draw?

What are the strengths and weaknesses of the two methods of displaying information?

Do you think the people you asked were typical of most people in your neighbourhood? If you have any doubts, how would you select a typical set of respondents?

Variables and Rounding Rules

In the above example about a traffic census, the measurement had to be a whole number (or 'integer'). We could observe 12 or 60 cars, not 1.75 or 34.81234 cars. A variable which can only take whole number values is called a discrete variable.

On the other hand, if we were asked to observe how many litres of fuel had been loaded into separate vehicles at a filling station, the number observed could have a value such as 34.81234; it would very much depend on the accuracy of the measuring instrument and the needs of the person requesting the series of observations. A variable which can have any value is called a continuous variable.

Continuous variables are 'rounded' to a value dictated by the needs of the information system. The rounding process is specified by stating the number of zeros before the decimal point or the number of numbers after the decimal point. For example, a continuous variable can be specified in thousands only (three zeros before the decimal point), and another variable can be specified to two decimal places (for example, 345.87 or 0.56 or 0.08).

Before a continuous variable can be rounded to a specified format, the rounding rules have to be clearly defined. For example, we are asked to round the number 23 478.97583 in thousands only, or the same number to three decimal points. What rules do we assume?

The most common rounding rule is to round up when the digit following the last digit of the required format is a 5 or more, and to round down when it is less than 5.

Rounding the number 23 478.97583 to thousands becomes 23 000 since the next digit representing the hundreds is 4 and is therefore rounded down to zero.

Rounding the number 23 478.97583 to three decimal places becomes 23 478.976 since the fourth digit after the decimal point is an 8 and therefore the 5 in the third digit is rounded up to 6.

One very common exception to the general rule is the classification of ages which are often rounded down whatever the value of the next digit. For example, if you are 18 tomorrow, you will give your age today as 17.

The rounding rule which this chapter will follow is: rounding up for 5 and above, rounding down if less than 5.

Frequency Distributions

When there is a large number of different values of a variable to examine, it is more informative to collect the numbers into manageable groups or classes. Figure 4.5 contains a table showing the number of absentees from work in a large business employing over 25 000 people, during a 100-day period. Absentees are people who have no valid reason for not being at work.

Figure 4.5 – ***Daily Absentees Over a 100-Day Period***

70	63	60	75	83	72	65	75	73	78
61	72	72	67	68	55	71	64	70	65
70	68	77	68	71	75	72	80	63	78
87	74	69	65	70	51	81	69	70	72
81	78	70	72	79	73	73	65	76	68
76	67	71	88	65	72	64	73	88	72
65	70	78	73	56	78	73	79	81	75
82	77	67	71	75	71	69	70	74	66
75	70	70	81	57	62	78	58	72	60
66	72	77	94	77	74	66	73	62	84

The data in Figure 4.5 conveys little or no information. We can see that all the numbers are two digit, and that the range (the difference between the highest and lowest values) is 94–51 which equals 43. Apart from these limits and spread, we can gain no other useful information from the numbers as they are presented in the table.

The best way of processing large sets of numbers is to arrange the numbers in an array which lists the numbers in order, from the lowest value to the highest. This array is then separated into sequential groups or classes, with each variable falling into one particular class.

For example, a small set of arrayed numbers such as:

2 5 7 8 8 9 10 13 15 15 17 20 20 21 22

could be put into classes:

Class A with class range from 1 to 6
Class B with class range from 7 to 14
Class C with class range from 15 to 23

Hence, there would be two variables in Class A, five in Class B and seven in Class C.

Such a classification is untidy and rules are required to give guidance on how best to define classes.

Generally, it is recommended that data is classified into six to twelve equal-sized classes with a class size in multiples of five (for example, 5, 10, 25, 100, etc), but this depends very much on the range of the variables.

The data in Figure 4.5 spreads from 51 to 94, giving a range of 43, which gives an initial indication of the class structure. There are a number of alternatives for splitting this range into six to twelve classes, but possibly nine classes of size five (a range of 45) would be appropriate, and would cover all the data.

It is important when defining classes that each value falls into one class only. This can be done by carefully defining each class limit. For example, a class could be defined as:

60 and above to under 65

This can be condensed to:

60 – u 65

In this case, the class size is five, which is the width of the class limits 60 and 65.

Using this description of class structure means that there is a unique class for each number, but care must still be exercised in order to prevent inaccuracies creeping into the process. For example, if it is known that a continuous variable such as 69.78kg has been rounded to 70kg, it is possible that the number could be included in a class defined 70 to under 75, whereas the number should be properly included in the class 65 to under 70. If such an event is rare, then only a small error is included. However, if the occurrence is common, significant errors could come into the process.

The guiding rule for determining the class structure is that the mid-point of the class, which will be used for representing the mean of all variable values located in that class, is not too dissimilar from the true mean of the numbers in the class.

For example, the numbers 10, 11, 12, 16, 16, are all the numbers located in a class, 10 to under 20. The mid-point of this class is 15. However, the mean value of the numbers in the class is actually 13, and the distortion of the processed data occurs. The distortion would be removed if the class size were adjusted to 10 to under 16, which has a mid-point of 13, but the affect on adjacent classes would need to be examined. Open-ended classes are sometimes useful when data at the top and bottom ends of the range are few and far between. It is often tidier to have open classes such as 75 and over or 50 and under.

FREQUENCY TABLES

The data in Figure 4.5 can be collected into nine classes, as shown in Figure 4.6

Figure 4.6 – ***A Frequency Table: Absentees Per Day***

Class limits	*Class mid-point*	*Frequency*
50 – u 55	52.5	1
55 – u 60	57.5	4
60 – u 65	62.5	9
65 – u 70	67.5	19
70 – u 75	72.5	35
75 – u 80	77.5	20
80 – u 85	82.5	8
85 – u 90	87.5	3
90 – u 95	92.5	1
Total		100

The frequency column indicates the number of values which appear in each class.

Since the total number of values is 100, the frequency column also indicates the percentage of numbers appearing in each class. For example, 19 per cent of the numbers are in the class with limits 65 inclusive up to but not including 70. Figure 4.6 is called a frequency table.

FREQUENCY HISTOGRAMS

The frequency table shown in Figure 4.6 can be displayed by means of a frequency histogram. This is a special type of bar chart, where both the horizontal and vertical axes are measurements. The vertical scale is the frequency, and the continuous horizontal scale is the number of absentees per day. Figure 4.7 shows the resultant histogram. In this case, the horizontal scale markings represent the mid-point values of the classes (for example, 62.5 is the mid-point of the class 60 to under 65).

Figure 4.7 – ***Frequency Histogram: Absentees Per Day***

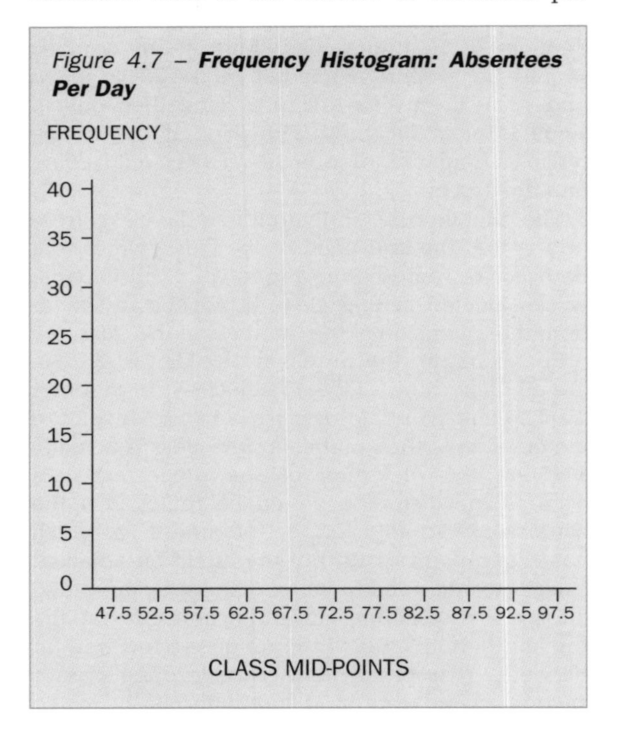

FREQUENCY CURVES

Connecting the mid-point of the top of each column in the histogram by means of a curve results in the frequency curve as shown in Figure 4.8. In drawing this curve, imaginary columns of zero height are presumed to exist at each end of the histogram. This enables the curve to be drawn to the base line at both ends.

Figure 4.8 – ***Frequency Curve: Daily Absentees***

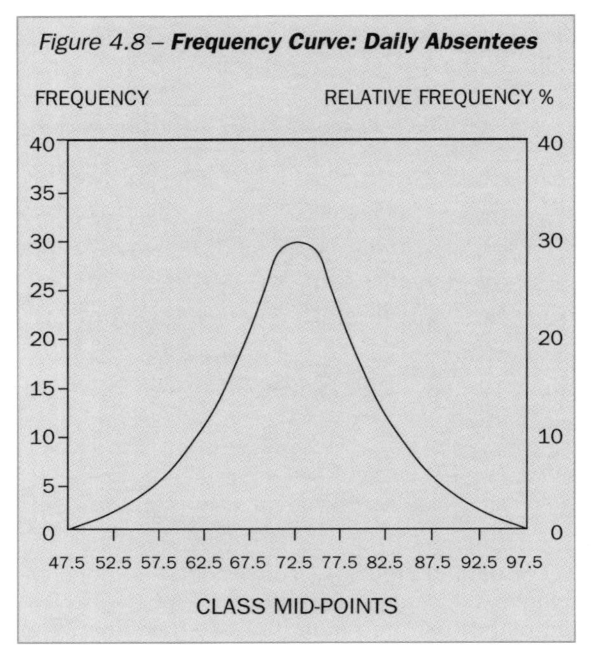

If the vertical scale is converted to relative frequency – that is, using the percentage frequency rather than the actual frequency – then all curves drawn from any data can use the same vertical scale. The horizontal scale depends on the value of the variable being investigated.

Figure 4.9 shows a number of different relative (%) frequency curves without specifying the horizontal scale. The absentee distribution curve is shown as (a). This is a fairly symmetrical curve, with a shape like a bell. Figure 4.9 (b) shows a curve skewed to the left (called 'positive skew'), (c) is skewed to the right ('negative skew'), whereas (d) is double peaked (or 'bi-modal').

Analysing different sets of data can be done by comparing the relative frequency curves of each set. If the absentee distribution is shown by Figure 4.9 (a) and the results of a similar investigation at another organization are shown by Figure 4.9 (d), what initial conclusion would you make? Is it possible that the other organization comprises two separate distributions, with distinctly different characteristics?

Figure 4.9 – ***Frequency Curve Shapes***

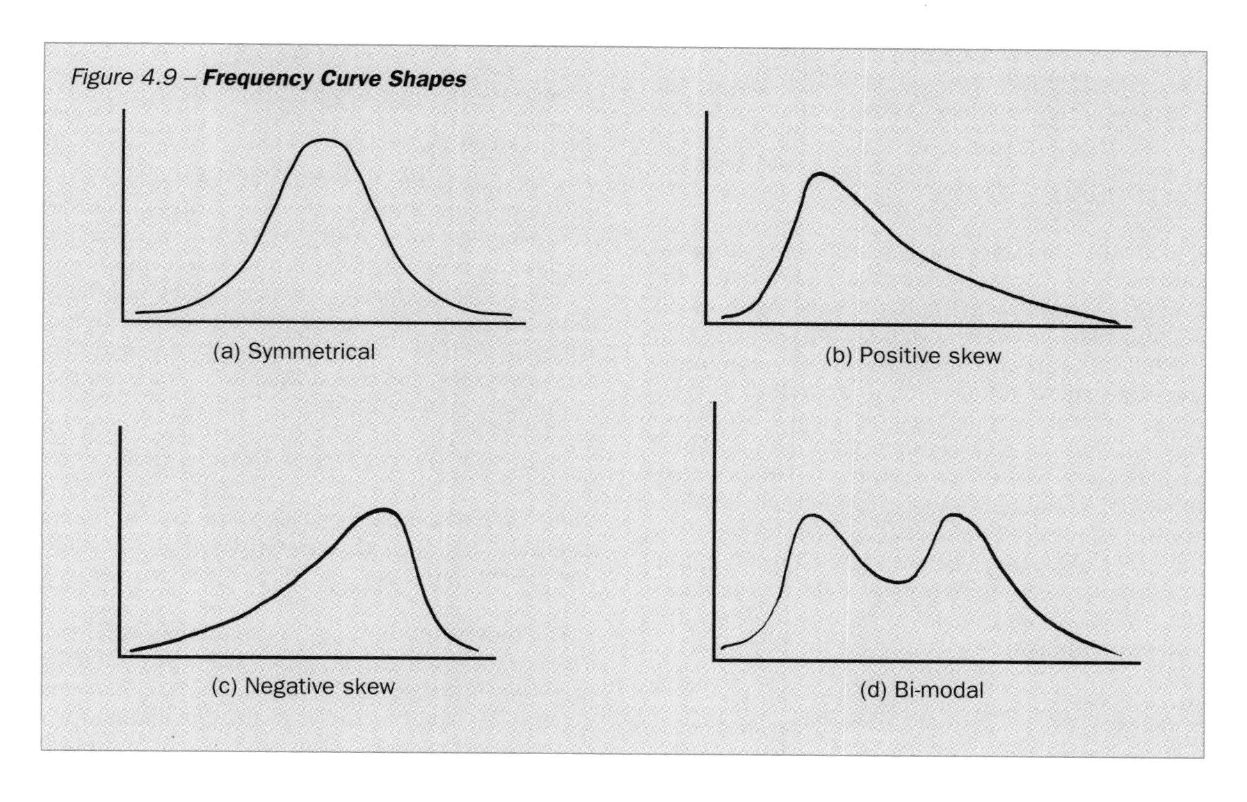

ACTIVITY 4.2

Find a 'service' point. This could be a self-service petrol station or a supermarket, and time how long it takes customers to be served. You may have to ask the manager to give you permission to do this. The service you will be timing has to be defined by you. In a supermarket, it could be the time from the pricing of the first item to the presentation of the bill. In a petrol station, it could be from the time when the driver finishes the filling process by replacing the fuel tank cap to the time the driver returns to the car after paying the bill. See if you can collect at least forty times.

Construct a frequency curve for the times you have collected by producing a frequency table and a frequency histogram. Is the shape of the curve similar to any one of those shown in Figure 4.9?

Repeat the investigation at another, similar service point.

Compare the frequency curves generated by both sets of data. Are they the same or are they different? What comments can you make to explain any significant differences in shape?

Could you use any other methods for presenting the information you have collected? When you have read

KEY POINTS 4.1

- **Pie charts, bar charts and histograms can be used to give meaning to information**
- **Data is either discrete or continuous. Continuous data is rounded to agreed rules**
- **Data classification improves understanding but reduces accuracy since the mid-point of the class is assumed to represent all data values in the class**
- **Classified data is used to construct frequency tables, histograms and curves**

the rest of this chapter, including the section on 'Deciles and Percentiles', come back to this Activity and have another go at answering this last question.

Processing Data

Up to this stage we have transformed numbers into pictures or graphs in order to generate information about the way numbers vary and how different sets of variables can be compared visually.

Processing is the application of a routine to generate more information from data. In business, there are a number of statistics which can be generated to give valuable information. These statistics are concerned with the average values of sets of variable numbers, termed 'measures of central tendency', and also how variable these variables are. Are they only just minutely different from each other, or hugely different? In statistics, the word 'dispersion' is used to measure this variation around the average value.

Measures of Central Tendency

THE AVERAGE

The average of a set of variable numbers measures the 'central value'. However, the average is not unique since there are a number of different averages which are used for different purposes. Consequently, it is important to make sure that the correct type of average is specified in business communications. Unfortunately, society as a whole does not appreciate such niceties and will persist in using the word 'average' when it should be more specific!

The most common averages are the mean, the median and the mode.

THE MEAN

The mean is what most people imply when they say the average. It is the value obtained by adding up all the values of a variable and dividing by the number of variables. The mean age of the people in your class is the sum of all the ages divided by the number of people. The mean value can give a wrong impression if by chance you have an 80-year-old in your class. All the ages must be included in the calculation – even untypical values.

The formula for calculating the mean value ($\bar{X}$) of a set of numbers is given by:

$$\bar{X} = \frac{\Sigma X}{N}$$

where:

Σ = the 'sum of all the . . . ' (and is called the 'sigma' operator)

X = the value of each variable

N = the number of variables in the set

THE MEDIAN

The median is the mid-point of the values of the variable when these values are arrayed in order from smallest to largest. Normally it does not matter too much if there are an even number of people in your class so that an exact mid-point does not exist – the one either side of the middle will suffice. If this is a problem, you can estimate the value from the two mid-values. For example, in the following numbers:

16 16 16 16 17 17 17 17 17 18 18 18 18 80

there is no middle number since there are 14 numbers. But we can see that since the seventh and eighth numbers are 17, the median value is 17.

The most important use of the median is to give a value for the average which is not distorted by extreme information. In the series, the extreme value of 80 is not included in the calculation as is done using the mean. However, if it is important to recognize the extreme values, the median should not be used.

THE MODE

The mode is the value of the variable which occurs most frequently. It is not necessarily unique since often more than one value occurs with the same frequency. If this happens, the mode loses some of its value as information.

In the series:

16 16 17 17 17 17 17 17 18 18 18 19

the value occurring most frequently is 17, which is the mode of this series of numbers.

In another series we might have the following numbers:

16 16 17 17 17 17 17 17 18 18 18 19 19 19 19 19 19

in which the numbers 17 and 19 occur with equal frequency. The series of numbers is called bi-modal with modes of 17 and 19.

The main use of the mode is in estimating the future values of the variable. We could say that the 'average' number of children in a family group is 2, rather than a mean of perhaps 2.453 which has a different meaning. 2 is the mode, the most frequent value and, thus, the most likely family unit to be met. 2.453 is useful for finding out how many bottles of milk have to be provided for 10 000 families if each child drinks one bottle. The answer would be 24 530 bottles.

ACTIVITY 4.3

Read a number of consecutive paragraphs totalling at least 100 words from a daily tabloid newspaper, such as the *Sun* or the *Daily Mirror*. Count the number of letters in each of the first 100 words. Calculate the mean, median and mode values of the average number of letters per word.

Repeat the exercise using an article from a quality or 'heavy' daily paper such as *The Times*, *Guardian* or *Independent*.

Compare the averages from one source with the corresponding averages from the other. Describe the differences in terms of the target readership and editorial policy of the different newspapers (for example, the time the reader may have for reading the paper).

How well are all the numbers in each group represented by these averages? Would full publication of all the numbers give more useful information than just the averages? If so, what information is missing?

Measurements of Dispersion

Dispersion means the spread of numbers around the centre (or average value). An example of a highly dispersed set of numbers might be the times taken by an inexperienced person to thread a needle! An example of a low dispersion of numbers might be the range of times it takes to sign your name. Dispersion is concerned with the degree of variability of a specified measurement.

Dispersion is also a measurement of risk. If an investment yields a wide range of possible returns, from zero to 'double your money', the variable return (or profit) is highly dispersed and would be considered a 'high risk'.

Dispersion is measured by calculating the variance of a set of numbers. The formula for calculating the variance (abbreviated to VAR) is:

$$\text{VAR}(X) = \frac{\Sigma(X - \bar{X})^2}{N}$$

where:

X = the value of the variable

$\bar{X}$ = the mean value of X

N = the number of values of X

Example

The number of bikes sold by five different stores during one week is: 12, 13, 14, 15 and 16.

The symbol X denotes the variable 'sales' at each store and N is the number of stores. Hence, the mean value of this set is $\bar{X}$, where $\bar{X}$ is given by:

$$\bar{X} = \frac{\Sigma X}{N} = \frac{70}{5} = 14$$

The value of VAR (X) is calculated as follows:

Data value X	$X - \bar{X}$	$(X - \bar{X})^2$
12	−2	4
13	−1	1
14	0	0
15	+1	1
16	+2	4
	Total	10

$$\Sigma (X - \bar{X})^2 = 10$$

Hence:

$$\text{VAR}(X) = \frac{10}{N} = \frac{10}{5} = 2$$

Often, the square root of the variance is used as a measurement of dispersion. This measurement is called the standard deviation. The symbol σ is used for this term.

$$\text{Standard deviation of } X = \sigma = \sqrt{\text{VAR}(X)}$$

$$\sigma = \sqrt{2} = 1.414$$

Deciles and Quartiles

It is possible to give information about the dispersion of numbers in an alternative way. If the numbers are arrayed it is possible to describe how many numbers are in the first 10 per cent, the next 10 per cent and so on. This is called a decile analysis. Instead of 10 per cent, we could break the arrayed set into quarters (25 per cent) and state how many numbers are in each quarter, called a quartile analysis. These methods are widely used by the government to illustrate huge numbers to as wide a range of people as possible. For example, a decile analysis of a large set containing the wage level of five million people may indicate that the top 10 per cent (the top decile equal to 500 000 people) of people earned over £400 per week, whereas the bottom decile earned less than £50 per week.

Figure 4.10 – ***Secretarial Salaries***

Salary	*% Secretarial staff*	*Cumulative % staff*
4 000–u 6 000	5	5
6 000–u 8 000	10	15
8 000–u 10 000	11	36
10 000–u 12 000	21	57
12 000–u 14 000	18	75
14 000–u 16 000	13	88
16 000–u 18 000	7	95
18 000–u 20 000	5	100

Descriptive methods such as deciles and quartiles are important in describing how a variable is dispersed or distributed to people who have no knowledge of variances or standard deviations.

Figure 4.10 shows the distribution of yearly secretarial salaries in a large organization. The number of staff earning a salary in each class has been converted to a percentage value. In addition, a column has been included to give the cumulative percentage distribution.

Figure 4.11 shows the information contained in Figure 4.10 by plotting the cumulative percentage population against the mid-point of the corresponding class.

Thus, the top 10 per cent, or top decile, of staff have salaries in the range £16 800 to £20 000. Whereas the bottom 10 per cent, or bottom decile, have a salary in the range £4 000 to £6 850.

Figure 4.11 – ***Cumulative Percentage Curve: Secretarial Salaries***

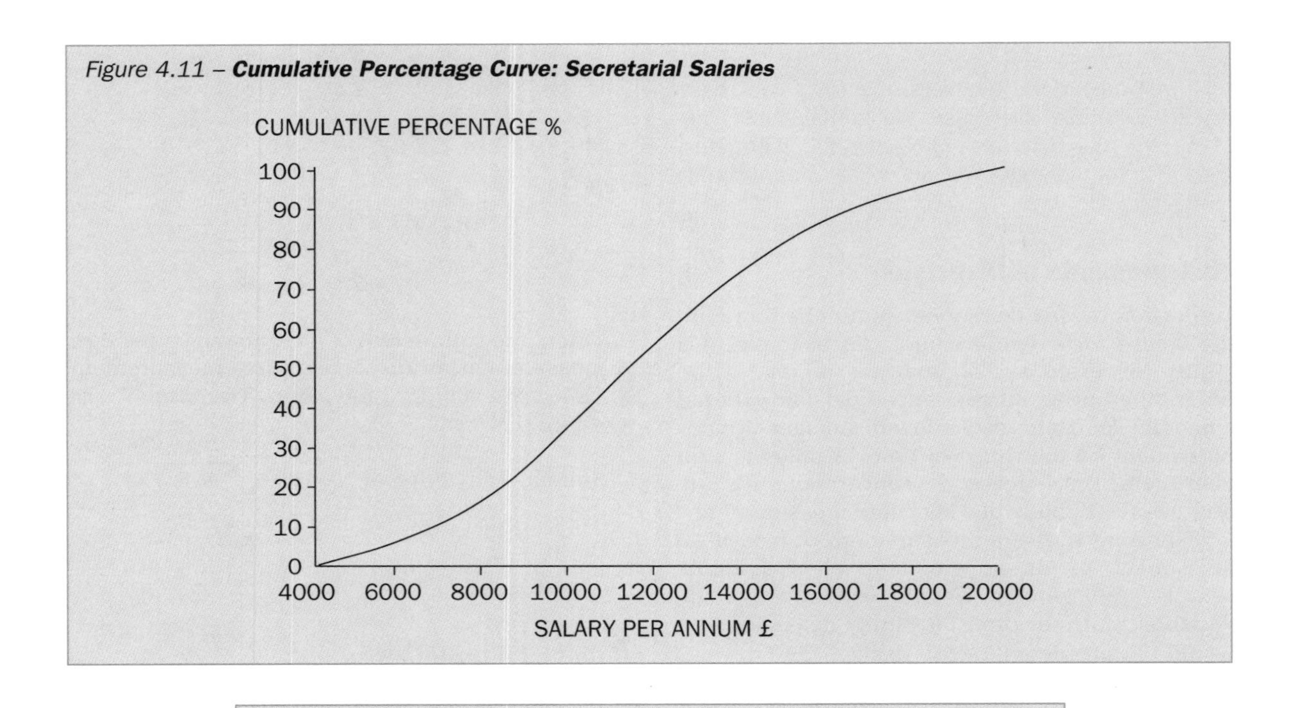

KEY POINTS 4.2

- **There is more than one average value for a set of data**
- **The mean value represents the 'centre of mass' of a set of data**
- **The median value represents the mid-point of arrayed data**
- **The modal value represents the most frequent value of the data**
- **The dispersion of a variable is measured by the variance or the standard deviation**

The Normal Distribution Curve

When there are a large number of reasons why a variable does vary, and the probability of each of these causes remains constant, and not too remote, then the variable will tend to have a relative frequency curve which is symmetrical and bell shaped, as shown in Figure 4.12. This shape occurs very often in business, and is called the normal distribution curve.

An example of a measurement in business which would vary 'normally' is the time taken to type manually a typical one-page business letter. There are many reasons why one letter should take longer to type than another, even a reasonably standard one. Most letters take about five minutes to type, a few as long as ten minutes, perhaps a few as little as one minute. In a normal distribution, most of the values of the variable are located near to the mean. Values of the variable further away from the mean occur with decreasing frequency. In a normal distribution, the rate of decrease is the same for values higher than the mean and for values lower than the mean. The distribution is symmetrical.

Properties of the Normal Curve

If a variable can be shown to vary 'normally' or assumed to vary 'normally', there are important properties of the normal distribution curve which can be used to help understand the variable. These properties relate to the area under the curve between points on the horizontal scale.

Calculation of the standard deviation of the data enables the horizontal scale to be transformed from a direct measurement of the variable (for example, time) to a non-dimensional scale indicating how many standard deviations any value is from the mean value. The name given to this new scale is the standard deviate, and is often referred to by the symbol Z.

For example, say a variable is normally distributed with:

Mean value	$\bar{X} = 15$
Standard deviation	$\sigma = 3$

A small table can be constructed to show this transformation, where:

$$Z = \frac{X - \bar{X}}{\sigma}$$

Value of X	$X - \bar{X}$	*Value of Z*
6	–9	–3
9	–6	–2
12	–3	–1
15	0	0
18	3	1
21	6	2
24	9	3

Since the normal curve is symmetrical, the mean (the 'centre of mass'), the median (the central number) and the mode value (the most frequent value) all have the same value of 15. This is equivalent to Z = 0.

Theoretically, the normal curve never quite touches the Z axis, and this is called 'asymptotic'. However, to all intents, contact is made around Z = ±4.

The properties of the normal curve relate to the areas in the curve between different values of Z.

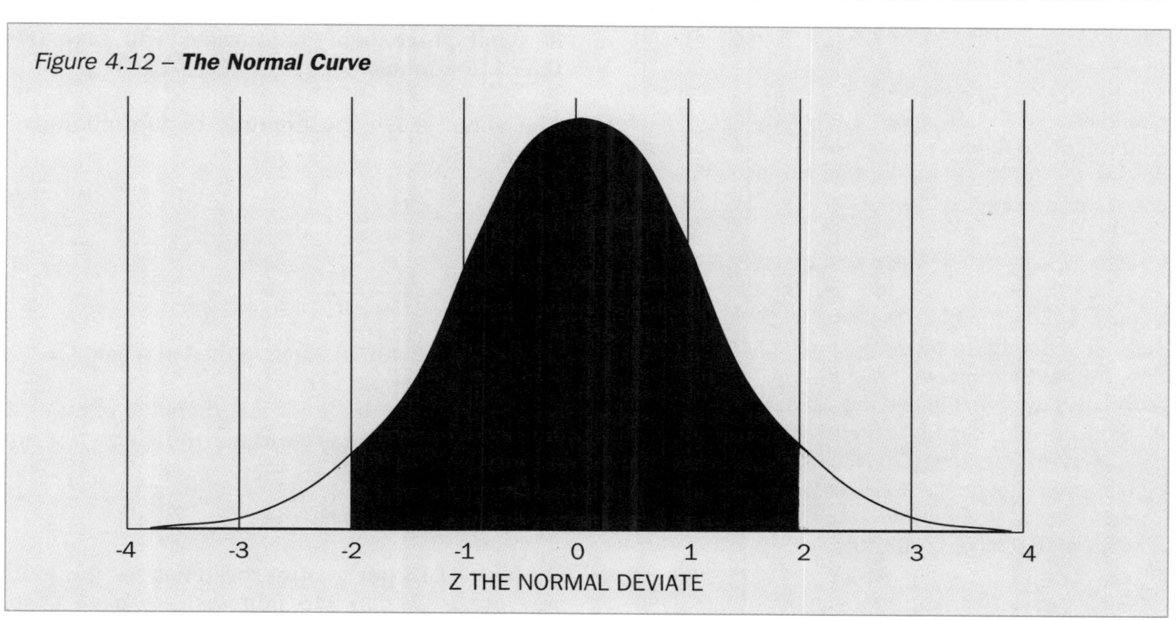

Figure 4.12 – ***The Normal Curve***

The most important values are as follows:

- The area between Z = +2 and Z = –2, shown shaded in Figure 4.12, contains approximately 95 per cent of the total area bounded by the curve and the Z axis
- The area between Z = +3 and Z = –3 contains approximately 99.75 per cent of the total area.

Since the total area between the curve and the Z axis contains 100 per cent of the information, or all the values of the variable, then :

- 95 per cent of the values of a normally distributed variable lie within ±2 standard deviations from the mean. This is the most important attribute of a normally distributed variable
- Similarly, approximately 99.75 per cent of all the values lie within ±3 standard deviations of the mean

This result enables the standard deviation of an assumed normal distribution to be estimated reasonably accurately. Since nearly all the values lie in a range of 6 standard deviations (+3 to –3), then approximately:

$$\text{Standard deviation} = \frac{\text{variable range}}{6}$$

Assume that a variable, such as the weekly demand for a stock item, varies normally and that the highest likely demand is 240 items per week and the lowest demand is 180. The range is therefore 60 items, and an estimate of the standard deviation of weekly demand is given by:

Standard deviation = 60/6 = 10 items per week

ACTIVITY 4.4

It is reasonable to assume that a variable is normally distributed, in the absence of any information to the contrary, if experience suggests a large number of causes for the variability, and each reason has a low chance of occurrence.

Repeat Activity 4.2. Measure the time taken for a 'service' to be given – that is, the time to pass through a 'check out' or the time to serve fuel. Measure at least thirty times and calculate the mean time. Repeat the measurements, but this time write down also why you think the time for consecutive times was not constant. From at least a total of one hundred recordings, including your initial thirty, construct a frequency table and frequency curve. To save some time, share your investigation with a number of friends or colleagues.

What conclusions can you draw from your investigation?

Using the Normal Curve

Appendix B contains a table of values of the areas in the tail of a normal curve. These values enable us to calculate the proportion of variables contained within any specified range.

Example
The time taken to travel by train to London from Norwich is assumed to be normally distributed, with a mean of 110 minutes and a standard deviation of 5 minutes.

1. What percentage of journeys will take longer than 120 minutes?

The first step is to transform the value 120 to the Z value using the formula:

$$Z = \frac{X - \bar{X}}{\sigma}$$

$$Z = \frac{120 - 110}{5} = 2$$

Using this value of Z, the area in the tail of the curve in Appendix B is shown as 0.0228, which is 2.28 per cent. This tail covers all the values of the variable which exceed Z = 2, and therefore the answer to the question is 2.28 per cent (or perhaps 2.3 per cent, to avoid criticism of false accuracy).

You can deduce from the values in Appendix B that 95 per cent of the values of the variable are contained within the range Z = ±1.96, as opposed to the approximation of Z = ±2. This small error is often ignored in business applications since the magnitude of error is small.

2. What percentage of journeys will take less than 115 minutes?

The value of Z corresponding to 115 minutes is given by:

$$Z = \frac{X - \bar{X}}{\sigma}$$

$$Z = \frac{115 - 110}{5} = 1$$

From Appendix B, the area in the tail when Z = 1 is 0.1587 or 15.87 per cent.

Therefore, all the times less than 115 minutes is represented by the area under the curve but not in the tail, as follows:

100% – 15.87% = 84.13%

Since 84.13 per cent of the times for the journey are less than 115 minutes, we have some realistic measurement of the likelihood of the next journey time taking less than 115 minutes.

3. What percentage of journeys will take between 120 minutes and 115 minutes?

We have already shown that the percentage of journeys greater than 120 minutes is 2.28 per cent. Therefore, the percentage of all journeys less than 120 minutes is given by:

$$100\% - 2.28\% = 97.72\%$$

We have also shown that the percentage of journeys less than 115 minutes is 84.13 per cent.

Therefore, the percentage of journeys less than 120 minutes but not less than 115 minutes is given by:

$$97.22\% - 84.13\% = 13.09$$, or sensibly rounded to 13%

As has been implied by the answers to these questions, the point of the exercise is not to confirm information generated from the past, but to give an understanding of expectations for the future on the assumption that a variable is normally distributed. This is covered in more detail in the next section on probability and expectations.

Probability

We all have some idea on the likelihood of an event happening. We often use subjective or non-numerate expressions to communicate our feelings about this probability. For example, we could say that Jill is a 'dead cert' for winning the 100m sprint this year (high probability), or there is 'no way' that Jack will pass his examinations (very low probability), or there is an 'evens chance' of the football match ending in a draw.

In business, it is important to be more precise when communicating probability statements so that it means the same to all recipients. Statements such as 'quite likely' or 'reasonably certain' have different values to different people. Probability is measured by a scale from zero (0) to unity (1), where 0 means that the event will definitely not happen and 1 means that the event will definitely happen.

Typical examples of business probabilities are:

- The probability of an error being found in the accounts is 0.01
- The probability of the sales exceeding 20 000 units next month is 0.90
- The probability of taking longer than five weeks to do the job is 0.2
- The probability of rejecting a batch of production is 20 per cent

On the basis that 1 or 100 per cent represents a certainty and that 0 represents the opposite, the values of the probabilities given above, whether they are expressed as proportions or percentages, should give you a 'feeling' for the outcome.

Some estimations of probability are based on logical reasoning, called *a priori* probability. For example, the probability of rolling a 'six' with one throw of a die is 1/6 or 'one in six'. Another example is the probability of drawing an ace from a full pack of well-shuffled cards. The *a priori* probability would be four chances in fifty-two, or 1/13.

Many estimations of probability in business are generated from experiments or past experience. This is called prior probability.

The prior probability of an outcome is calculated by observing the number of occurrences of the outcome and dividing this by the number of observations.

For example, if 30 per cent of past sales are to people younger than twenty-one, the prior probability is 30 per cent or 0.3 that any future sale will be to a person under twenty-one. This can be represented by the formula:

$$\text{Probability of sale to under 21} = \frac{\text{Number of sales to under 21s}}{\text{Total number of sales during period}}$$

The evidence was that during the period, 400 sales were made, and of these 120 sales were made to people under twenty-one. Therefore, the prior probability is given by:

P(sale to u21) = 120/400 = 0.3 or 30%

Example

A production manager, given the responsibility of establishing a reasonably constant flow of work in a clothing factory, is worried about the variability in the time taken to fold, pin and pack a

Figure 4.13 – ***Time to Pack a Shirt***

Time in seconds	Frequency	% Frequency	Probability
11	40	8	0.08
12	40	8	0.08
13	60	12	0.12
14	60	12	0.12
15	70	14	0.14
16	80	16	0.16
17	100	20	0.20
18	50	10	0.10
Totals	500	100	1.00

man's shirt into a cardboard box. Observations of five hundred packing operations have been made and the times recorded. These times are shown in Figure 4.13 (previous page). Figure 4.14 shows the same information in a cumulative format, where the cumulative frequency column indicates the number of shirts packed at the corresponding time or less. For example, in Figure 4.14, 40 per cent of the shirts were packed in a time of fourteen seconds or less.

Figure 4.14 – ***Time to Pack a Shirt: Cumulative Values***

Time in seconds	*Cumulative frequency*	*% Cumulative frequency*	*Probability of time or less*
11	40	8	0.08
12	80	16	0.16
13	140	28	0.28
14	200	40	0.40
15	270	54	0.54
16	350	70	0.70
17	450	90	0.90
18	500	100	1.00

The estimated, or prior, probability of an operator taking any specified time is the frequency expressed as a proportion rather than a percentage (see Figure 4.13). For example:

- The probability of an operator taking thirteen seconds to pack a shirt is estimated at 0.12 because this time occurs 12 per cent of the time
- The probability of an operator taking seventeen seconds to pack a shirt is 0.20
- The probability of an operator taking sixteen seconds *or less* to pack a shirt is 0.70 (Figure 4.16)
- The probability of an operator taking more than sixteen seconds to pack a shirt is 0.30. (The reason for this is that since the probability of taking sixteen seconds *or less* or taking *more than* sixteen seconds must be a certainty (probability equals 1), then the probability of taking more than sixteen seconds is 1 minus 0.7)

Expectations

If it is possible to estimate the probability of an event occurring, we can calculate the expectation of the number of events happening over a large number of attempts.

For example, assume the probability of selling a set of books is 0.01. This probability was perhaps calculated from historical figures by finding out how many people were asked to buy a set of books, and how many people actually bought a set. If we now plan to approach two hundred people in a week on a door-to-door selling operation, we can say that:

Expected number of sales
= prob. of sales $\times$ no. attempts to sell
= $0.01 \times 200 = 2$ sets of books

In the above example, the outcome was either a sale or a refusal. Expectations can also be calculated from group data by using the following formula:

$$\text{Expected value} = \Sigma\,(T \times P\,(T))$$

Where:

T = value of the outcome
P(T) = the probability of the outcome

By applying this formula to our previous example of packing shirts, we can work out the expected time to pack a shirt, as follows:

Time in seconds (T)	*Probability P(T)*	*T × P(T)*
11	0.08	0.88
12	0.08	0.96
13	0.12	1.56
14	0.12	1.68
15	0.14	2.10
16	0.16	2.56
17	0.20	3.40
18	0.10	1.80
	Total	14.94

The expected time to pack a shirt is, therefore, 14.94 seconds.

And Or Probabilities

The words 'and' and 'or' have mathematical meanings in information processing and are often called 'logic operators'. Although the meanings of these words are what you would expect, they can also be represented by symbols.

The 'and' operator can be replaced by the multiply symbol $\times$. The 'or' operator can be replaced by the addition symbol +. This is the start of a subject of mathematics called Bolean Algebra which will not be pursued in this text. Bolean Algebra is the logic language of computer theory.

Example
A factory production manager has recruited two hundred staff to work on an electronic circuit board assembly line. The end product is used in the construction of a colour television set. The work comprises picking up small coloured electronic components from a box situated to the

Figure 4.15 – ***Probability Tree***

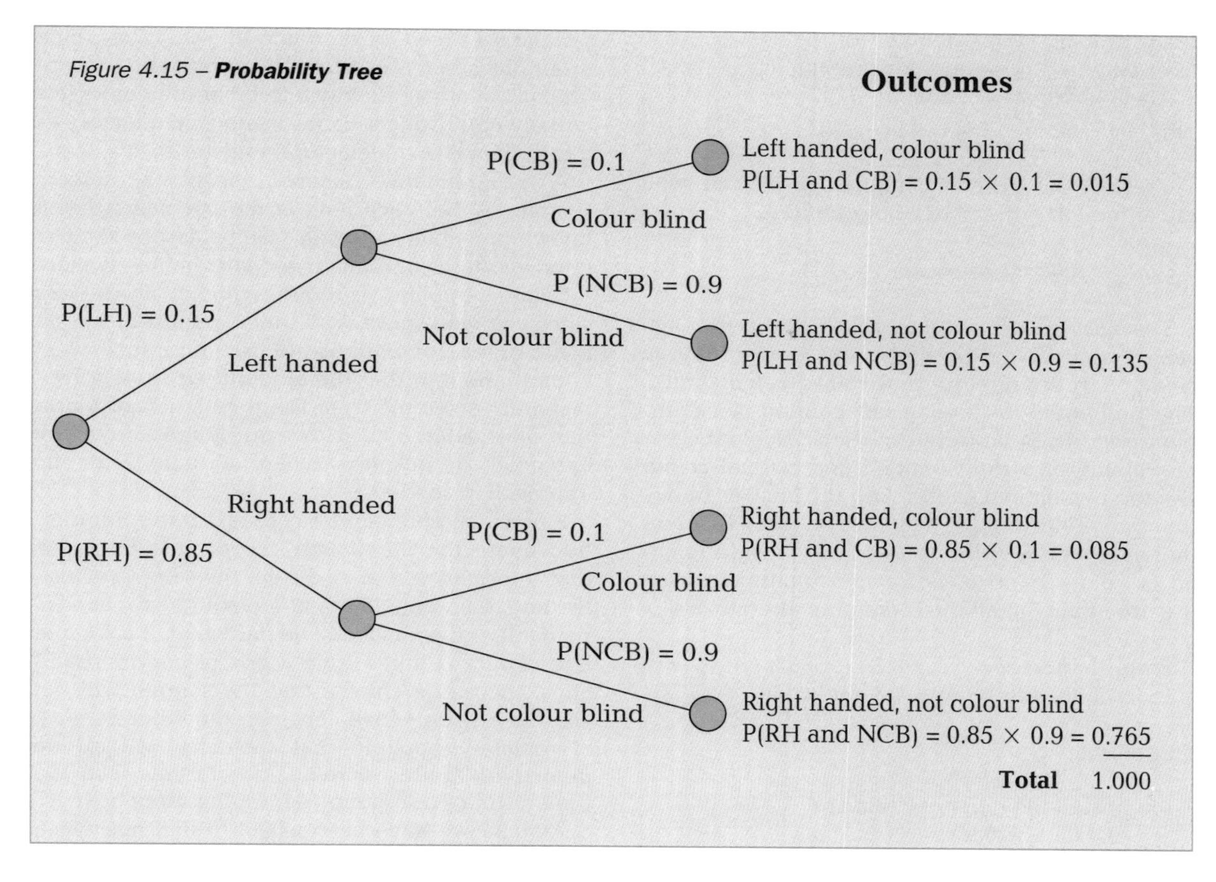

right side of the assembler, and accurate, quick work is required.

The factory manager later realizes, to his horror, that although good eyesight and dexterity tests were part of the recruitment procedure, test for colour blindness and knowledge of whether the staff member was left handed or right handed were missing.

How the manager is going to cope with the problem is another matter, and you might have some thoughts on it. What the manager wants to know now is how many of the two hundred recruits are expected to be either colour-blind *or* left handed, and how many are expected to be colour-blind *and* left handed. The manager has found out that 10 per cent of people are colour-blind to some degree, that 15 per cent of people are left handed to some degree, and that there is no connection between being left handed and being colour-blind.

Probability (left handed) = 15% or 0.15
Probability (colour-blind) = 10% or 0.10

The probability of being both left handed *and* colour blind is:

Prob(l'hand) *and* Prob(c'blind)
= Prob(l'hand) × Prob(c'blind)
= 0.15 × 0.1
= 0.015 or 1.5%

Therefore the expected number of recruits who are both left handed and colour-blind is:

Expected (l'hand *and* c'blind)
= 0.015 × 200
= 3

The probability of a recruit being left handed *or* colour-blind requires a little thought, a logical challenge which often occurs in probability calculations. The temptation is to assume that the answer is just the sum of the basic individual probabilities, but this is not the case. We should really restate the problem as:

> What is the probability of a recruit being left handed, whether or not he/she is colour-blind or the probability of being colour-blind given that the recruit is right handed. This latter statement is a conditional probability statement.

Restated like this, we have the following:

Prob(l'hand or c'blind)
= Prob(l'hand) *or* Prob (c'blind *and* r' hand)

= 0.15 + (0.1 × 0.85)
[note: Prob(r'hand) = 1 – Prob(l'hand)]
= 0.15 + 0.085
= 0.235

Therefore, the expected number of recruits who are either left handed or colour blind is:

0.235 × 200 = 47 recruits

The answer to the second part of the problem can be approached by a different logical route (a common procedure in probability calculations). The probability of finding left handed or colour-blind recruits is no different from calculating the probability of a right handed and normal colour sighted person and subtracting the answer from 1 (the probability of a 'dead cert'). This assumes that everyone is either left handed or right handed or colour-blind or not colour-blind. We want the probability of all the remaining alternatives.

Prob(r'handed) = 0.85 (or 85%)
Prob(not colour blind) = 0.9 (or 90%)

Therefore:

Prob(r'handed *and* not c'blind)
= 0.85 × 0.9
= 0.765

Therefore:

Prob(l'handed *or* c'blind) = 1 – 0.765
= 0.235 as before

Figure 4.15 (previous page) shows a probability tree, the 'branches' of which signify a particular state. The outcomes are all the possible combinations of states, such as right handed and colour-blind (abbreviated to RH and CB in the diagram). Down the right hand side of the diagram are all the possible combinations with the probability of each outcome. For example, the probability of being right handed and colour blind is shown as a unique branch and is 0.85 × 0.1 = 0.085, the product of the individual states.

Hint: You have probably(!) found that this section on probability needs quite a lot of concentration. It is often possible to use probability trees to clarify the logic of the problem.

Sampling

It is often the case that there is not enough time, money or information available to find all the members of a set and, therefore, a representative sample is chosen. In sampling, the set from which a sample is taken is called the population. A population is not necessarily a number of people; it is equally applicable to items in stock in a factory as it is to names on an electoral register.

A representative sample means a random sample, so that each item in the population has a known probability of being selected for the sample. Random samples are discussed later in this chapter.

Some sampling is done without much fuss since common sense is all that is required. We sip a cup of tea, for example, to find out if it is sweet enough, hoping that the amount we sip is a representative sample from the population of tea in that particular cup! However, there are many examples in business where a more scientific approach is needed.

Since a sample cannot contain all the information about the population, there must be a risk that information deduced from the sample is misleading. Of a population of a box of paper clips, 5 per cent of the clips may be defective. If a sample size of fifty is taken from a box of one thousand clips, there is a chance that the sample will not contain any defective clips. On the other hand, it is remotely possible that the fifty will all be defective. Quite extreme conclusions can be drawn from these samples from the same box!

Assume we have been asked to find out which political party people intend to vote for in the next election. It would be too expensive and take too long to ask everybody listed in the electoral rolls. So we could ask a sample of about two thousand voters for their opinions. The answers would give an indication of voting preference but not an absolute answer since there must be a risk in accuracy in any sample. The smaller the sample, the greater the risk that the sample is not a fair one.

In a population of equal numbers of males and females, it would be most unlikely that ten males and ten females would always appear in a random sample of twenty from the population. In order to make the sample more accurate, a stratified sample survey could be undertaken so that the proportion of males in the sample was the same as the proportion of males in the population. Stratified samples are very common when surveys are conducted through street interviews. If the planners of the activity know that in a city, 25 per cent of the population is aged over sixty-five, they will try to make sure that 25 per cent of those interviewed are aged over sixty-five.

SAMPLES IN BUSINESS

Samples are used in business for two purposes:

- To estimate the statistic for a defined group or population by using a corresponding sample statistic

- To check whether or not a group still has a known statistic – this is called testing an hypothesis.

An example of the first use is when a company takes a large sample of bottles of salad cream from its production line (may be about fifty bottles) and measures the weight of the contents of each bottle. This will give an accurate estimate of the mean contents weight of all bottles being filled. The machine operator can alter settings on the machine to control the 'fill weight' until a further large sample gives an estimated mean which is acceptable. This process is called 'machine setting'.

An example of the second use is when the company checks whether the contents of a bottle of salad cream being filled at a rate of a hundred bottles per minute contains more or less than the acceptable 'fill weight'. A sample size of about five would be appropriate for this analysis.

More detailed explanations of estimation, hypothesis testing and sample sizes are given later in this chapter.

Random Numbers

A random number comprises digits, each of which has an equal probability of occurrence. Each digit in the range 0 to 9 has a probability of 0.1. We can select how many digits to use in constructing the random number.

For example, say you want to generate a random number in the range 000 to 999 – a range of 1 000 numbers including the 000. You can do this by writing the numbers 0, 1, 2, 3, 4, 5, 6, 7, 8 and 9 on ten identical cards. Next, shuffle the pack and select the top card. Say it is a 4. Replace the card into the pack.

Shuffle the pack and again turn over the top card. This time it is a 3. Repeat the procedure once more. This time it is a 0.

Your random number is 430.

Computers generate random numbers either by measuring minute voltages above a radio active source (an exact physical phenomenon) or more commonly by using an approximate formula, which is accurate enough for most applications.

ACTIVITY 4.5

A useful and simple way of generating your own random numbers is to use an area telephone directory of private subscribers. Open the directory at random, start at the top left hand column and copy down the last two digits of the private subscribers's telephone numbers. Avoid business names or names in bold type since there is a chance that these subscribers have chosen a special number, perhaps ending in 00, to make it easier for customers to remember.

List your two-digit numbers in a continuous sequence of thirty numbers across the page, with a gap after every fifth number, and thirty rows with a gap after every fifth row (similar to the format shown in Figure 4.16). You will have a total of nine hundred individual numbers. Since there is no reason why any one digit should occur more regularly (or less regularly) than any other, you would expect to have ninety of each single numeral from 0 to 9 (inclusive). How many have you got?

You can use this random number table in any way you like, but in order to avoid using the same set of numbers you must have a random start. Do this by closing your eyes and marking a point on the paper with a pencil. The nearest numeral to your mark gives you the row number, and the second nearest the column number.

For example, say we want a selection of three-digit random numbers, and with the 'blind pencil' test we hit the number 45. Therefore, our three-digit random number starts at the fourth row and fifth column, which is the number 7 and the random number sequence is 790. If we had arranged to go down the sheet, the next number is 654 and so on. When we get to the bottom of the sheet, we start again at the top with 722, 245 and so on. This selection of numbers is shown in Figure 4.16

Figure 4.16 – ***Random Number Selection***

56078	54**772**	23098	12376	54387	6...
68094	73**245**	09853	71674	93457	7...
12936	12097	58775	62857	54626	4...
9081**7**	**90**517	97382	37498	23741	2...
5647**6**	**54**872	38234	76523	47652	3...
0912**3**	**98**762	34876	18773	45876	1...
7681**6**	**38**273	46867	24870	18763	6...

Sequence of three-digit random numbers:
790, 654, 398, 638, 722, 245 . . .

Now you can use your random number table to select eleven matches in a football pools competition from a list of, say, fifty-eight. Make a random start and select the next two-digit random numbers from a pre-planned sequence. If the first digit is a zero, say 07, this means the number is 7. If the two-digit number is greater than 58, ignore it, and use the next one. If the number has already been selected, select the next one until you have eleven different random two-digit numbers in the range 01 to 58.

Random Samples

Random numbers should be used for selecting random samples if there is a danger of taking a biased sample. A biased sample is one that does not allow each member of a population to have a known chance of being selected for the sample. A good example of a biased sample are the apples used for display on a market stall. These apples are usually the best available and often do not reflect the quality of apples kept in the back and sold by the stall holder!

Random numbers are also used to select a random time for observing and recording the activity of a person or group of people. The activities recorded are a sample of the 'on going' activities.

For example, assume we wish to find out what percentage of time a person is working or not working. We would construct a random sequence of times and observe the activity. This can be done by selecting two-digit random numbers and using these values as the 'between observation' times in minutes. Typical random numbers could be: 34, 07, 23, 96, 45, 21 . . .

If the work starts at 9.00am, the first recorded observation would take place at 9.34am, the next 7 minutes later at 9.41am, the next 23 minutes later at 10.04am and so on. The proportion of observations when the person is working is an estimate of the total working time.

Estimating the Mean

Before a random sample is taken to estimate a population statistic, it is necessary to state the accuracy limits and confidence required for the estimate.

Suppose we want to estimate the mean bursting pressure for a type of motor tyre (a good example of a situation where sampling is necessary, since the product has to be destroyed to measure the pressure). The accuracy required would be suggested by the design department – on this occasion, assume that it is ±1 per cent of the bursting pressure. The confidence required is a way of measuring the risk due to sampling, and is usually expressed as a percentage (for example, 95 per cent).

The requirement is to find out the mean bursting pressure of the tyre type with a 95 per cent confidence and an accuracy of at least ±1 per cent. This means that the information given by the sample test has only a 5 per cent chance of being wrong (or, if you prefer, a 95 per cent chance of being right). In probability terms, this would be expressed as a 0.05 chance of being wrong (or a 0.95 chance of being right).

95 per cent confidence in an answer in decision-making in business is quite common, unless there is a danger to life. In this case, the smallest risk possible would be taken.

The formula for estimating the mean value from a random sample is given by:

$$\bar{X} = \bar{x} \pm \left(\frac{2\sigma}{\sqrt{n}} \right)$$

where:

$\bar{X}$ = population mean
$\bar{x}$ = sample mean

The part of the formula, σ/n, is called the standard error of the mean, where:

σ = the population standard deviation
n = the number in the sample

The value of 2 in the formula represents a confidence of 95 per cent. This comes from the properties of the normal curve, and a theorem called the Central Limit Theorem, which states that the means of samples are distributed normally with a standard deviation equal to a standard error.

Since the standard deviation of the population is not known, the standard deviation of the sample is assumed to be a good approximation, providing a good representative sample is used.

Hence, 95 per cent of the sample means are within ±2 standard errors of the true mean.

Returning to our tyre example, an initial sample of thirty-six measurements are taken (36 randomly selected tyres are destroyed), and from this sample can be found the mean value and the standard deviation of the bursting pressure. Let us assume the sample statistics are:

$\bar{x}$ = 250kg/sq.cm
σ = 6kg/sq.cm

Therefore:

$$\bar{X} = 250 \pm \left(\frac{2 \times 6}{\sqrt{36}} \right)$$
$$= 250 \pm 2$$

The accuracy is within the 1 per cent allowed. If it were outside these limits, more samples would have to be tested to increase the sample number. Accuracy can only be improved by taking larger samples. Similarly, confidence can only be increased by taking more standard errors. A value of 3 instead of 2 would increase the confidence to 99.75 per cent .

This would have the effect of changing the formula to:

$$\bar{X} = \bar{x} \pm \left(\frac{3\sigma}{\sqrt{n}} \right)$$

Substituting the test values into this formula yields:

$$\bar{X} = 250 \pm \left(\frac{3 \times 6}{\sqrt{36}}\right)$$

$$= 250 \pm 3$$

This now exceeds the accuracy requirement and can only be reduced by a larger sample. Note that with a fixed sample, confidence only increases by widening the accuracy limits of the estimate (for example, from 250 ± 2 to 250 ± 3).

Estimating the Proportion

Estimating the proportion of the population which has a specified attribute (for example, a desire to purchase a particular product) can also be estimated from a random sample. The formula for calculating the population proportion, P, is:

$$P = p \pm 2 \times SE\ (prop)$$

where:

SE(prop) = the standard error of the sample proportion
p = proportion of sample
the value '2' = a confidence of 95 per cent

$$SE(prop) = \sqrt{\frac{p(1-p)}{n}}$$

n = number of items in the sample

This formula is not of acceptable accuracy if either the sample size is less than thirty or the sample proportion is in the range 0.4 to 0.6. In the latter case, larger samples have to be taken. In general, when estimating proportions, samples of at least one hundred are typical.

Example
2 500 voters were randomly selected from the electoral roles and 10 per cent implied that they would vote for the White Party in the forthcoming election.

The 95 per cent confidence estimate of the total electoral population who will vote White is given by:

$$\text{Population proportion} = p \pm 2\sqrt{\frac{p(1-p)}{n}}$$

$$= 0.1 \pm 2\sqrt{\frac{0.09}{2\,500}}$$

$$= 0.1 \pm 0.012$$

The conclusion is that the best estimate of the total population proportion who will vote White is 10 per cent plus or minus 1.2 per cent, or in the range 8.8% to 11.2%

ACTIVITY 4.6

Conduct a survey to determine what percentage of students would favour a four-term academic year with each term lasting about ten weeks. Restrict your survey to a randomly selected group of at least one hundred fellow students. You could share this survey with others and pool your results.

The answer to your survey question must be a straight 'Yes' or 'No'. From the results of your survey, estimate the population response.

What are the limitations and sources of inaccuracy in your survey?

How could you make the results of your survey more accurate to reflect all students? How much do you think that an accurate survey would cost?

Do you think there is a connection between the costs of a survey and the accuracy of it?

Testing an Hypothesis

Instead of trying to estimate the mean value of a variable, it is possible to do the sums backwards! We can suggest or, in statistical terms, make an hypothesis, that the mean value is 250kg/sq.cm in our tyre-bursting example, and then take a sample to test this hypothesis. When testing an hypothesis, a much smaller sample is needed than when estimating a population statistic.

Hypothesis testing is a relatively complex mathematical process, but basically it takes the estimation formula and asks the question:

> 'I know that the bursting pressure of tyres is a variable, and I think the mean value is 250kg/sq.cm which is acceptable. A small sample of five tyres gave a mean of 240kg/sq.cm. Is this difference between expectation and sample mean too big to be explained by sampling error?'

If the answer is yes, the hypothesis that the mean bursting pressure is 250 kg/sq.cm has to be rejected, and another sample of thirty or so tyres has to be tested to find the new mean estimate.

Exactly the same reasoning can be applied to the proportion estimation. For example, it might be suggested that 5 per cent of the output of a factory is defective.

KEY POINTS 4.3

- **When a sample is taken to estimate a statistic of a population, an error is introduced (a risk of being incorrect) and this is measured by the 'standard error'**
- **The probability that the population statistic estimated from a sample is within a specified range is called the 'degree of confidence'**
- **Samples taken in order to estimate population statistics must be randomly selected**

This hypothesis can be checked by taking a small sample and finding out if the sample proportion lies within an acceptable range, or if there is a significant difference between the suggested proportion and the sample proportion.

Testing hypotheses such as these is called significance testing.

Forecasting

There are two extreme types of business. The managers of the first type continuously try to forecast what is likely to happen over the next week, month, year and possibly the next five-year period. On the basis of these estimates, the managers plan activities to try to make sure that their objectives in business are met. Managers involved in rapidly changing high technology businesses, such as computer manufacturing, are of this type. It is essential that change is anticipated continuously or the business will become 'out of date' and fail.

The managers of the second type do not forecast at all. The business progresses from day to day, and there is very little planning. Businesses of this type do not change much, but in an unchanging business environment, survival is quite possible because operations are performed very efficiently. Such businesses like insurance companies, banks, fish and chip shops and even schools existed quite happily without much forecasting in the 1970s and 1980s. However, there are not many businesses or organizations today which can survive without some form of forecasting. Schools must now try to forecast the likely number of pupils in the future; fish and chip shops must forecast 'take away' eating habits and likely competition; and insurance companies must forecast likely increases in thefts from cars and other rapidly changing statistics.

There are two main methods of forecasting. The first method, and the only one we shall consider in this text, is extrapolative forecasting. This method analyses past performance of a variable and extends, or extrapolates, this performance into the future. A 10 per cent increase in sales each year over the last five years, for example, will be extrapolated as a 10 per cent increase in the future.

The other method of forecasting is one which analyses associations with factors that might change. A good example is the possible existence of a relationship between an individual's personal income and the purchase of a package holiday. Although past performance might suggest that package holidays were increasing at, say, 20 per cent per year, a prediction that rising unemployment will reduce personal incomes by 10 per cent could indicate a fall in purchased holidays. This information is essential for planners of package holidays who might easily be misled by constantly increasing annual holiday figures. Factors such as these are considered more fully in another book within this series, *The Business Environment*.

Extrapolative Forecasting

Extrapolative forecasting techniques are used for both short-term (months ahead) and long-term (several years ahead) forecast. The restricting assumption behind extrapolative forecasting is that a pattern is found by analysing past performance and it is assumed that this same pattern will take place in the future.

Extrapolative forecasts are at risk when major changes in customer behaviour occur in the short term. It is doubtful if patterns in international trade found by analysing performance in the early 1990s will be repeated in the mid-1990s due to immense changes in the political world.

The main difference between short-term and long-term forecasting is the consideration of trend – the projected growth or decline rates. In the short term, a stationary forecast is predicted – that is, the forecast for next month and the month after, and the month after that, are the same until more information is available (seasonal factors apart). Long-term forecasting includes a trend rate which in many cases is assumed to be a straight line growth or decay. This trend rate could be expressed as a 10 per cent growth.

Seasonal factors which indicate significant regular increases and decreases at certain seasons of the year are included in both short-term and long-term forecasts.

Moving Averages

The forecasting technique of moving averages is very simple. If the value of a variable such as demand for sales is known over, say, the past five weeks, then the average of these sales is used as the forecast for future short-term sales.

The word 'moving' means that when a new, and most recent, demand is known, a new average is calculated by including the new figure and discarding the oldest figure.

Example
On 1 July, the previous five weekly sales in a supermarket of jars of a popular brand of instant coffee were listed. Week 5 is the latest week's figure.

Week number	*Sales in 000s*
1	13
2	15
3	12
4	14
5	16

The average sales over the five weeks is:

(13 + 15 + 12 + 14 + 16)/5 = 70/5 = 14

Consequently, on 1 July the weekly sales forecast for the next few periods is 14 000 jars.

On 8 July, the sales figures for Week 6 were available, showing sales of 18 000 jars. This means that a new average has to be calculated for the latest five weeks. The new average over weeks 6 to 2 is:

(15 + 12 + 14 + 16 + 18)/5 = 75/5 = 15

Therefore, on 8 July the weekly sales forecast for the next few weeks is 15 000 jars.

An easy way of calculating the moving average after the first calculation is simply to add to the old total the difference between the new sales value and the discarded sales value. In the coffee jar example above, the new value was 18 and the old value was 13, so 5 is added to the old total of 70.

The decision that needs to be made when using the moving average forecasting method is how many values to include in the average calculation. Five as in the last example, or six, seven or four. The greater the number of terms in the average calculation, the less sensitively the moving average forecast responds to sudden changes in demand. The smaller the number of terms in the average calculation, the greater the response.

This sensitivity to individual values can be shown in the table below, where the sales figures of coffee have been increased to a period spanning twelve weeks. The moving average at Week 12 can be calculated over both a twelve-week period and compared with that for a four-week period.

Week number	*Sales in 000s*
1	13
2	15
3	12
4	14
5	16
6	18
7	13
8	11
9	16
10	16
11	18
12	18

The average over 12 weeks = 180/12 = 15

The average over 4 weeks = 68/4 = 17

The twelve-week forecast of 15 000 jars a week tends to smooth out the fluctuations over Weeks 7 and 8. Whereas the four-week forecast of 17 000 jars tends to give more importance to the increases which have occurred recently. More numbers making up the moving average tend to smooth out short-term, perhaps seasonal, variations. An example would be the sudden increase in the sales of ice-cream over a 'mini' heatwave. Such a short-term increase would not influence the long-term forecast significantly. If the moving average comprised only two time periods, the ice-cream manufacturer could mistakenly double production!

Z Charts

Z charts are very useful annual control and forecasting displays. They can best be described by means of an example. Figure 4.17 contains a

Figure 4.17 – ***Monthly Sales of Cars***

Month	*Monthly sales (units)*	*12-month total*	*Cumulative total*
January 90	140		
February	120		
March	120		
April	160		
May	180		
June	150		
July	80		
August	220		
September	190		
October	180		
November	170		
December	160	1870	0
January 91	160	1890	160
February	150	1920	310
March	140	1940	450
April	190	1970	640
May	200	1990	840
June	170	2010	1010
July	130	2060	1140

table of monthly sales demands over an eighteen-month period of car sales by a large area distributor. Figure 4.18 shows an incomplete Z chart for the year 1991. Figure 4.17 also shows the rolling twelve-month total sales and the cumulative sales so far for 1991.

In Figure 4.18, the top line shows the rolling annual total sales, which is the sales of the previous twelve-months at the end of each month. The diagonal line is the cumulative sales so far over 1991, and the lower line is the sales of each month.

Figure 4.17 shows how car sales increased dramatically in August as a result of the new registration rules. However, the twelve-month moving total does not reflect a significant increase in August since it always has only one August value included in its calculation.

Although the Z chart in Figure 4.18 only presents part of 1991, a reasonable indication is provided of expected sales for the rest of the year. These expectations are shown by the dotted line. Seasonal variations in sales do not distort longer-term forecasts.

Time Series Analysis

Time series analysis (TSA) is the name given to a long-term forecasting technique which examines components of past information in significant detail, and extrapolates these components into the future. It is often used to analyse the components of past data of demand. These components are:

- The long-term cycle, C, which is a measurement of the rise and fall of annual sales over a number of years. Many industries have found that business follows a regular cycle of high/low activity spanning five to fifteen years.
- The trend, T, which is the steady, straight line sales growth or decline
- The seasonality, S, which reflects the rise and fall of sales over a twelve-month period due to seasonal factors (such as Christmas, etc)
- The irregularities, I, which indicate the likely error, or differences, between predicted and actual performance

Figure 4.18 – ***Z Chart of Car Sales***

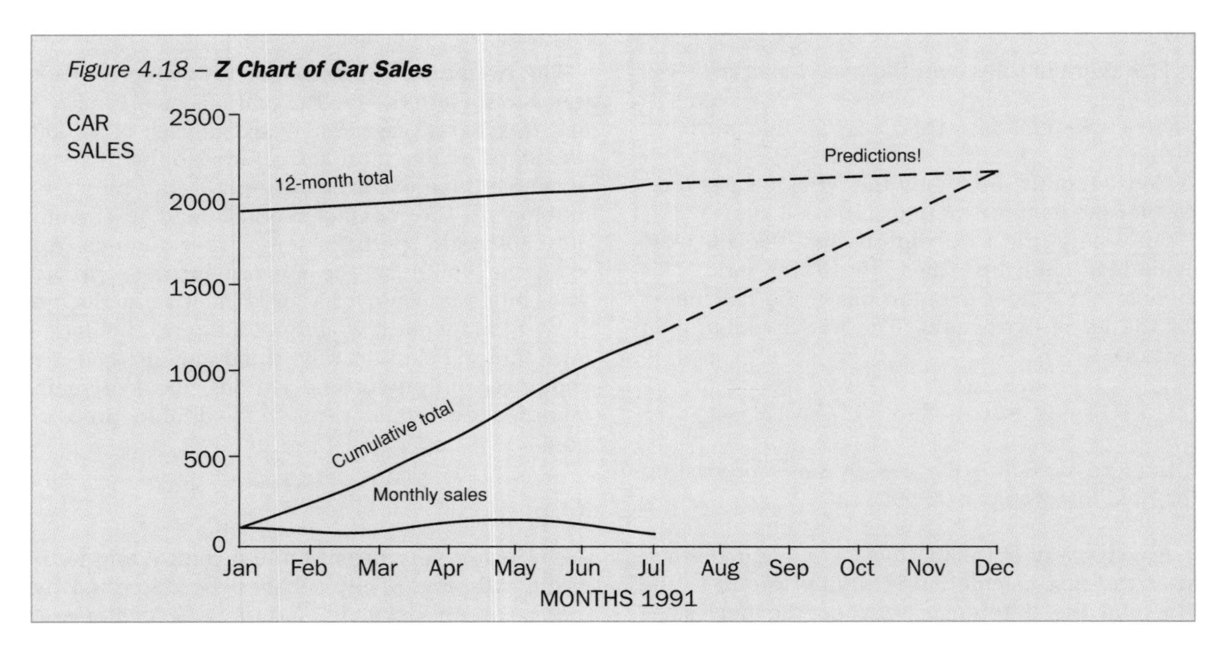

TSA suggests that a forecast, F, for any period in the future is given by a combination of these components, as follows:

$$F = C \times T \times S \times I$$

In the following text, we will assume that long-term cyclic behaviour, seasonal factors and short-term irregularities are small components compared with the trend, T. That is, we will assume:

$$F = T$$

where T is equivalent to a straight line demand or a constant growth or decline rate.

SCATTER GRAPH

Before any analysis is undertaken to understand time series data, it is important to construct a scatter graph to 'get the feel' of the data and to be reasonably confident that a prediction can be made from the data supplied. A scatter graph is simply the data plotted on a graph without any assumptions on how the data points are to be connected.

Many forecasting methods are based on a straight line trend equation, and it is important to see if a straight line is indeed a realistic base for further work. Figure 4.19 shows the trend line drawn through the scatter of data points. If the straight line were withdrawn, this would leave the initial scatter graph.

CALCULATING TREND

A common method for calculating the trend, T, is by using the method of 'least squares' (see below) to determine the line which best fits the data supplied.

The equation of a straight line is given by:

$$Y = a + b X$$

where:

Y is the dependent variable (for example, sales)
X is the independent variable (for example, time)
a is the intercept on the Y axis
b is the slope of the line

This is illustrated in Figure 4.19.

The principle of the method of 'least squares' is to find the line which best fits the data point according to the following test:

Plot the data points on an x–y graph and draw any line adjacent to the data points. Measure the vertical distance between a data point and the line. Square this distance and repeat for all data points. Add up all these squared values. Reposition the line so that this sum of the squares is a minimum.

The test is carried out theoretically using calculus, but this technique is outside the scope of this book. The results of these calculations give the following equations:

Figure 4.19 – ***The Straight Line***

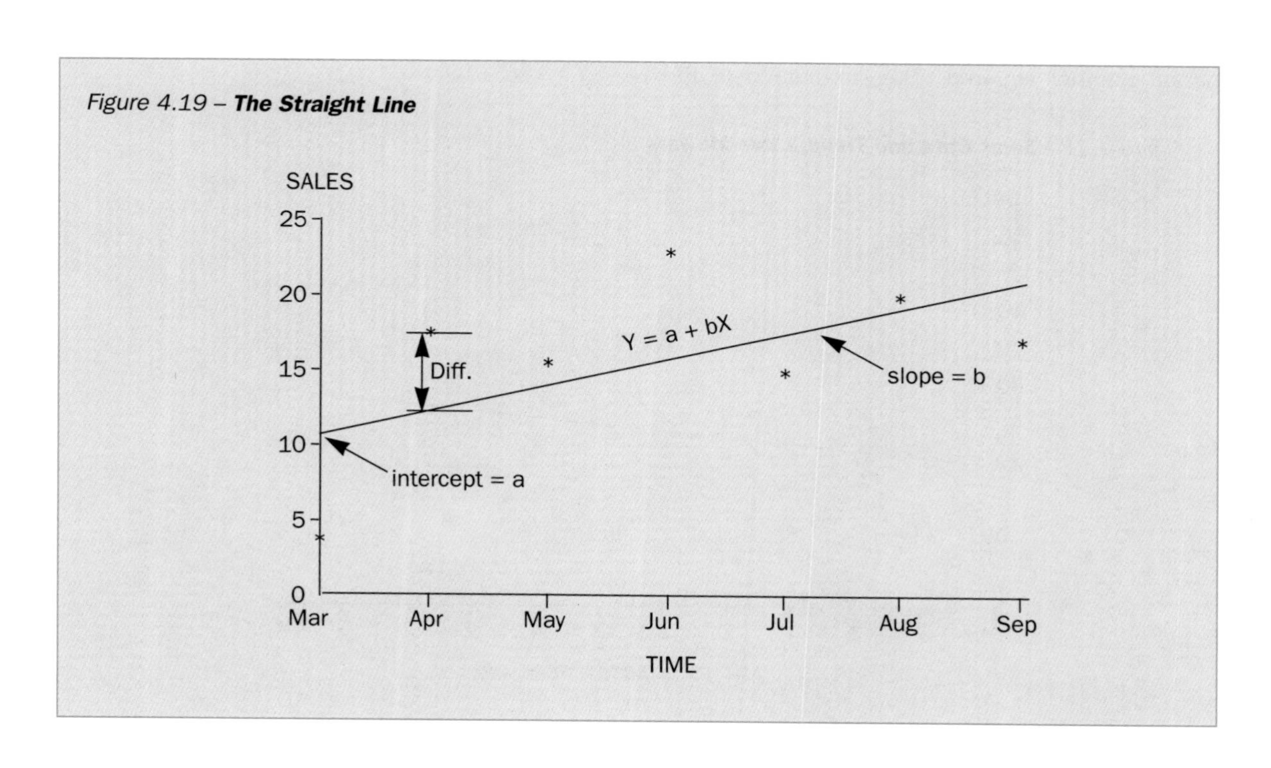

$$\Sigma Y = an + b\Sigma X$$
$$\Sigma XY = a\Sigma X + b\Sigma X^2$$

where:

ΣY is the sum of all the Y values
ΣX is the sum of all the X values
ΣXY is the sum of all the XY values
ΣX^2 is the sum of all the X^2 values of independent results
n is the number of independent results

Figure 4.20 – ***Quarterly Sales of Lawn Mowers***

Year	*Quarter*	*Sales (Y) (units)*	*Period ref: (X)*	*X.Y*	*X*
1	1	15	1	15	1
	2	30	2	60	4
	3	20	3	60	9
	4	10	4	40	16
2	1	20	5	100	25
	2	35	6	210	36
	3	25	7	175	49
	4	15	8	120	64
3	1	25	9	225	81
	2	40	10	400	100
	3	30	11	330	121
	4	20	12	240	144
Totals		285	78	1975	650

Example
Figure 4.20 shows the sales of lawn mowers for each quarter of a year over the last three years, together with extra columns showing the values of sales multiplied by period number and the period number squared. The summation of the appropriate columns gives the following results:

n =12, $\Sigma X = 78$, $\Sigma Y = 285$, $\Sigma XY = 1975$ and $\Sigma X^2 = 650$

By inserting these values in the 'least squares' equations, we get:

$$285 = 12a + 78b \quad \text{(i)}$$
$$1975 = 78a + 650b \quad \text{(ii)}$$

These simultaneous equations are solved by multiplying (i) by 78 and (ii) by 12 to obtain:

$$22230 = 936a + 6084b \quad \text{(iii)}$$
$$23700 = 936a + 7800b \quad \text{(iv)}$$

Subtracting (iii) from (iv) gives:

$$1470 = 1716b$$

Hence:

$$b = 1470/1716 = 0.86$$

By inserting this value in (i) we get:

$$285 = 12a + 66.8$$

Therefore:

$$a = (285 - 66.8)/12 = 18.2$$

Hence, the trend equation Y = a + bX is given by:

$$Y = 18.2 + 0.86X$$

Figure 4.21 – ***Sales Data and Trend: Lawn Mowers***

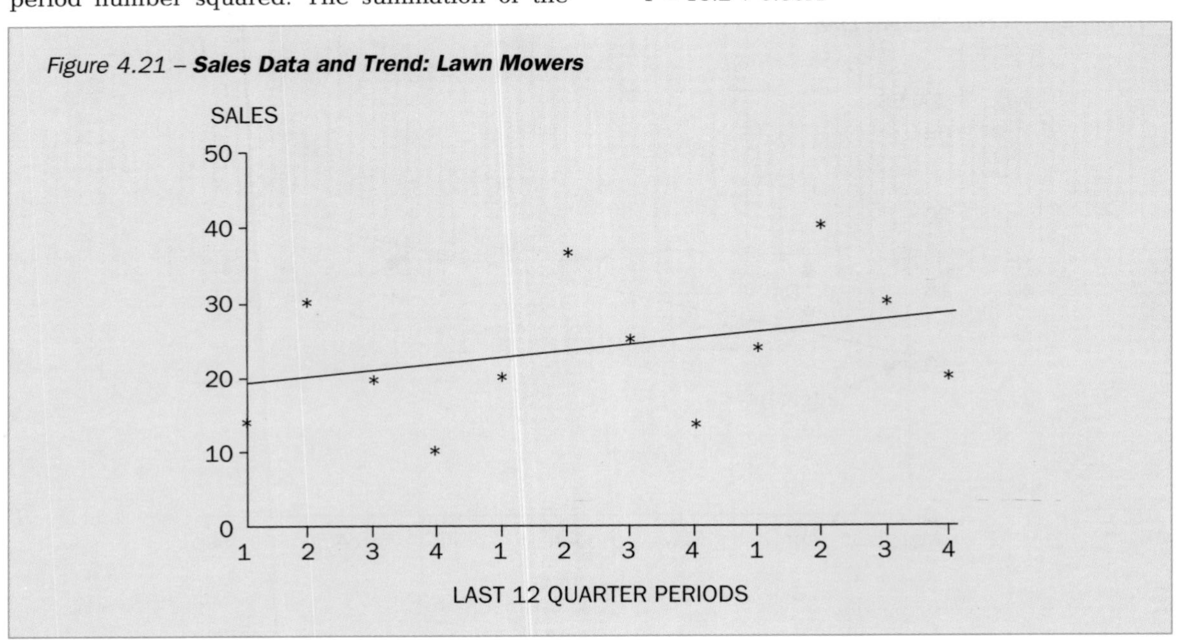

The trend equation will give the 'base' forecast for any period in the future.

For example, the base forecast for the last quarter of next year (period 16) is:

$$Y = 18.2 + 0.86 \times 16$$
$$= 18.2 + 13.8 = 32 \text{ units}$$

The base forecast is not adjusted for any long-term cycle or seasonal factor.

Figure 4.21 is a graph showing the sales data and the calculated trend equation.

ACTIVITY 4.7

In the UK, Post Offices sell an inflation-linked bond so that savers can make sure that their money does not decrease in value over the savings period. In order to give such savers an indication of the current value of their savings, a list of the inflation indices over the last few years is displayed in the Post Office. The index started with a value of one (100 per cent), and each month a new index is displayed.

Find the last twelve monthly inflation indices as published by the government and calculate the trend line.

Using the trend line, estimate the inflation index in six months's time.

Use the trend line to calculate the indices you used in the first twelve months. What is the difference between each actual index and the calculated value? This difference is called the 'error'. What is the mean error and the standard deviation of the error?

Is the 'error' normally distributed? If it is approximately normal, calculate the error on all estimates of the inflation index within a confidence of 95 per cent or ±2 standard deviations.

The Cost of Information

Time costs money in business, and so generating information means increasing costs. For example, most of this chapter involved you in a significant amount of time. How much would it have cost you to employ someone to do this work for you? The costs incurred have to result in better information for better decisions and eventual savings higher than the costs involved.

An example of costly information is obtaining market research information from an external agency. Charges of the order of £5 000 may have to be paid for information on the likely sales of a product over the next twelve months. Is it worth it? To find out, you must compare how much profit would be made using an internal guess and how much profit would be made using an external expert. This is not easy.

Often, when consultants are asked to give advice on the running of a business, they find that very little relevant information is available on such topics as the time for carrying out a job, the cost of a product or even the amount of material in stock. Such basic information will need to be generated before any valid advice can be supplied by the consultant. There has to be a minimum investment in information to operate any business efficiently.

KEY POINTS 4.4

- **Forecasting solely on the basis of past information is only justified if the environment within which the data was collected remains fairly constant**
- **The moving average method of forecasting is sensitive to the number of periods within the 'average' calculation**
- **A Z chart is a useful and important way to present visually data for forecasting, which is not sensitive to seasonal variations**
- **The trend factor is the most important part of long-term forecasting**
- **Information costs money and, therefore, its value must be greater than the cost of generation**

EXAM PREPARATION

DATA RESPONSE QUESTIONS

1 Observations have been made on the time taken to serve customers at a Post Office counter queue. The results of the two hundred observations have been recorded in a frequency table:

Time of Service	*Frequency*
under 1 minute	15
1 min – under 2 min	34
2 min – under 3 min	93
3 min – under 4 min	33
4 min – under 5 min	20
over 5 minutes	5

(a) Draw the relative frequency histogram for this data.
(b) Draw the approximate relative cumulative frequency curve.
(c) What is the probability that a customer will have a service time in excess of 3 minutes?

2 The sales of swimming costumes at a large London departmental store are recorded weekly as follows, with week number 1 being the first week in April:

Week no.	*Sales of costumes*
1	234
2	216
3	209
4	320
5	298
6	435
7	567
8	590
9	789
10	876
11	990
12	854

(a) What is your forecast for the sales of costumes in week 13, using:
(i) a four-period moving average method
(ii) a straight line trend calculation.
(b) Which of these different techniques do you think is most appropriate and why?

3 A sample of two hundred readers was taken by a newspaper editor to find out how many agreed with a national referendum in favour of an European Community resolution concerned with whale hunting. Readers were invited to phone in, and the first two hundred were questioned. The results published by the newspaper showed that 80 per cent were in favour of a complete ban on whale hunting.

(a) Do you think the sample selected was a fair sample or did it contain bias?
(b) On the assumption that the sample was fair, what is the estimation of the population's percentage in favour of banning whaling at a 95 per cent confidence level?

4 The data given below refer to a manufacturing company, XYZ Ltd. In 1970 the company employed a workforce of 2 000, but by 1983 this number had dropped to 1 000.

Figure 1 – Analysis of XYZ Ltd workforce, by occupation

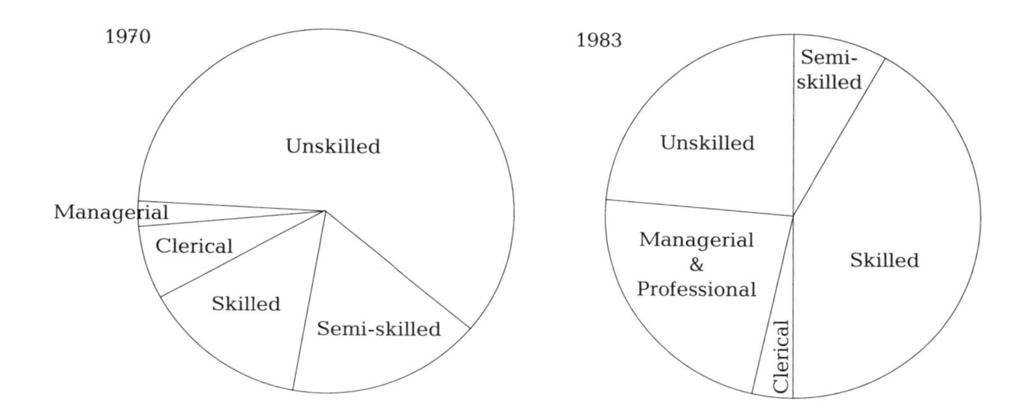

Figure 2 – Indices of Real Net Investment and Gross Profits for XYZ Ltd

(Industry average = 100)

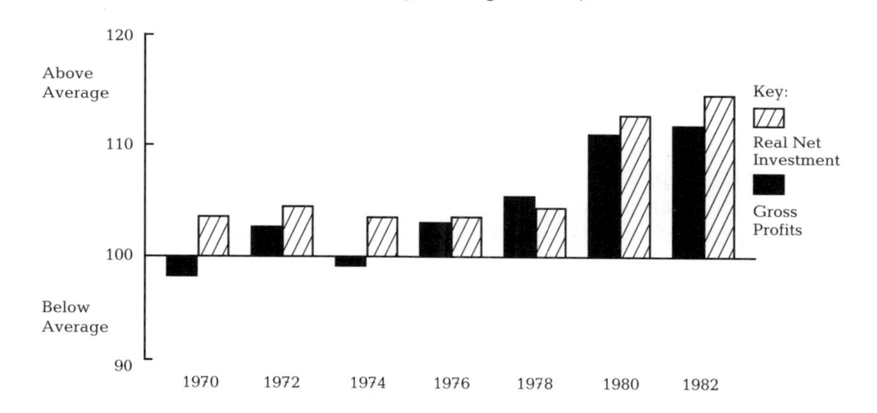

(a) State **one** advantage and **one** disadvantage of presenting data in the form of a pie chart. (4)
(b) Give **one** reason why the pie charts in Figure 1 are of different sizes. (3)
(c) Describe briefly the changes that have taken place in Company XYZ between 1970 and 1983. (5)
(d) Using the data given above, state and explain **one** possible reason for the decline in the number of people employed by XYZ Ltd. (4)
(e) Outline **three** problems the company might have faced as a result of the changing occupational structure of the workforce. (9)

(AEB June 1985)

5 **(a)** (i) Three companies, A, B and C, have roughly the same number of employees, and the distributions of their salaries have the same modes. The distributions for A and B are approximately normal, but that for B has half the standard deviation of that for A. The distribution for C is positively skewed, but with the same range as that for A. Sketch the three distributions using the same axes for all three. (3)
(ii) If you were an ambitious 'high-flier', which company would you prefer to work for and why? (2)

(b) The distribution of A's salaries is shown below:

Salary range (£)	*No. of employees*
7 000–7 999	9
8 000–8 999	33
9 000–9 999	285
10 000–10 999	433
11 000–11 999	192
12 000–12 999	39
13 000–13 999	9
	1 000

(i) Estimate the median salary.
(ii) The mean salary is £10 500 and the standard deviation is £1 000. (There is no need to confirm these values). Determine whether the distribution is approximately normal. What assumptions have you made? (8)
(iii) If the total wage bill for the same size of workforce one year earlier was £10 000 000, calculate the percentage increase in total salaries over the year. (3)

(Cambridge June 1988)

7 Cooksons plc is a large Midlands-based company producing and distributing packet food stuffs. The company was set up in the 1920s and is proud of the fact that it has kept abreast of current developments in the industry. Its current product range includes condiments and spices, baby foods and instant convenience snacks which merely require the addition of boiling water.

One problem faced by Cooksons is the cost of the sales force. The following distribution relates to the number of miles travelled by Cookson salesmen in one week.

Miles travelled	*Number of salesmen*
500–599	10
600–699	20
700–799	24
800–899	0
900–999	26
1000–1099	40
1100–1199	24
1200–1299	0
1300–1399	26
1400–1499	0
1500–1599	20
1600–1699	10

(a) Assuming the distribution is approximately normal, find the probability of a salesman travelling:
(i) between 600 and 1150 miles
(ii) between 500 and 600 miles
(iii) between 1150 and 1600 miles. (23)

(b) (i) Explain how Cooksons can use this information to determine the likely costs of its salesforce. (5)
(ii) What limitations may arise from reducing the data to one or two measures? (5)

Cooksons are concerned that some lorries are underutilized. The following figures show the percentage capacity used on seventy journeys by Cookson lorries.

37	82	70	58	25	24	81	12	68	32
78	87	27	58	57	67	51	63	29	38
52	43	61	76	61	72	87	67	89	52
59	74	30	57	53	67	60	78	51	71
18	26	76	27	90	29	88	76	23	84
28	76	87	48	76	64	80	55	81	91
11	12	79	90	99	33	51	45	66	96

(c) Compile a grouped frequency distribution from which you can estimate the following:
(i) the average percentage capacity used
(ii) the proportion of journeys which are unprofitable, if 65 per cent is the smallest profitable load. (18)

(d) How can Cooksons use this information and what can they do to improve the situation? (14)

8 The following data has been obtained by the Marketing Manager of a Midlands Safari Park. The data relates to the number of miles travelled from home by people using the Park.

Frequency	*Miles travelled to reach Safari Park*
10	1–10
20	11–20
50	21–30
40	31–40
30	41–50
25	51–60
15	61–70
10	71–80

(a) Construct a histogram to illustrate this data. (12)
(b) According to the data, which of the groups contains the modal distance travelled to the Safari Park? (2)
(c) What percentage of visitors travelled more than fifty miles to reach the Safari Park? (3)
(d) State **two** methods that might have been used to collect this information. (2)
(e) The above information is an example of 'primary' data. State and explain **one** advantage and **one** disadvantage of this over 'secondary' data. (4)
(f) State **two** promotional methods that could be used to encourage more local people (ie, those living within a twenty-mile radius) to visit the Safari Park. (2)

(AEB June 1988)

ESSAYS

1 What are the value of opinion polls, when on the basis of the 1992 General Election, the polls seem to get it so wrong?

2 'A picture is worth a thousand words' is a well-known statement. Do you think that it is also true to say that 'a histogram is worth a thousand numbers'?

CHAPTER 5

Operations in Business

▷ ▷ **QUESTIONS FOR PREVIEW** ▷ ▷

1 *How does a business produce goods and services of the right type and quantity?*

2 *How does a business produce goods and services on time?*

3 *Why is it necessary to stock materials and how much should be stocked?*

Information for Operations

IN TODAY'S modern office there is a lot of equipment ranging from facsimile (fax) machines to quite complicated computer systems. In advanced manufacturing businesses, there are less people employed in the production process and more computer controlled machines such as industrial robots. Consequently, the differences between the modern service business and the modern manufacturing business are getting less and less.

One major difference which exists between service and manufacturing businesses is that in a service business the customer often forms part of the operations environment. For example, in a service business such as an accountancy practice, an accountant gives advice to a client in his or her office. In manufacturing businesses the customer usually only sees the product when all the manufacturing and delivery systems have been completed. Another significant difference is that in manufacturing businesses the operation's process is to 'add value' to materials. For example, an engineering business adds value to a sheet of steel plate by forming it into the shape of a car body. In service businesses, the operation (the giving of the service) does not usually add value to any material.

Although some differences between service and manufacturing do exist, the term 'operation' will be used to mean either a manufacturing or service activity. The term 'production' will also be used to include both the production of goods and the supply of services. However, it will occasionally be necessary to refer to manufacturing systems or service systems specifically.

What is Production?

It will be useful if we examine the full production process by considering the preparation of something which happens daily. Could you, for example, prepare an evening meal for paying customers?

Before answering this, there are a few other questions that need to be answered:

- Do you know exactly what is required and when?
- Do you know how to produce what is wanted?
- Do you have the appropriate skills?
- Do you have the right resources (materials, equipment, etc)?
- Do you have the time?

Exactly the same questions must be answered if the problem was to produce an airliner or clean an office or write a book. In a business, the cost of production must also be calculated with an emphasis on producing goods as efficiently as possible and consistent with the requirements of the customer. The customer should be delighted with the goods or service provided.

What is Required?

Suppose an engineering company has been asked to produce twenty identical excavator buckets for fixing to large mechanical diggers, as shown in Figure 5.1. The customer has provided a set of drawings showing the design of each bucket and the type of materials to be used in their construction. The customer has asked for all buckets to be delivered within six weeks.

What the customer has supplied is a product specification. The drawings and any notes relating to them specify exactly what is required. Information is presented as follows:

- **Dimensions:** each dimension on all the drawings is clearly shown and given a tolerance (for example, 25cms ± 0.1mm). Any curve shown on the drawing is marked with the exact centre and radius
- **Materials:** all materials of construction are given the correct type specification, which in the UK would be a British Standard (BS) reference, or to a European (EN) reference, or to an International (ISO) reference. In many cases, all three references are identical. Any small components, such as bolts or screws, would be fully described in a parts list, giving a supplier's reference or a standard reference
- **Assembly:** if parts of the bucket have to be bolted or welded together, the drawings would show how this should be done – how tight the nuts on the bolts have to be, and what type of welding has to be performed
- **Finish:** the drawings would also clearly show the smoothness of finish required on metal parts, and the type and specification of finishing materials (such as paint)

The product specification is more than a list of ingredients. It concentrates on what the finished product should look like in addition to specifying

Figure 5.1 – ***An Excavator Bucket***

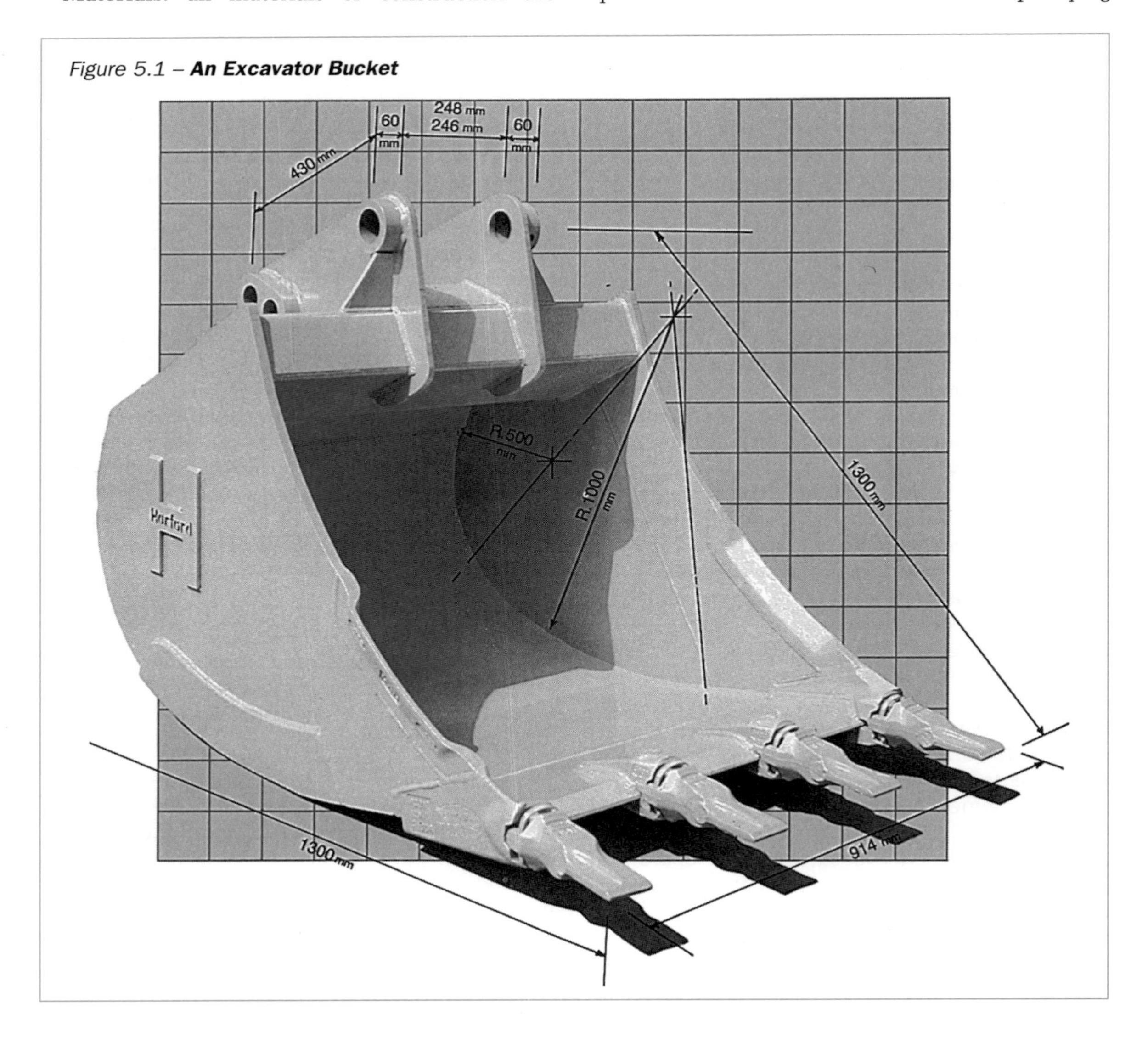

the type of basic materials. Sometimes, before an order is placed, a potential customer will circulate to a number of potential suppliers details of what is required in order to find the best. The best supplier can only be the cheapest supplier if each is capable of supplying exactly what is required in terms of conformance and reliability. That is, it conforms to the production specification and will continue to conform for an agreed period under normal conditions of use. The agreed period is often written into a contract of sale by the supplier or conditions of purchase by the customer.

How is it Produced?

What is not specified by the customer is the detailed production specification – that is, how each bucket must be built. Although this is often left to the supplier, there is little doubt that the customer would like to know that the supplier is capable of producing the bucket using conventional engineering equipment. In some cases the customer will insist on seeing the supplier's production specification before releasing an order, and even visiting the supplier to see the equipment to be used and the premises where production will take place. If food preparation is part of the production process or, indeed, if food is to come into contact with the product being produced (such as packaging materials), very strict regulations are imposed on the cleanliness of the production environment.

The production specification is similar to cooking instructions found in any popular cook-book. What is required is a step-by-step list of instructions stating the operations to be performed (for example, cutting steel plate), what machine to use, how to prepare the material for the next operation, how to remove sharp edges and how to clean surfaces.

It should be possible for any manufacturing organization to have a complete set of instructions of how specific products are made before manufacture commences. This is the case in large organizations which produce many products in large numbers. However, in many other organizations, the method of production is in the operator's 'head' and seldom recorded in any detail. Recent requirements relating to quality standards are insisting that production specifications are written down to recognized levels of detail.

Do You Have the Skills?

If the product and the production specification are available, and also the right equipment and materials, does this mean that the product can be made to satisfy the customer's requirements at a planned cost?

Say you have been asked to produce a birthday cake with icing and fancy decorations. You can read, and you are given the product specification, production specification, all the materials and all the equipment you need. What might stop you from making the cake as specified? Your skill?

Many production processes require input from skilled operators who have been trained in a particular process and can perform that process to a specified competence level. Welders working on important structures, such as offshore drilling rigs have to be formally approved by an internationally recognized agency. They have to produce test pieces of their welding which then undergo strength tests. A novice welder with little experience would not be allowed to work on the major parts of such a structure. Sometimes, production specifications also detail the competence levels of the operators involved.

Do You Have the Resources?

One major consideration is how to obtain the materials required for the product specification. Should these materials be ordered specially, which might incur a long delay, or should they be bought in bulk and placed in stock, to be 'called off' when required? If stocking materials is the answer, how should the stock be controlled? What quantity should be stocked? How often should it be re-ordered? These questions will be answered later in this chapter.

The other consideration relates to the machines or equipment required. Does the company know what machines it has available and what performance it can expect from them? Many businesses now have an assets register which lists all equipment individually, together with the current value, depreciation history, current performance, latest maintenance and repair requirements and the present location of the equipment. In large factories, it is surprising how easy it is to forget where some items are located.

Do You Have the Time?

It would be pointless to agree to take on work which requires quick delivery when it is known that many weeks of other work have to be completed first. In many cases involving engineering products, there can be an agreement over the delivery time. The supplier states the best that can be achieved, and the customer either accepts or rejects this.

Most suppliers realize that quick and reliable delivery dates give them a marketing edge over their competitors, even though the quoted price might be higher. It is therefore very important that the time taken to complete the order is carefully estimated and followed. Time is money in many cases and, therefore, long times usually mean more expense. Planning production is covered in more detail later in this chapter.

Push and Pull Production

There are two basic types of production: 'push' and 'pull'.

In a 'push' production system, the owners decide to make a certain range of product – for example, garden furniture. The design of the furniture dictates the machinery to be used and the skills needed by the operators. Salespeople travel to shops and large stores which sell this type of product to pick up orders which are sent back to the factory. The factory will produce garden furniture even though orders have not been received, and this production is held in stock to await expected future orders. The salespeople are constantly being 'pushed' to sell more of the standard products to keep the factory busy and to keep stock low. It is rare for this type of business to produce variations of the standard range of products described in its catalogue. Product designs do change as customers's needs change and as better materials become available; but change is a long-term process rather than an overnight occurrence.

In a 'pull' production system, the business is set up to respond to customers's requirements as quickly as possible. There is often no standard product, but there is usually a well-defined production process. Products can only be made within this production process. For example, the owners of a business may decide to make plastic mouldings which can be used by other manufacturers who make cars, household appliances or even garden furniture. Such a business will only make mouldings to meet specific orders, and often does not have any stock of finished items, since the product is unique to the customer. Production processes do change over a time period to meet new types of moulding and new plastic materials, but often the cost of new machines is extremely high.

The ultimate type of 'pull' system is called 'Just in Time' (or 'kanban' in Japanese). Just in Time (JIT) is discussed in more detail later in this chapter.

Some businesses have a combination of 'push' and 'pull' production systems. As well as producing a standard range of products, they produce variations on these standards for special customers. This is often not a good combination, since the production process can become inefficient if not controlled well. For example, say you ran a business making scissors and produced 10 000 pairs of identical right-handed scissors per week. What would be your reaction if a customer asked for twelve pairs of left-handed scissors? Do you think you could make them for the same cost? Would it be fair to charge left-handed people more than right-handed people? Would you be tempted to state that you *only* produce right-handed scissors as shown in the catalogue?

ACTIVITY 5.1

Write a product specification for a birthday card. The design is yours, but do not make it too dissimilar from the designs you might expect to find in a card shop. Only specify reasonably common and easily obtainable materials. Your specification must be such that if you gave it to two different suppliers you would receive nearly identical products. Do you need to produce a pre-production model (called a 'prototype')? If not, you need to specify the size, the colour and weight of the cardboard, the colour and style of the wording, and the style of any illustrations.

Write a production specification for the manufacture of the birthday card. List, in order, all the operations required. Again, you may have to make a model yourself to help design this specification. How is the card cut and folded? How are the words and illustrations added? How is the quality checked?

If possible, give the product specification and the production specification to two different people. Compare the final products. How long did each person take to produce the product? What were the reasons for any differences in time? Is there a requirement for training?

Continuous and Batch Production

Continuous production means that the production process remains constant, and continuously produces identical goods with very little 'down time' (a name given to a process which has been halted). Operators perform the same activities on the same products all the time, although some type of 'job rotation' is often included in order to maintain the motivation of operators. Asking one operator to change with another doing a different job helps to maintain interest.

Continuous production also means that attention can be given to making the production process extremely efficient. Machines are purchased to do defined operations; the flow of materials both into the process and from the process can be well planned; and the training of operators is quite specific. Costs of production are low if the line is kept going because there is very little waste. Continuous production is appropriate when large volumes of output of constant product specification are required. However, difficulties and extra costs will arise if there are frequent interruptions in the flow due to poor machine maintenance, changes in product specification or high labour turnover. An example of a continuous process is the production of packets of crisps.

Batch production means the manufacture of a product in comparatively small quantities. In batch production, the demand for the product is lower than the cheapest continuous production rate. For example, one hundred items per week might be needed from a production process which is capable of producing four hundred per week. Therefore, in this case, it would seem appropriate to run the line for one week and make a batch of four hundred. The extra three hundred items are then for supply over the following three weeks. The production line can then go on to produce some other item.

An example of a batch process is the manufacture of shoes. The shoe factory makes such a large range of shoes that batch production is the only possible production method. Batch production is often found in industries where the customer is given a wide choice of product variations. It is usually more expensive than continuous production because of the need to store products, and to change the production line from making one item to another. This change not only means resetting and often cleaning the machines, but also there is a learning loss – the time lost in restarting the process. For example, an operator may have to revise the production specification and this will take time.

ACTIVITY 5.2

To illustrate the advantages of continuous production over batch production, try the following exercise:

(a) See how many times you can sign your name in one minute – for example, Susan Popple
(b) See how many times you can sign your name using alternate letters only in thirty seconds – for example, Ssn Ppl
(c) Repeat (b) using the other alternate set of letters – for example, ua ope

(b) plus (c) is the batch production version of (a). Even with a lot of practice, the chances are that you would have produced more full signatures in one minute using method (a) than the equivalent method of (b) plus (c).

Jobbing Production

Jobbing production occurs when a business only manufactures one complete product at a time. This is either because the product is unique and is different from any other product, or because the product is so large or complex that resources only exist to produce one item at a time. Costs of production per product are higher for jobbing production than for batch or continuous production (if this were possible), because of the difficulty in balancing job skills. For example, say the job requires the services of a welder for three hours for a production process lasting twelve hours. What does the welder do for the other nine hours? Perhaps the welder can be hired at high cost from a separate welding company?

KEY POINTS 5.1

- **Manufacturing businesses and service businesses both require product specifications and production specifications. The product in a service business is the service itself**
- **Production processes of the 'push' type tend to have higher stocks of finished goods than processes of the 'pull' type**
- **Continuous production processes tend to be more efficient than batch production processes**

Work Study

Work study is the name given to a technique for finding the best methods (method study) to use in the production process and the expected times (work measurement) needed to complete these methods. Often the best method is also the shortest in terms of time, since labour costs relate to time and the criterion for deciding what is best is often least cost. However, quality of conformance must also be considered – that is, making sure that the designer's requirements for quality are continuously met. Does the final product conform to the product specification?

All good designers, before fixing the design specification, will have discussed the likely production methods with the appropriate staff, which may influence the design itself. Design is a very challenging and creative process. The designer may be working from a concept or from customers's specifications, and has the job of writing a full product specification which will result in a product which is made with the minimum amount of effort and used with the maximum amount of satisfaction.

Product reliability is the name given to the probability of the product still performing at the end of a specified time period, and it is the designer's job to make sure that the customer's requirements for use and reliability are met.

Method study is concerned with finding the best method for the manufacturing process and is achieved by breaking the existing process into small sections and critically examining each one. This is called 'analysis'. Since this analysis is undertaken in an office environment, well away from any actual or potential production facility, flow diagrams are often used to illustrate the manufacturing process. This is no different from having a music score to represent a piece of music. Skilled musicians can correct, replace and create new notes, and the skilled production designer can view the flow chart in the same way. An example of a flow chart showing the most common symbols used is given in Figure 5.2.

Figure 5.2 – ***A Simple Production Flow Chart For Frying Fish***

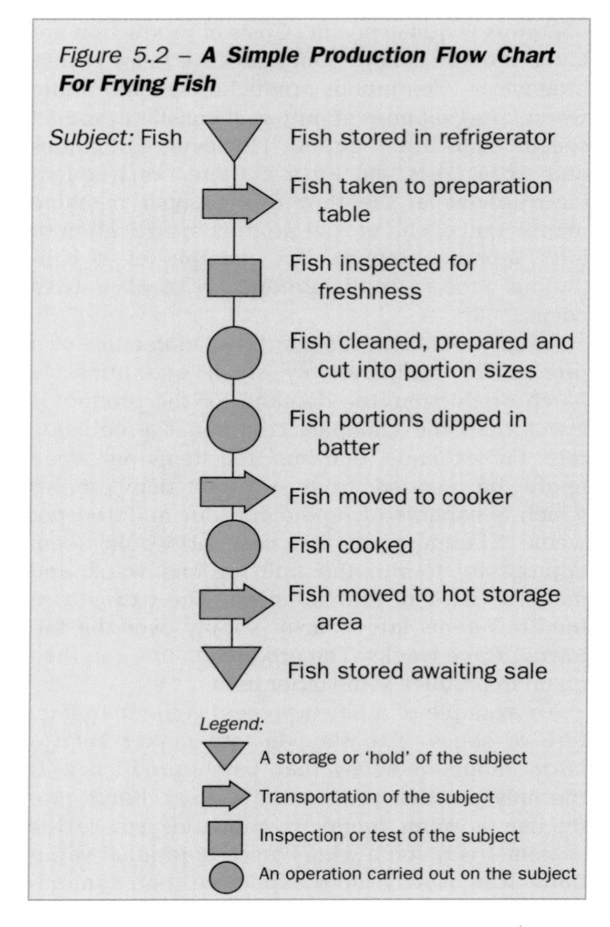

Once the production flow chart has been completed, the times for the operations are calculated or estimated. Establishing these times can be the subject of detailed discussions between operator and planner. The planner may feel that the operator is not working hard enough and wants a 'tight' time. The operator, on the other hand, may feel that the planner is making unreasonable demands.

A skilled work study planner has to be trained to recognize 'standard' work – that is, the output rate of a suitably skilled and motivated operator working in good conditions and using the appropriate resources. Once the standard time for a job, or a part of a job, is defined and agreed, allowances can be made for specified individuals working under known conditions.

When the times and methods of manufacture have been agreed, it is possible to work out how long it will take to produce the completed product, how much it will cost in terms of labour, how much labour is required to meet selected production rates, and what training might be required.

Example

It has been agreed that the time taken to interview social security claimants is twenty minutes, given that the interviewer has been properly trained. It has been forecast that 1 800 claimants will require an interview each week. Currently, there are fifteen trained interviewers available.

How many trained interviewers are needed to meet demand?

The first step is to calculate the real capacity of each interviewer, who arrives for work at 8.30am, has a one-hour lunch break and finishes work at 5.00pm. The total time the interviewer is available for work, the capacity of the interviewer, is thirty-seven and a half hours per week. It is highly unlikely that the whole of the capacity could be spent on interviews. Time would be needed for receiving instructions, comparing notes, drinking tea and all the other normal demands. Often, in business, a figure of 80 per cent of capacity is used as a measurement of the actual capacity. If we use this as a guide, the actual capacity of the interviewer is thirty hours or 1 800 minutes per week.

If each interview last twenty minutes, then each interviewer could see ninety claimants per week. In order to see a total of 1 800 claimants per week, twenty trained interviewers would be required. There are at present only fifteen.

The answer to the problem is either to recruit an extra five trained interviewers or to reduce the interview time to fifteen minutes. Could the methods of work study help to make this reduction and still maintain the quality of the service? Are there better methods? The next section on brainstorming examines problem-solving of this type in more detail.

It is very important in production to make sure that the times for the operation and the methods required to perform the operation are as carefully, or as scientifically, worked out as possible. It must not be a guess based on past methods and times for similar jobs, since this can perpetuate a bad method and an excessive time for manufacture.

Value Analysis and Brainstorming

Value analysis has grown out of work study and concentrates on finding the right materials for the product specification. The main principle of value analysis is to find the lowest cost material which satisfies the customer's requirements. Value analysis was introduced in the USA in the 1950s to check that existing purchasing requirements were appropriate – that is, buyers were obtaining the best value materials and components. The technique has since spread to an analysis of all materials used in an existing and proposed product.

Both work study and value analysis use the same critical examination procedures based on the following check questions:

- What material is being used for this product?
- Why is this material being used?
- What alternative materials could be used?
- What alternative materials should be considered?
- What alternative material is recommended?
- How is this change to be implemented?
- How is this change to be monitored?

Although much of the work study and value analysis procedures require trained production and material procurement staff, there is plenty of opportunity to involve other staff in the creative part of the programme, especially in answering the third and fourth questions.

Brainstorming is the name given to a group creativity session and this is described in *The Business Environment*, another book in this series. Basically, a team of individuals are asked to suggest as many ways of solving a problem as they can without interruption or comment from any other team member. The problem to be solved is stated as simply as possible – for example, how can the cost of making a bicycle pump be reduced? The ideas generated are submitted for later examination both in terms of feasibility and cost. The cheapest, feasible ideas are short-listed for further examination, and a final decision is then made after other criteria which usually involve commercial reasons (such as reliability of supply) have been considered. One of the answers to the bicycle pump problem could be to make it smaller!

Productivity

The design of the production process requires as much skill as the design of the product itself, and the production specification must be considered by the designer at all times. Some designers receive criticism because their initial elegant design cannot be made on the equipment available to the firm.

This suggests that there are two production specifications. The first states how a product should be produced in the most efficient manner. The second states how the product should be produced with the resources within the firm in terms of skills and machines. In practice the ideal specification is not often written down: it remains as a goal for the future. However, the gradual reduction in the production costs as they approach the lower costs of the ideal method represent improvements in productivity.

Productivity is the ratio of the actual work produced in a time period to the theoretical amount of work that could be produced. For example, say that it takes forty hours to make a car and it is known that, theoretically, it could take only thirty hours if all the factors were right. 'Factors' include the correct working methods, the right degree of motivation by the car workers, or the availability of the right materials. In this case, in forty hours, only one car is made whereas one and one-third cars could have been made. Hence:

$$\text{Productivity} = \frac{\text{Actual work produced per operator per time period}}{\text{Theoretical (ideal) work produced per operator per time period}}$$

$$= \frac{\text{1 car in 40 hours}}{1\tfrac{1}{3}\text{ cars in 40 hours}} = \frac{3}{4} \text{ or } 75\%$$

Alternatively:

$$\text{Productivity} = \frac{\text{Theoretical time for producing ouput}}{\text{Actual time for producing output}}$$

$$= \frac{\text{30 hours}}{\text{40 hours}} = \frac{3}{4} \text{ or } 75\%$$

Or, in terms of cost:

$$\text{Productivity} = \frac{\text{Theoretical labour cost}}{\text{Actual labour cost}}$$

For example, if the current cost of labour in producing a car is £400, and the labour cost of producing the same item in the best possible way is £300, then:

$$\text{Productivity} = \frac{300}{400} \times 100$$
$$= 75\%$$

Production specifications should contain all the information needed by the operator to make the item in the prescribed way (method), and to realize how long it should take (time). All this information could be made available in flow chart format (as in Figure 5.2) with additional detailed descriptions of complex operations.

Flow charts are useful for improving the productivity of manufacturing processes. Operations to a material, in this case the fish, add value to the material. For example, cleaning the fish is a valuable activity for which the customer is prepared to pay. On the other hand, transporting and storing the material does not add any value as far as the customer is concerned. No-one is going to pay more because the fish has been waiting to be cooked! A flow chart can show the relationship between valuable activities and wasteful activities. Maximizing value and minimizing waste is an on going operation in business.

Production Times

The production specification requires information on the time taken to complete a job, or the activities comprising the job.

The time for a job obviously depends on the method to be used, and usually the method selected is the one which takes least time. Basically, the production method is selected first since this comes from experience, and the appropriate time is then calculated. However, new methods of manufacture which could cut production costs without increasing total costs should always be examined.

The time used for a job must be the time expected from a motivated person, trained to carry out the job and given the correct equipment. This is called the standard time. It is possible sometimes to calculate this time from manuals, but often it is calculated by staff who have been specially trained to recognize standard performance when they see it, or who can predict what it should be if it is a new way of working. The time given for a job should not be the average of all the times taken in the past because there is a danger of compounding an error.

ACTIVITY 5.3

How long should it take to mend a puncture on a bicycle?

The easiest way to answer this is to average out all the times it took in the past to mend punctures and say 'about ten minutes'. But perhaps in the past there has been no motivation to do the job with any relish, the right equipment was not available, and the procedure followed was copied by observing someone else doing the job many years in the past. Hardly the right way to develop a standard time for an operation!

Your task is to find out how a bicycle tyre 'inner tube' puncture is repaired, and to produce a 'method' for doing it, together with your estimation of the 'time' it should take. The task will be performed by only one person.

After you have understood the procedure, draw a flow chart of the major operations, with a description of each operation, and a time estimate for each operation. A typical part sequence of operation could be:

- Partially inflate inner tube without increasing the normal diameter or causing any local bulges (time: 15 seconds)
- Submerge sections of tube into bowl of water to find air leak from bubble formation (time: 1 minute)

When you have finished your work study project, ask a friend to follow your instructions and time the process. Does your estimated time equate with your friend's time?

Would your friend get better at mending punctures if he or she repeated the process a number of times?

What conclusions can you draw from this?

Do you think that a fully trained and well motivated person could do the job much faster? If yes, what conclusions can you draw?

Network Charts

The flow chart as shown in Figure 5.2 is a sequence of activities which need to be followed given the resources available. A network chart is different from a flow chart in that it shows the logical sequence of activities to achieve an end result, initially without regard to any resource limitations.

A network chart is a 'logic' chart, and flow charts are constructed from the logic network after considering any resource limitations. Figure 5.3 illustrates a network showing what happens when a car stops at a service station for fuel, water for the screen washer, and a cleaned windscreen. Theoretically, all three activities could be performed at the same time as shown by the network. However, if resources were limited to one driver, the activities would have to be performed consecutively and would be shown by a flow chart as a 'string of sausages'.

In Figure 5.3, the operations are shown as boxes rather than circles (as in Figure 5.2). Boxes are the only symbols used in networks and are called 'nodes' and are linked by arrows, as in flow charts. The arrows are called 'precedence' arrows since they link one operation which precedes another operation. In networks, operations are usually called 'activities'.

The basic logic rules of a network are:

- No operation can start until all the preceding activities have finished (a preceding activity is one which is at the tail end of a precedence arrow)
- Networks have only one start and one finish. Usually, dummy activities called 'start' and 'finish' are introduced to emphasize this point. Apart from the 'finish' activity, all other activities *must* precede another activity

Critical Path Analysis

One of the major reasons for constructing a network of a set of operations (usually called a project) is to find out how long the project will take to complete. This is achieved by adding the times to each activity and seeing what sequence of activities would control the overall time.

Figure 5.3 – ***An Example of a Network Diagram Showing Logical Sequence of Activities at a Service Station***

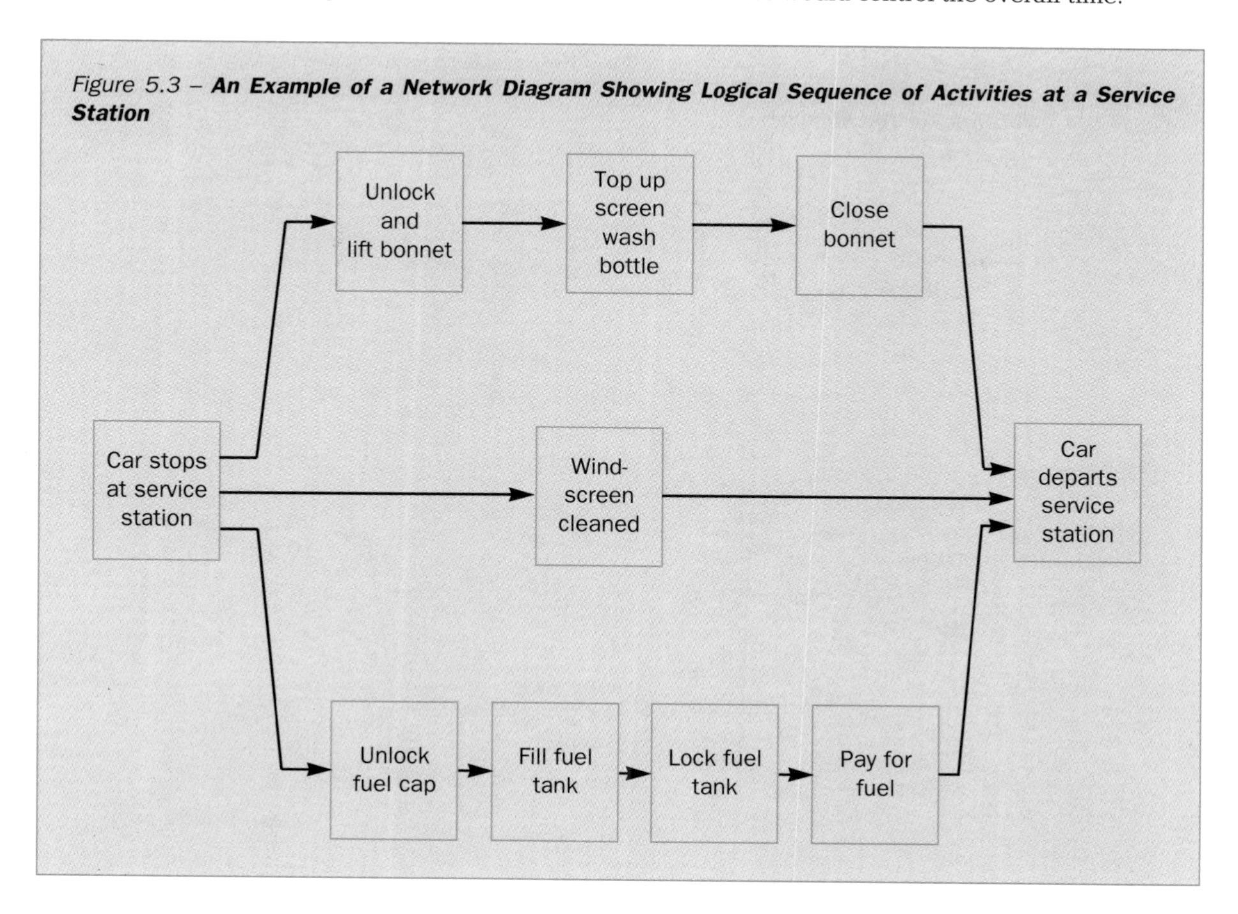

The following example is a simple one relating to the making of a cup of tea. The list of activities and associated times is given in the table below, and the network is shown in Figure 5.4. The logic of the method for making a cup of tea is from personal experience.

Activity	*Time (seconds)*
Fill kettle	10
Boil water	180
Prepare crockery	60
Add milk to cup	5
Add tea leaves to teapot	10
Pour water into teapot	10
Allow tea to infuse	60
Pour tea into cup	10

The sequence of activities which is the longest (timewise) controls the overall time for pouring a cup of tea and can be deduced from Figure 5.4. This is the sequence of activities shown by a 'crossed' arrow line and is:

Fill kettle → Boil water → Pour water → Wait 60 seconds → Pour tea

The sum of the activity times in this sequence is four minutes and thirty seconds. This sequence is called the critical path, and each activity in this path is called a critical activity.

If the time taken to complete a critical activity changes, the time for the whole process changes. For example, if the time for waiting for the kettle to boil increases from three to four minutes the whole tea-making process increases by the same duration. In a major project the identification of the critical path is extremely important, since the delay of any activity in this sequence can cause a delay to the project.

The other, non-critical activities such as 'prepare crockery', 'add milk to cup' and 'add tea leaves to pot', are important but not critical as regards the time duration. For example, if the time for 'prepare crockery' increased from ten seconds to thirty seconds, the overall time for making a cup of tea would not change.

Each non-critical activity has a float which is the amount of increase in time allowed before the activity becomes 'critical'. For example, the 'prepare crockery' activity has a float of two minutes, which means that if the time for this activity increased by more than two minutes, to give a total time of more than three minutes, this activity would become critical and there would be a new critical path. The method for calculating the float of activities is shown below.

The network assumes that there are sufficient

Figure 5.4 – ***Network For Tea Making***

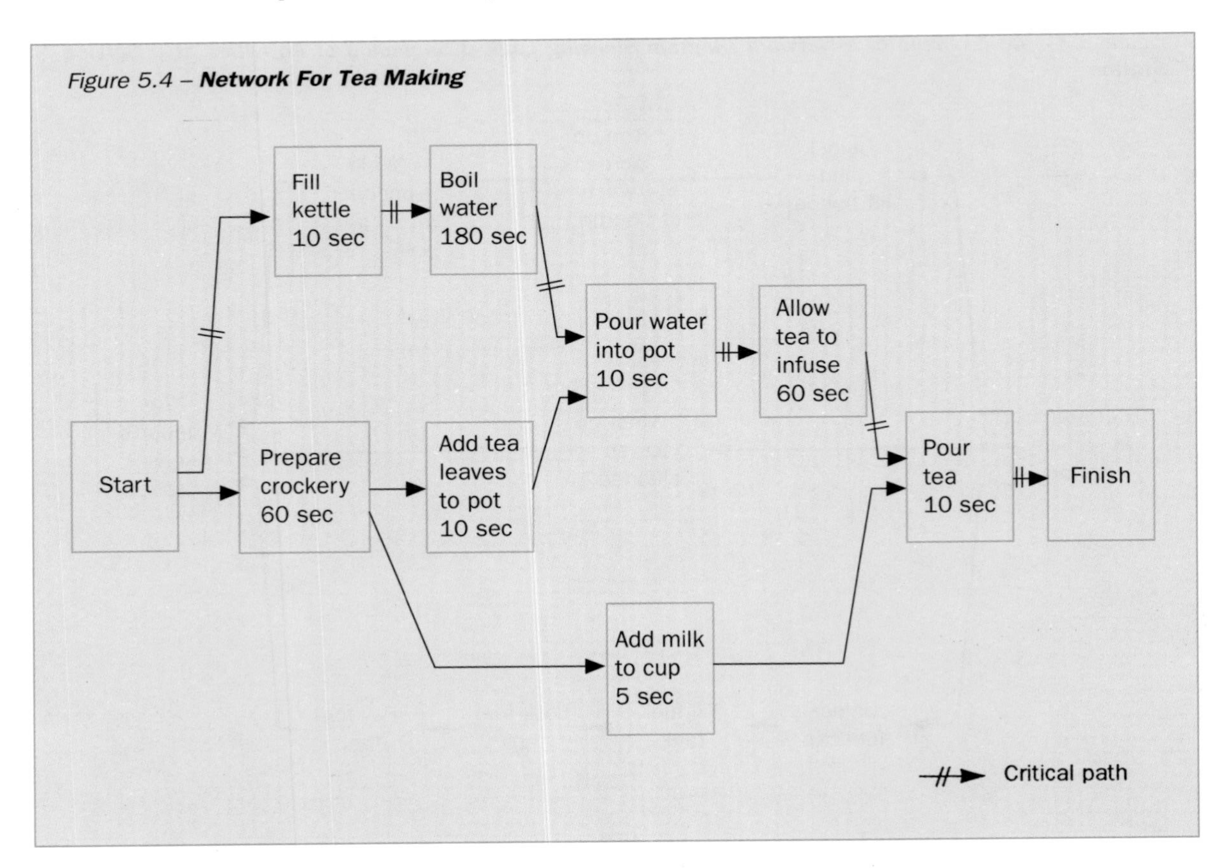

resources available to carry out parallel activities if needed. In the tea-making example, the non-critical activities could be done while waiting for the kettle to boil, so only one person (a major resource) is required.

Levels of Networking Complexity

Networks are extremely important in describing the production process, and are used at different levels of complexity in business:

- **Level 1:** a simple logic diagram showing the natural sequence of the production process. If you find it difficult to construct this network, the chances are that you are uncertain of the right way of doing the job
- **Level 2:** as Level 1, but with the addition of times for each activity so that the critical path can be calculated and priorities noted
- **Level 3:** as Level 2, but with the addition of resource requirements for each activity showing the people required, the cash required, the space required and any other resource
- **Level 4:** as Level 3, but with modifications to the network in order to balance resources. For example, the network may indicate that eight skilled workers are required if all activities which could be done at the same time are so planned. If the firm only has six such skilled workers, then the network must be adjusted to allow for this short fall

Levels 1 and 2 are the only levels considered in this text. Except in small networks containing less than thirty or so activities, planning networks at Levels 3 and 4 is usually undertaken with the help of a computer program.

The following Level 2 networking problem shows the usual conventions used in preparing precedence network diagrams. Unfortunately, these conventions are not universal, nor is the method of drawing networks.

Example
The table below shows the activities involved in erecting a pre-fabricated garage on a prepared site: the estimated time for completion of each activity and the reference number of the activity which must be completed before the current activity can start (called the 'precedence'). How long will it take to erect the garage?

Ref. no.	*Activity*	*Time (hrs)*	*Precedence*
1	Prepare site	2	start
2	Lay concrete foundations	5	1
3	Dig water drainage pit	3	start
4	Erect garage	8	2
5	Fix garage doors	2	4
6	Fix drainage pipes	2	3,4
7	Connect electrical supply	2	4
8	Paint garage doors	3	5

To find out, you must draw the network and

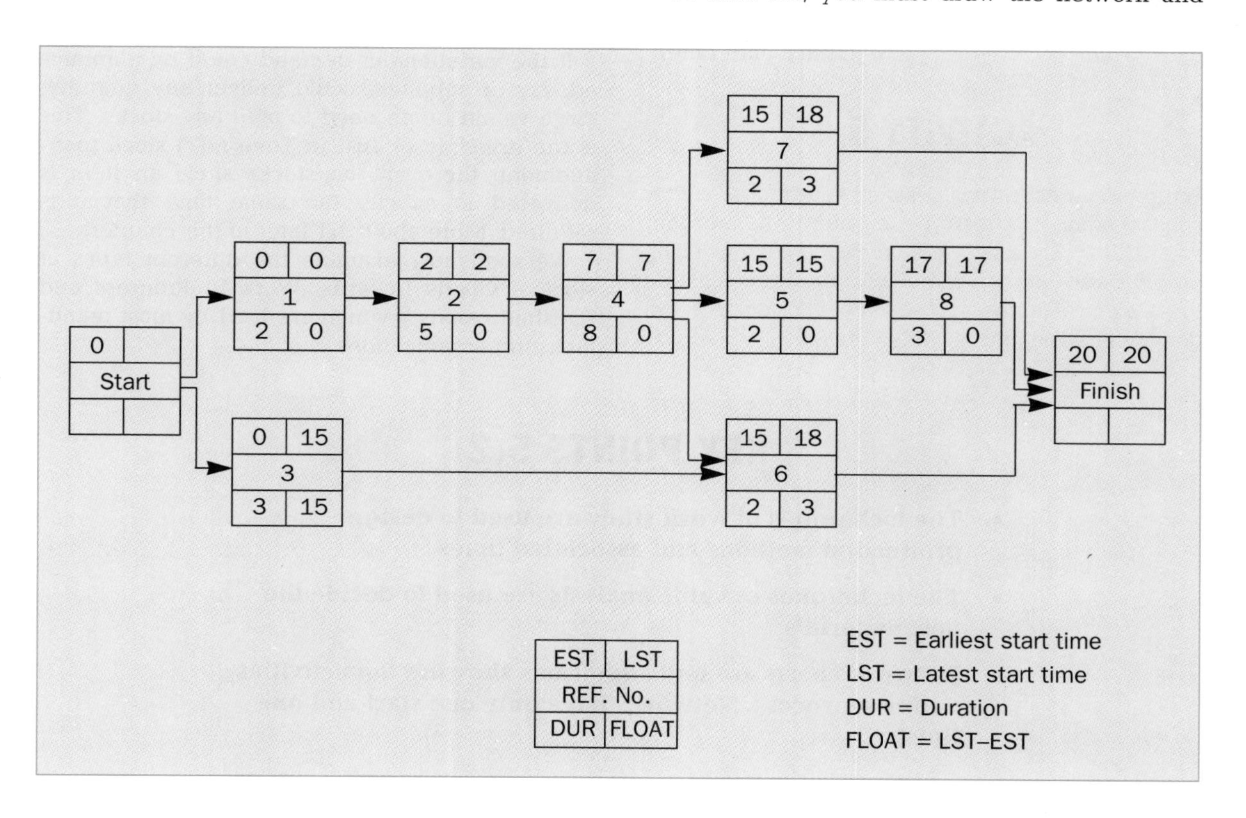

then complete the 'earliest start time' (EST) and the 'latest start time' (LST) for each activity. The float for each activity is the difference between these times, and the critical path is the sequence of activities with zero float. Float is the amount of time any one activity can expand in duration or delay in starting before there is a change in the overall time of the project. Float is shared by all activities in a non-critical sequence of activities.

The EST for any activity is the EST for the preceding activity plus the duration of the preceding activity. If there is more than one directly preceding activity, the latest EST is used. This method requires a 'forward pass' through the network, starting with 'Start' and working towards the 'Finish'.

The LST for any activity is the LST for any directly following activity less the duration of this activity. If there is more than one directly following activity, the earliest LST is used.

The resultant network and the analysis are shown in Figure 5.5 (previous page).

The activities with zero float make up the critical path. These activities are:

Critical activities	*Time (hrs)*
Prepare site	2
Lay concrete	5
Erect garage	8
Fix doors	2
Paint doors	3
Total	20 (critical path time)

ACTIVITY 5.4

The previous Activity (5.3) asked you to draw a flow chart showing how a bicycle puncture was mended. Your task in this Activity is to draw the corresponding logic network for the same problem assuming that there are no shortages of resources for doing activities at the same time.

Attach your estimates of the time for each activity and from these figures find the critical path and calculate the overall time for completion.

If resources were restricted to two persons, would the time for completing the job be changed?

What do you think are the major advantages or disadvantages between flow charts and networks?

Stock Control

There are many separate areas in a manufacturing organization where stocks of materials, part finished materials and finished materials are stored. The purpose in holding stocks is to create a buffer between the irregularities of supply and demand. If a customer requires ten units per day, every day, it would be possible to make ten units a day and there would be no finished goods in stock. However, although the average might be ten units a day, the actual number could vary between five and fifteen units a day. If the customer is to be kept satisfied, stocks of at least twenty units might be required to cover periods when demand is at its peak.

Similarly, if a supplier could deliver two hundred units a day to meet a steady production request of two hundred a day, there would be no need for Goods Inwards Stores. However, some suppliers may only deliver in batches of, say, two thousand units. There is therefore a need for stocks.

If the variations of demand could be eliminated, and if suppliers could deliver any quantity, there would be no need to hold any stocks. This is the principle of Just in Time (JIT) stock management; there are no stocks since an item is delivered at exactly the same time that it is required. More about JIT later in this chapter.

We shall now examine the different types of stock – Goods Inwards, Work in Progress and Finished Goods – which are held by most manufacturing organizations.

KEY POINTS 5.2

- **The techniques of work study are used to design production methods and associated times**
- **The techniques of value analysis are used to decide the best materials**
- **Network charts are logic diagrams showing the activities within a process. Networks have only one start and one finish**

Goods Inwards Stores

Materials are received from an external supplier and placed in the Goods Inwards Stores (GIS). Materials are withdrawn from the GIS on presentation of a requisition which has been issued by the production control department. This is a request for a certain quantity of items, probably comprising several different types of material or 'bought in' items, to be collected at a production point for a specified operation. The production control department obtains this information from the parts list which is attached to the production drawing of the component to be manufactured. The parts list contains all the material specifications for making one item, and the controller only has to multiply this list by the number of items to be made. The process of collecting all the items together is called 'despatching'.

Work in Progress Stocks

Products usually proceed through a number of production stages, such as cutting, machining, welding and assembly. Each stage may be a different department in a factory, although it is now quite common to see one group of workers carrying out the whole production process at one location.

Volvo, for example, is famous for its methods of car production which broke away from the classical assembly line methods. The company introduced a number of teams which produced a significant component of the car, such as a suspension unit, which it passed to another team for further assembly work. Teams became efficient production units and jobs were rotated within each team to encourage skills and motivational development. The 'Volvo experiment' has now become a common method for describing this type of work structure.

When production occurs at different locations, it is usual for a batch to be produced and passed on when it is finished. Alternatively, it may be possible to match exactly the production rate at one stage with the production rate at the following stage.

Products which are waiting to be worked on by the next production stage are called Part Finished Stock. The actual materials or part-finished product which is currently being worked on is also 'stock' and this together with the Part Finished Stock is called Work in Progress (WIP). WIP is therefore made up of two different types of stock: that which is waiting to be worked on and that which is currently being worked on. It may be possible to reduce Part Finished Stock by better planning.

Finished Goods Stock

At the end of the production process, the goods are placed in the Finished Goods Stores (Goods Outwards) to await delivery to the customer. Sometimes a customer already exists and the product moves straight from the production department to the waiting lorry. At other times, a customer does not yet exist and the finished goods wait for the sale to take place.

The Costs of Stock

It is agreed by many specialists involved with stock control that the cost of holding stock, whether as Goods Inwards, WIP or Goods Outwards, amounts to approximately 25 per cent of the value of the average stock level each year. This includes all those costs which vary with stock level: insurance, obsolescence, limited shelf life, heating or cooling, pilfering, damage in store, control (for example, measuring and counting) and, most importantly, the cost of the money needed to produce the stock. Perhaps the business borrowed £100,000 to pay for stock, and has to pay 12% interest charges per year. This is called an opportunity cost. The more stock the more the money borrowed and the more the interest charge.

Although the figure of 25 per cent of average stock value is a good approximation for calculating storage costs per year, some types of stock are more expensive than others. The storage of frozen meat is significantly higher than 25 per cent because of the extra refrigeration costs, whereas the storage of large industrial steel tubes is relatively low since any type of outdoor site is acceptable.

Holding stock is a very expensive business and often implies 'waste'. Every effort must be made to reduce this waste to the minimum level necessary for efficient operation.

Example

A business produces a number of different products, and maintains high Goods Inwards, WIP and Finished Goods Stock levels in order to provide quick delivery times for its customers. Although materials and products are constantly moving through the production process, the average levels of stocks in the various locations are as follows:

- The average Goods Inwards Stocks are valued at purchase price at £40 000
- The average WIP stocks are valued at material costs and labour costs at £60 000
- The average Finished Goods Stocks are valued at material, labour and production overhead at £100 000

(See Chapter Six on stock valuation methods.)

Figure 5.6 – **The Simple Stock Replenishment Model**

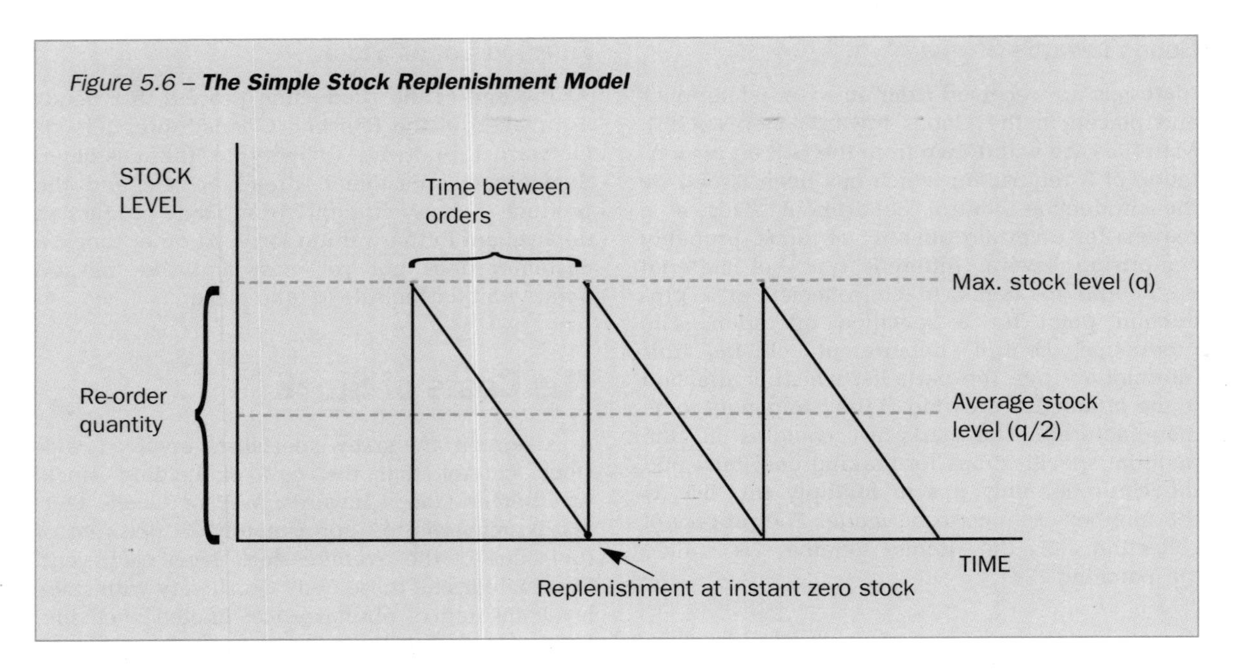

The average total value of all stock is £200 000. Hence, the estimated cost to the business of holding these stocks is: 25 per cent of £200 000 per year, or £50 000 per year.

If it is possible to reduce the average stock levels to £100 000 per year by getting rid of unnecessary stocks, then a saving of £25 000 could be achieved. Not only that, but in times of difficulty in borrowing cash, the cash saved could be used for other pressing needs, such as paying wages.

This example confirms that every effort should be made to keep stock levels to a minimum. However, there is a problem which has to be considered: the cost of ordering stock.

We will assume that the forecast demand for a stock item is 120 000 units, or approximately 2 400 per week, and that the company purchases this item from an external supplier at a cost of £1 each. Every time an order for resupply is placed, there is a cost of £100 which could have been avoided if the order had not been placed. This cost relates to time taken for preparing the order, postage and telephone, the time taken to check a sample of item when they are received and any fixed transport costs (ie, irrespective of order size). These costs could all have been avoided, since they are directly related to placing an order.

There are, however, an infinite number of alternatives regarding the ordering process.

Figure 5.7 – **Acquisition Costs at Different Order Levels**

Numbers of orders/yr	*Amount ordered*	*Average stock*	*Average value £*	*Holding cost/yr £*	*Order cost/yr £*	*Acquisition cost/yr £*
1	120 000	60 000	60 000	15 000	100	15 100
3	40 000	20 000	20 000	5 000	300	5 300
6	20 000	10 000	10 000	2 500	600	3 100
12	10 000	5 000	5 000	1 250	1 200	2 450
25	4 800	2 400	2 400	600	2 500	3 100
50	2 400	1 200	1 200	300	5 000	5 300
250	480	240	240	60	25 000	25 060

Notes: a No. of orders per year × amount ordered equals 120 000
b Average stock equals half amount ordered
c Average value equals average stock × £1
d Holding cost/year equals 25 per cent average stock value
e Ordering cost per year equals no. of orders × £100
f Acquisition cost equals holding cost plus ordering cost

Which one of the following ordering strategies should the company follow?

- Order 120 000 units once a year
- Order 10 000 units once a month
- Order 2 400 units once a week (assume fifty working weeks per year)
- Order 480 units every day

or anything in between.

The costs of acquiring stock is called the acquisition cost, which is the sum of the cost of storing stock and the cost of ordering stock:

Acquisition cost = holding cost per year + order costs per year

Assume that stock is consumed at a steady rate and that a replenishment of stock occurs at the moment stock is used up. Figure 5.6 is a typical stock level graph and shows the average stock as equal to half the amount of stock received during each order.

Figure 5.7 is a table showing the acquisition costs at different order levels, where the holding cost is assumed to be 25 per cent of the average stock value, and the ordering cost is £100 per order.

ACTIVITY 5.5

A large toyshop has a standing order with a 'teddy bear' manufacturer to supply two hundred and forty bears per fortnight, the average fortnightly demand.

The daily demand for bears is variable and there are six selling days per week. Obtain a single dice (die) with numbers one to six and throw the die to simulate the daily demand. The number of bears sold each day is equal to the value of the top dice face multiplied by ten. If you throw a six, for example, this represents a daily demand of sixty bears.

At the beginning of a six-week period, you have two hundred and forty bears in stock. Throw the dice to find the daily demand. Show the following values for each day:

- Stock at start of day
- Delivery of new stock (two hundred and forty items every twelve working days)
- Day's demand for stock
- Stock at end of day (equals next day's starting stock)

If you find that the demand in the fortnight is less than the average, the new delivery will add to the stock remaining. If the demand is higher than average over the fortnight, there will be a 'stock out' and you will have to wait for the next delivery.

From the table you have produced over the six-week period, show a graph of stock levels (as in Figure 5.6).

What conclusions can you draw from your simulation? Could you use similar types of simulation for other business activities?

Using your 'expected probability' skills developed in Chapter Four, discover why the average stock demand is thirty-five bears per day.

The Economic Order Quantity (EOQ)

In Figure 5.8, the holding cost, the order cost and the acquisition cost have been plotted against

Figure 5.8 – ***The Economic Order Quantity Graph***

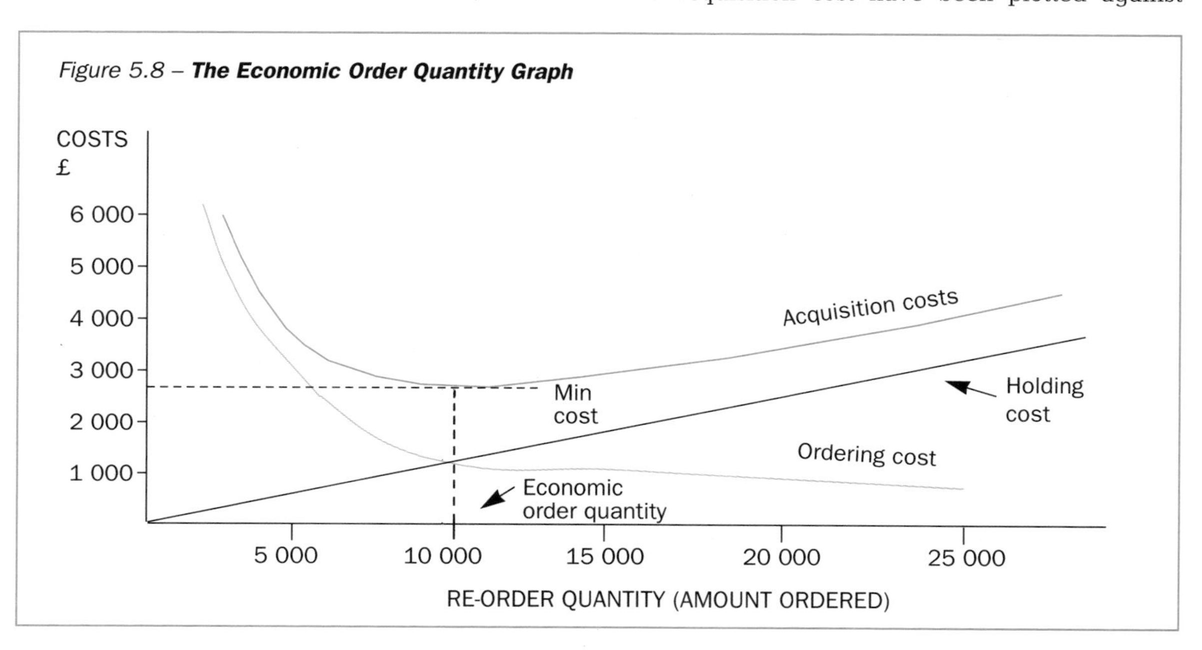

different order quantities per order (as shown in Figure 5.7).

The minimum acquisition cost occurs when the order quantity is 10 000 units, equivalent to an ordering frequency of twelve orders per year. In fact it is possible to prove, with this model of the stock supply, that the minimum occurs when the annual ordering cost equals the annual holding cost. This value of order size which minimizes the acquisition cost is called the economic order quantity (EOQ) and is clearly shown in Figure 5.8.

Economic Batch Size

It has been assumed in the example that the item is purchased externally. However, exactly the same analysis applies to stock which is ordered from an internal production system. This enables the most economic batch size (EBS) to be calculated. Exactly the same methods are used for calculating the EBS as for the EOQ.

The ordering costs for an internal order differs significantly from the costs for an external order. The paperwork costs, and also the costs of stopping and starting a production process which results in expensive learning costs, form part of the order costs. These learning costs relate to the time taken to build up a production process to the most efficient level.

For example, assume you were asked to mark one hundred examination papers. Would you prefer to mark them in one batch of one hundred, or mark two a day over fifty days? Think of all the extra time you would need to get ready (learning time) if you marked only two a day! The cost of the time you spent, compared to the scripts you marked, would be very expensive because of this 'learning loss'.

Economic Order Quantity Formula

A formula can be developed for the calculation of the EOQ. The formula is:

$$EOQ = \sqrt{\frac{2DC_o}{C_H}}$$

where:

D = the forecast demand of the item over a time period (T)
C_o = The cost of placing one order
C_H = The cost of holding one item in stock over period T

If the values used in Figure 5.7 are substituted in the formula, so that:

D = 120,000 per year
C_o = £100
C_H = 25% of £1 = £0.25

the EOQ would be:

$$EOQ = \sqrt{\frac{2 \times 120\ 000 \times 100}{0.25}}$$

$$= \sqrt{96.10^6}$$

$$= 9\ 798 \text{ (approx.)}$$

Just In Time

In the advanced manufacturing countries of the world, the trend is towards a 'pull' system for all production. That is, towards a production system which responds quickly and easily to different customers.

One way of doing this is to have high stocks of everything, so that a customer just selects what he or she requires. However, although this might be possible on a supermarket shelf where sales promotion is often associated with high stock levels (have you noticed how some supermarkets place mirrors behind shelves to give the impression of more stock?), it would be extremely wasteful in a production business.

You will remember from the previous section that the cost of holding stock is on average 25 per cent of the average stock value per year. However, you will also remember that average stock levels of essential items can only be reduced by increasing the frequency of ordering, which leads to higher order costs per year.

But what if it was possible to reduce the cost of placing an order? If it was possible to reduce the cost of ordering to zero, there would be no need to hold any stock. Instead, the production company would just order the item for a known fixed 'delivery time' ahead. This delivery time is called the lead time. If the lead time is not constant, there is a danger of either waiting for a delivery and holding up the production process, or there is a danger of stock arriving before it is needed. Although this latter condition is not often met, when it does occur it can cause problems for businesses who have nowhere to store items.

Just in Time (JIT) is a Japanese philosophy which is aimed at reducing waste in the form of unnecessary stocks. It does not demand that stocks be removed completely, but it does question the reasons for stock holding:

- Can the demand for products be matched with the supply of products to eliminate the need for stocks to buffer the variations between demand and supply?

- Can the cost of ordering stock be reduced significantly, especially for items made internally?
- Can production processes anticipate orders by better forecasting so that components are just available for customers when they arrive?
- Can suppliers deliver in smaller quantities to match demand rates?

JIT is part of a new attitude within business to reduce waste and to improve quality. However, very high investments in capital equipment are required in order to produce items for the customer on demand.

Imagine a machine which will, in one second, produce a bicycle because a customer has just walked into a shop and asked for one! This example is deliberately futuristic and nobody has suggested that such a possibility could currently exist. However, if instantaneous production is not yet possible for anything except very simple items, the only alternative is to have an extremely accurate forecasting system.

Figure 5.9 – ***European Car Manufacturing***

Car makers must join fast lane

EUROPE's car industry must prepare to revolutionise the way it does business if it is to fend off the challenge of rapidly increasing competition on world markets.

The Community has pledged to gradually open its market – the largest in the world – to Japanese cars once internal borders come down next year.

But it is woefully ill-prepared for the competition this will bring to the still closeted markets of Spain, Italy and France.

Having persuaded the motor industry to accept in principle an opening to Japan, the European Commission is preparing a strategy to help Community manufacturers take on their rivals on an equal footing.

The strategy, being drafted by Industry Commissioner Martin Bangemann and due to be endorsed by the Commission later this spring, focuses on increased competition, higher productivity, more and better quality training and a narrower focus for R&D.

EC production grew rapidly during the 1980s – up from 10.7 million vehicles in 1982 to 14.3 million in 1989 – but has slowed more recently. Despite the boost given by German unification, output dropped to 13.7 million last year.

Growing demand also shows signs of slowing. EC experts say that new registrations, which rose 30 per cent between 1980 and 1990, will continue to grow – but at a much slower rate.

Production – including output from Japanese plants in the Community – is forecast to increase by 16 per cent between 1991 and 2000, bringing annual production to 16 million vehicles.

Despite improvements, the Commission says, productivity remains worringly low. Although 400,000 jobs were shed across the industry during the 1980s, construction still employs 1.2 million people directly and a further 950,000 in the components sector.

Overall employment in manufacturing and related areas is estimated at 2.5 million, or one in ten of the Community's total workforce. 'In the Community it takes on average 35.3 hours to build a car, more than double average production time in Japan,' explained one EC official. At some of the least efficient plants, production time stretches to 56 hours. At 23 hours per vehicle, the Community's best compares more favourably with the average production time of 20 hours in Japanese-owned plant in the US, the Commission notes.

A rapid shift to lean production and 'just in time' production processes established by the Japanese are essential if the industry is to survive.

Against this backdrop of increased competition and falling productivity, the Commission warns against the dangers of spiralling state subsidy.

'National governments are in danger of engaging in a subsidy war, using higher and higher levels of support to try to give their manufacturers an edge over the rest,' EC sources said.

The Commission is convinced that the Community must improve the skills of its workforce. Illiteracy and a poor general level of training are proving a serious handicap, the Commission notes. The average age of the workforce – 45 compared with 28 in Japanese plants in the EC and 30-40 in Japan – also hampers retraining.

The Commission suggests that a comprehensive retraining programme will increase annual training costs for the average Community car maker by Ecu25 million, equivalent to 30 to 50 per cent of their current training budget. EC officials say the Commission will later this year unveil a scheme to help workers affected by new technology across the industrial spectrum.

According to a study prepared for the Commission by Boston Consulting Group, the European car industry must embark on deep-rooted structural reforms – including a reduction in the number of components suppliers and higher levels of specification if the EC is to bridge the productivity gap separating it from its main rivals. This means fewer suppliers and closer vertical integration, mimicking Japanese car makers' company structures.

Source: *European*, 2–8 April 1992

In this case, it is predicted that at 3.00pm on a Tuesday in four weeks's time, a customer will walk into a shop and ask for a particular type of bicycle with specific 'extras'. The bicycle is now produced in the four weeks available and, remarkably, the customer turns up as predicted and gets the bicycle just as it has been finished. Is this a plausible situation?

The only possibility that such an event could take place is if only one type of product was produced and if customers made a fixed appointment to arrive with their request. Perhaps then the only way to have any degree of product variability would be to have 99 per cent of the components identical, with the customer choosing the remaining 1 per cent which can be incorporated very quickly? For example, a motor car with red seats instead of grey seats? This is certainly possible, but a good forecasting system would still be needed.

Figure 5.9 (previous page) contains a report on the European car manufacturing industry and the need for manufacturers to adopt the JIT philosophy.

KEY POINTS 5.3

- **Stock is used to buffer the variations of supply and demand**
- **Stock costs about 25 per cent of the average value each year**
- **Stock costs are minimized if the economic order quantity is used**
- **Just in Time methods are aimed to reduce waste in holding stocks**

EXAM PREPARATION

SHORT QUESTIONS

1 What are the principle components of work study?

2 What is the difference between a product specification and production specification?

3 Define a Just in Time production system.

4 (a) Differentiate between job and batch production systems.

(b) How might a biscuit manufacturer benefit from changing production processes from batch to flow (continuous)?

(c) Discuss the potential problems that might arise from such a change.

5 Discuss whether value analysis is important when developing a new product.

6 Name three ways in which the production department is influenced by the activities of the marketing department.

7 Why is an efficient stock control system important to a manufacturing business?

8 What do you consider to be the main problems likely to be caused by the introduction of a work study unit to a manufacturing firm?

9 List the factors which contribute to the cost of holding stock.

10 What is the value in calculating the float of an activity in network analysis?

DATA RESPONSE QUESTIONS

1 Harrison Gear Manufacturers buy in 12 000kg of special steel each year to manufacture small precision gears for bicycles. Until recently, the business has been purchasing 2 000kg every two months in order to take advantage of a supplier's discount which reduces the basic price of £5 000 per 1 000kg by 2 per cent.

Recently, a consultant has informed the purchasing manager that the cost of placing an order is approximately £20, and that the storage cost of all materials is approximately 25 per cent of the purchase price per year.

Questions

(a) If the demand for steel remains constant, and the supplier maintains a 2 per cent discount on orders of 2 000kg or more, would you advise the managers of Harrison to change their purchasing policy?

(b) A new supplier of special steel informs the managers of Harrison that it can supply to specification at a price of £5 200 per 1 000kg at instant call off. That is, the new supplier will deliver steel daily as requested from a local warehouse. Would you advise Harrison's managers to consider changing suppliers?

2 **(a)** Cooksons decide to build a new factory and use critical path analysis as a management tool. You are required to construct a network from the following data and from it identify the critical path.

Activity	*Code*	*Estimated duration (weeks)*
laying foundations	A	2
sewer connections	B	6
construction of walls and roof	C	10
plumbing	D	9
laying floor boards	E	6
electrical installation	F	8
plastering	G	5
fitting of window frames	H	4
internal fittings	J	6
glazing	K	2
painting	L	3

Precedence relationships

B and C	follow A
D	follows B
E	follows D
F	follows C
G and H	follow F
J	follows E and G
K	follows H
L	follows J and K

(17)

(b) Discuss problems which may arise in the sequencing of activities. (8)

(c) Suggest, with reasons, another model which may be useful to Cooksons in its current situation. (10)

ESSAYS

1 Is stock control theory an outdated technique now that Just in Time theory suggests that stock levels should be zero?

2 'Critical path analysis is only useful for large projects such as building a bridge or designing a large ship.' Do you agree?

CHAPTER 6

Costs in Business

▷ ▷ QUESTIONS FOR PREVIEW ▷ ▷

1 *What is the difference between a revenue cost and a capital cost?*

2 *What is depreciation and how is stock valued?*

3 *What is the difference between absorption costing and variable costing?*

4 *What are standard costs and variances?*

Information on Costs

IN CHAPTER THREE, we examined the financial accounts published by businesses on a regular basis (usually once a year, but sometimes more frequently). These accounts contained references to costs, but no attempt was made to determine how these costs were calculated. The costs shown were based quite broadly in that production costs, rather than, for example, how much it cost to make a specific product, were considered.

Year-ending accounts which are available for public examination do not disclose a great deal of information since this could be helpful to competitors. Consequently these accounts are of limited use to those people who are responsible for running the business profitably. They need to know, more frequently than once a year, how activities are progressing, usually by reference to the costs and revenue over which they have some influence.

An 'activity' in business terms is anything that has a cost attached to it. For example, a workman building a wall, a clerk preparing an invoice or an engineer designing a new boat are all activities. Each of these activities costs money because resources such as wages, materials, office rent and so on are 'used up'.

In this chapter, we shall examine activities which are costed and used to construct a more detailed profit and loss account. Such information is usually restricted to senior staff in an organization or others who have a 'need to know'. This information is called management accounting and is an aid to decision-making.

There are several ways of costing which generally lead to different reported profits. It is often thought that establishing the cost of an activity, such as the cost of making a product in a factory, is known with the same precision as the cost of the train fare to travel from London to Newcastle. This is not the case: two professional accountants can view exactly the same activities and calculate two different costs. This is because they may each have a different idea, or concept, of the fairest method to be used to calculate these costs.

Why Cost a Product?

If at the end of a time period, all the revenue from sales exceeds all the costs involved, so that a profit is made, why is there a need to find out how much each product or service costs? There are a number of businesses which agree with this statement, but they are usually small, one-person businesses where the need for paperwork is low because most product costs and sales are remembered.

However, this is not a proper state of affairs for any type of business which is being operated efficiently (lowest costs) and effectively (the right product to the customer at the right time).

The selling price of the product (which is examined in more detail in *People, Marketing and Business,* another book in this series) is decided by many factors which are usually outside the control of the supplier. Naturally, the whole point of being in business is to make sure that the selling price of the product exceeds the total costs of producing the product – that is, to make a profit. It would be foolish not to have worked out beforehand the expected costs of producing the product. The profit generated by each product could then be planned in advance on the basis of the sales forecast. Figure 6.1 is a report on the cost of a compact disc and an LP record.

After production, the actual costs incurred could be compared with these planned costs to see where improvements need to be made. Did the product take the allowed time to make? Did wages remain at the same level as originally thought? If costs are getting out of hand, corrective action must be undertaken quickly. In the ideal situation, the costs need to be examined during the course of production, not afterwards, so that corrections can be introduced as soon as possible.

Figure 6.1 – ***Cost of a Product***

Music industry defends high price of compact discs

PRICES of compact discs in the high streets are set to remain at current high levels, while the price of discs leaving the factory has fallen to less than £1.

Premium disc prices, which are between £10 and £12, leave no further room for price cuts, and cannot come down more than a fraction over the next few years, according to the British manufacturer Nimbus.

Many CDs are sold at £9.99, but the final end price is actually down to individual retailers, and can be considerably higher. The industry, however, is arguing that consumer perception in some quarters that CDs are overpriced is fundamentally misplaced.

According to the chairman of Nimbus, Peter Laister, none of the companies in the CD industry are making an unreasonable profit from the CD boom. "Nimbus this year is all right 'just'. It is certainly not making the sort of profit that allows us to reap adequate rewards."

The CD industry breaks into three tiers of supply before the product gets to the consumer: the music companies (some of which also press their own CDs); the companies which specialise in pressing CDs; and the retailers.

The "ex-factory" price of a disc (fully boxed and printed) has fallen from £1.80 to under £1 over the last few years. But it notches up a few pounds or pence as each part of the chain takes its cuts, as royalties are paid to the artists and as publicity takes its toll. The end price to the consumer for a new recording often manages to creep up to about £11.

Peter Scaping, of the British Phonographic Industry, said any suggestion that CDs are too expensive is "a lot of nonsense".

Although there are less expensive products selling for £6 or £7, these are invariably reruns of old songs available previously only on records. While they are cheaper for the consumer, there are also fewer underlying costs for the music industry.

While these mid-priced CDs are welcomed even by producers of new recordings as being "good for the market" there are serious worries in the classical music industry about cheapies coming in from the Eastern Bloc.

In the US, sales of "super-budget" CDs costing as little as $3.50 have boomed at the expense of the main CD companies. These cheap CDs are originated in the East, but often not pressed there, and they are beginning to make an impact in the UK as well.

Suppliers of prime classical titles argue that their customers will stop buying full price products. The knock-on effect is a squeeze on the industry's return on investment which, it is claimed, will stem investment in new titles.

When asked how and why these CDs can be made so much more cheaply, the answer from the western music executives is that "the economics are different". They argue that the countries where the music originates need hard currency, and will cut prices to the bone accordingly.

Justifications for keeping prices high also tend to hide behind the mystery of high technology. Making compact discs, Mr Laister says, is "just like making a semiconductor. It is a very advanced electronic product."

CD manufacture is very expensive to get into — requiring clean rooms where the impurities in the atmosphere must be minimal, and extremely sophisticated production equipment.

Nevertheless, the cost of making electronic chips falls dramatically as each new generation of chip matures. No such dramatic fall in manufacturing costs, however, is seen by Mr Laister. He says that as CDs are relatively new, and as they never started at the esoteric level of old electronic chips, neither will they enjoy the same dramatic drop in the cost of production.

Source: Independent, 8 November 1989

In many cases, the expected costs of producing a product or a service are derived from past experience. For example, the cost of materials may be estimated at £25 because over the last one thousand items produced, a total of £25 000 was spent on materials. However, is there not a danger of 'compounding a felony'? Are the right materials at the right quality and right price being used? The results of a 'scientific' investigation into the materials needed for production using method study and value analysis (as described in Chapter Five) might yield an ideal or standard material cost of £20 per unit. The same ideas apply to methods of production, skills needed from production personnel, methods of administration, marketing and other activities. This is called establishing a standard cost for the product or service.

Finally, costs are needed in advance of production to determine how much cash might be required before any income from sales is received. In a simple example, if a businessperson decided to sell computers it would be essential to know how much money would be needed 'up front'. Many new businesses find it difficult to obtain sufficient credit from suppliers to enable them to produce and sell products in sufficient time and quantity to repay the suppliers. The process of money going out of and coming into the business is called the cash flow.

In summary, costs are needed to carry out the following activities:

- **a** To plan future profits of each product or service
- **b** To calculate actual profits
- **c** To see if actual production is to 'standard'
- **d** To find better methods
- **e** To plan cash flows

Five examples are listed below showing the uses for cost information for a company producing a small item, a pen.

a Costs are needed to plan future profits

The expected cost of making the pen is £3, and the expected selling price is £5. Therefore the expected profit is: £5 – £3 = £2.

b Costs are needed to calculate actual profits

The actual cost of manufacturing the pen was £3.50, and the actual selling price was £4.95. Therefore the actual profit was: £4.95 – £3.5 = £1.45.

c Cost information is needed to compare 'what should be' with 'what is happening'

The difference between expected and actual costs is: £3 – £3.50 = (£0.50). The brackets indicate that the difference is negative. Negative means that more is spent than was estimated. A positive answer would mean that less was spent than was estimated. In accountancy this difference is called a variance.

d Costs are needed to find better methods

Experts have said that if better manufacturing methods were used, the minimum cost of making the pen could be reduced to £2.50.

e Costs are needed to plan cash requirements

If all costs had to be paid at the beginning of production, and if the customer did not pay until ten products had been made, the company would have estimated that it needed to borrow £30 (10 × £3). During the production process the company would have noticed that it was likely it would require more cash than expected and would have notified its lender (possibly the bank) accordingly.

What Are Costs?

It is important not to confuse the everyday meaning of the word 'cost' with the business meaning of 'cost'.

In everyday speech, a cost is used to describe an exchange of money for a product or a service. For example, a new car may cost £6 000, or a take-away meal may cost £3. We sometimes reply to a question using the words, 'It hasn't cost me anything yet, I don't have to pay till next February'.

The most important cost classification in business is the distinction between capital costs and revenue costs. This is like comparing the cost of building a theatre, a capital cost, and the cost of putting on a play, a revenue cost.

The theatre audience would not be expected to be charged a ticket price which for the first few performances included the total capital cost of building the theatre. However, the audience would be expected to pay for all the costs directly associated with that performance, such as wages, heating, costume hire, cleaning, advertising and so on. These are revenue costs; they have been 'used up' by the performance.

In addition to the costs directly relating to each performance, revenue costs would also include a charge to cover the estimated wear and tear, or depreciation, of the building. If the theatre cost £30 000 000 to build and had a life expectancy of one hundred years, somewhere along the line, £30 000 000 has been 'used up'. A proportion of this cost should be attributed to each year. How exactly this is done varies on several factors and we shall look at this in more detail later in this chapter.

There are other revenue costs which cannot be directly, or totally, allocated to any single performance. These are the periodic, or annual, costs of building maintenance, the salaries of staff, local taxes, telephone charges and so on.

Revenue costs are the costs of the resources which have been 'used up' within an accounting period. Generally, the period is twelve months, but other periods can be used provided that it is clearly defined.

The easy way of classifying a cost as a revenue cost or a capital cost is to use the idea of 'used up' or 'not used up' respectively. However, it is slightly more elegant to use the accountancy versions of these words, which are 'expired' and 'unexpired' costs.

If the cost is a revenue cost, then it is included within the profit and loss account for the time period. If the cost is a capital cost, then it is included in the balance sheet at the end of an accounting period.

The following examples illustrate how costs are classified into revenue or capital costs. All the examples relate to one firm which manufactures and sells brooms and dustbins. Each section deals with one particular issue.

COST A: MATERIALS FOR MAKING PRODUCTS

£30 000 was paid in January for materials for making brooms in a year. Each broom used £1 worth of materials. 20 000 brooms were made in the year, and of these, 16 000 were sold at £6 each. The rest stayed in stock.

The materials which have expired, or left the business, are solely those in the brooms which were sold to the customers – that is, the expired material costs are £16 000. This is a revenue cost. The remaining part of the costs of material is an unexpired or capital cost of £14 000. This is made up of £10 000 of material remaining in the material stores room and £4 000 as part of the finished but unsold brooms in the finished goods store room. These capital costs are recorded in the year-end balance sheet as current assets and form part of the working capital.

COST B: OPERATORS'S TIME FOR MAKING PRODUCTS

£60 000 was spent on paying wages to the people who made the 20 000 brooms during the period.

Each broom, on average, cost £3 in wages. Since only 16 000 brooms were sold, the expired operator cost for the year is 16 000 × £3, or £48 000. This is a revenue cost. The balance of wages paid, £12 000, is unexpired and is recorded in the finished broom stock. This is a capital cost as described above. Although the wages themselves have all been paid, value has been added to the broom material equal to the wages. Can you see that if no brooms had been sold then none of the wages of the broom makers would be a cost in the time period?

COST C: SALES FROM STOCK

4 000 dustbins were made in the previous year, and 3 000 have been sold this current year at £8 each. No dustbins have been made this year.

At the end of the last year, the unsold dustbins were valued at £4 each and put into stock as a capital cost. This year, the 3 000 sold dustbins (valued at £12 000) are a revenue cost while the remaining 1 000 unsold dustbins (valued at £4 000) remain in stock as part of the working capital of the business.

COST D: PRODUCTION STAFF SALARIES AND OTHER PRODUCTION MATERIALS

This year £20 000 has been spent on salaries of all the people who helped in the production process, but who were not directly engaged in making brooms. These people included organizers and people who moved boxes around and looked after stores and so on. £5 000 has also been spent on packaging materials, cleaning materials and other materials used in the production process, but which did not form part of the brooms.

It is normal to apportion the indirect costs of production (indirect costs are covered in more detail later in this chapter) uniformly over the items produced. In this case, the total indirect production cost of £25 000 is allocated to the production of the 20 000 brooms (that is, £1.25 each broom). Therefore, £20 000 of indirect production cost has expired with the sale of the 16 000 brooms (£1.25 × 16 000), and the balance of £5 000 is unexpired and carried forward as a capital cost.

COST E: COSTS OF SELLING AND ADMINISTRATION

£15 000 has been spent during the year on running the business and trying to sell the products.

All these costs are considered to have expired during the year and are therefore revenue costs. These costs include administration and salespeople's salaries, advertising, rent for the premises and so on. Unlike the production indirect costs, there is no argument about proportioning some of these costs as capital costs. All accountants are agreed that these are revenue costs.

COST F: CAPITAL EQUIPMENT

During the year, the business paid £10 000 for a fork-lift truck to make transportation methods more efficient. At the end of the year this truck was valued at £9 000.

Only the loss in value of the fork lift truck, the depreciation, is a revenue cost for the year. The unexpired part, £9 000, is a capital cost and is recorded as part of the fixed assets of the business at the end of the year.

There are other costs in a business besides those included in the brief list above, but all of them have to be considered as having expired or not, so that the total revenue costs for the year can be calculated. As indicated, there are areas of costing where universal agreement is not apparent and, therefore, differences in calculating costs will occur.

Revenue Costs

Revenue costs are those costs which are transferred to the profit and loss account for the time period.

Figure 6.2

PROFIT AND LOSS ACCOUNT FOR PERIOD Sales and expired costs	£	£
Sales		
Brooms	96 000	
Dustbins	24 000	120 000
Costs		
Cost A: Materials	16 000	
Cost B: Operators's wages	48 000	
Cost C: Sales from stock	12 000	
Cost D: Production salaries, etc	20 000	
Cost E: Sales and admin. costs	15 000	
Cost F: Depreciation	1 000	
Total costs		112 000
Profit for period		8 000
ADDITIONS TO BALANCE SHEET		
Capital costs		
Additions to working capital		
Basic materials stock		10 000
Finished goods stock		
Materials in unsold brooms	4 000	
Wages in unsold brooms	12 000	
Prodn. salaries, etc	5 000	21 000
		31 000
Additions to fixed assets		
Capital equipment		9 000
Total addition		40 000

We can see from the statements A to F that the broom manufacturer had a lot of expenditure during the year. However, not all the expenditure related to revenue costs or expenses: quite a significant proportion were capital costs.

The sales of brooms (16 000 at £12) and dustbins (3 000 at £8) give the total sales income, or revenue, for the year. In Figure 6.2 the costs to be set against revenue, the revenue costs, are shown in a profit and loss account together with the appropriate statement reference (A to F). These are the expired costs.

Capital Costs

In Figure 6.2 the capital costs are shown as additional entries in the balance sheet produced at the end of the period. These are primarily the unexpired costs and form part of the working capital for the next period. The exception is the cost of the new fork-lift truck which forms part of the fixed asset capital.

Not included in Figure 6.2 are the withdrawals from stock of the dustbins sold during this period.

The Timing of Costs

It is always important to know the exact time at which a cost has been incurred. This is because financial accounts are prepared for defined periods, usually twelve months long, with the starting time and finishing time precisely defined (for example, from midnight on 31 December 1990 to midnight on 31 December 1991).

The administration rule is that a cost has been incurred when the ownership or beneficiary of the asset or resource has been agreed. In many cases this time is the point at which cash is 'handed over' in exchange for services, or more likely at the time an invoice, or bill requesting payment, is made out.

However, it is quite possible for a bill to be delayed until well after the period when the asset or resource was 'used up'. For example, a business hires a person to do some work for a day, and receives the bill from the person three months later. In this case the cost has 'expired' when the work was carried out. The cost, even an estimated one in the absence of a bill, is dated at the time work was done. This is in accordance with the Accrual Concept discussed in Chapter Four.

It is not often that a business has the time and staff available to work out when resources or assets actually expired, so for convenience the date of the bill is used. How precise this is when considering small amounts is not very important, but it is more so when considering large costs.

ACTIVITY 6.1

A business, which cans vegetables for sale to large supermarket stores throughout the country, calculates a monthly profit figure by deducting revenue costs from the revenue income.

In one particular month, the business sold 150 000 cans of carrots which it held in stock from previous months's production. The business received 60p for every can of carrots sold (total revenue equals £90 000), and the agreed stock value of each can was 30p.

In the same month, £20 000 had been spent on operator wages, £2 000 on cans and £60 000 on fresh peas. In addition to the operator wages, £40 000 had been spent on other wages and salaries connected with production. The other non-production costs, such as administration, marketing and services, amounted to £30 000. 150 000 cans of peas were produced, but none were sold this month.

In calculating the profit for the month, the accountant assumed that stock is valued at material plus operator wages plus all the production costs.

Therefore, the value of the 150 000 cans of peas in stock is:

£ 20 000 on wages
£ 2 000 on cans
£ 60 000 on peas
£ 40 000 on production costs
£122 000 which are all 'unexpired' costs

The expired costs are:

£ 45 000 for expired stock
£ 30 000 for expired non-production costs
£ 75 000 total expired costs

The profit for the period is revenue minus 'revenue costs' (expired costs):

Profit = £90 000 − £75 000 = £15 000

Although the business failed to sell a single can of peas, it still made a profit through selling from stock. This is because all the production costs had been added to the stock valuation of the canned peas.

Repeat the profit calculations with (a) all production costs regarded as expired, and (b) with 50 per cent of all production costs regarded as expired.

Remember, the production costs do not include the wages of the operators who actually can the peas. What would the profit for the period be if all wages and production costs were assumed to have expired? That is, the unsold canned peas are valued at material cost only.

What method do you think is the fairest one for calculating the profit for the period? Can you see how different accountants using different assumptions can make very different profit calculations?

Depreciation

Depreciation is the loss in value of an asset over an accounting period, and the term is reserved for fixed assets which have a life expectancy exceeding the accounting period. Normally, the accounting period is one year.

For example, if the business owned a computer which had a value of £1 000 at the beginning of the year and a value of £600 at the end of the year, the depreciation of the computer is £400.

The residual value of an asset is the expected value at the end of the planned usage. The total capital lost when an asset is disposed is the purchase price less the residual value.

Depreciation is a fair charge on the user of an

KEY POINTS 6.1

- **In a defined period, such as twelve months, all costs are either expired or unexpired**
- **Any cost which has expired is a 'revenue' cost and set against the sales value in that period**
- **Unexpired costs are regarded as 'capital' and make up the wealth of the business. This wealth is available for the start of the following period. Any loss of this wealth over the next period is an expired cost for the next period**

asset for the loss in asset value during the accounting period, but it is important to realize that the depreciation cost does not involve a flow of cash like the cost of other consumables (like electricity). For this reason, depreciation is called a provision and not an expense. The latter term implies a flow of cash.

For example, the cost of running a car is approximately £50 per week: £30 on running costs and £20 on depreciation (most new cars lose value at the rate of approximately £1 000 per year). However, although the total costs are estimated at £50, the only cash costs are £30 to cover running costs. The depreciation charge does not involve a cash transfer; the cash transfer occurred when the car was purchased.

There would be no problem in calculating the depreciation cost if the starting value at the beginning of the period and the finishing value at the end of the period were known. Simple subtraction would suffice. However, this is rarely possible since there is seldom a known 'second hand' market except for vehicles, some types of office equipment and the more common types of machine tool such as a lathe. Even then, the true value is the selling price and it is not often the case that a business wants to sell the asset.

Some businesses own unique types of equipment, specially made for the production process. For example, a business which makes and wraps chocolate sweets may own a very special packing machine which costs £250 000 at the beginning of the accounting period. How can the depreciation be calculated if the only way of calculating the end-of-period value is to try to sell the machine? Clearly this is unacceptable, and a reasonable estimate of the loss in value must be made.

Depreciation methods

The depreciation of assets is dependent on a number of different factors, including:

- Time: the older an asset the less its value
- Usage: the more the use of an asset the higher the loss in value

There are a number of depreciation methods which are based on either time, usage or combinations of both. It is always important to select the 'fairest' method of depreciation. An illustration of the use of different depreciation methods is given in the following example.

Example
A toy company salesperson has been given a car which is now one year old having been purchased for £8 000 when new. The car is expected to be resold after four years or after covering about 100 000 miles, whichever happens first, for approximately £2 500, the expected residual value.

At the end of the first year the car has travelled 30 000 miles. What depreciation charge should be applied to the car after the first year?

DEPRECIATION BASED ON TIME

There are two methods of calculating the depreciation using time as the controlling factor.

a The straight line method
This time method assumes that the value of the car decreases by the same amount each year. The depreciation cost each year is simply the total loss in value divided by the number of years:

Depreciation/yr = loss in capital value/life in years
= (£8 000 − £2 500)/4
= £1 375 per year

b The reducing balance method
Depreciation is assumed to be a constant percentage of the value at the start of each year. A percentage appropriate to the asset has to be chosen and 25 per cent is often used for cars.

Depreciation in Year 1 = 25% × £8 000 = £2 000

Value at start of Year 2 = £6 000 (called the written down value)

Depreciation in Year 2 = 25% × £6 000 = £1 500

Value at start of Year 3 = £4 500

Depreciation in Year 3 = 25% × £4 500 = £1 125

Value at start of Year 4 = £3 375

Depreciation in Year 4 = 25% × £3 375 = £844

Value at end of Year 4 = £2 531

It was necessary to continue the depreciation calculations down to the end of the fourth year in order to make sure that the resultant value is not too far away from the estimated value. In this example, an appropriate 'reducing balance' percentage was estimated, since the calculated value at the end of Year 4 is very nearly the same as the estimated value. If the values were different, it would have been necessary to modify the percentage to be more accurate.

It is theoretically possible to calculate the reducing balance percentage rate if the value at the end of a time period is known by using the following formula:

$$r = \left[1 - \left(\frac{S}{P}\right)^{1/n}\right] \times 100\%$$

where:

r = reducing balance percentage
S = the expected residual value
P = the initial purchase price
n = the number of years of expected life

Such a procedure is rarely followed in published accounts. Accountants tend to use typical percentage values for different types of asset. For example, computers tend to be depreciated at 33 per cent, industrial buildings at 5 per cent, machinery at 10 per cent and so on.

The advantage of the straight line method is its simplicity when dealing with individual items. However, the reducing balance method is relatively simple for dealing with groups of similar assets. For example, if all the cars in a business were valued at £120 000 at the start of the year and a 25 per cent depreciation rate was used, the depreciation for the year is simply 25 per cent of £120 000, or £30 000, and the written down value at the end of the year is £90 000. All this is calculated without a detailed examination of each car.

The reducing balance method is most appropriate when repair and maintenance costs tend to increase with the age of the asset, with very little, if any, maintenance costs in the early time period. The reducing balance method gives a depreciation which, when added to the maintenance costs, remains fairly constant with time.

Thus, in the above example, let us assume that maintenance costs are zero in Year 1, but are £1 200 in Year 4. If we add the depreciation costs we get:

Year 1 = £0 maintenance + £2 000 depreciation
= £2 000

Year 4 = £1 200 maintenance + £844 depreciation
= £2 044

This means that the cost of using the machine remains reasonably constant irrespective of its age. This procedure would be appropriate if we are comparing the performances of two managers by comparing their costs of operating their similar departments. Let us assume that one manager has a brand new machine with no maintenance costs, and the other manager has an identical, but much older, machine with high maintenance costs. If the depreciation provision was constant with age, the second manager would have higher total costs than the former. On the other hand, if a reducing balance method was used, the total costs of each manager for using the machines would be roughly the same.

*Figure 6.3 – **Depreciation Policies of Airlines***

GPA faces storm over jet assets

GUINNESS Peat Aviation, the world's largest aircraft leasing company that plans to come to the stock market in a $3bn (£1.7bn) flotation next month, depreciates its assets over a much longer period than leading airlines.

According to the company's preliminary prospectus filed in the United States, GPA writes off 85 per cent of the value of its aircraft over 25 years.

The company's SEC Form F1 says: "Depreciation is calculated on a straight line basis. The estimates of useful lives and residual values are reviewed periodically, and at present stand at 25 years from manufacture and 15 per cent of cost respectively."

Singapore Airlines writes off 80 per cent of the value of its aircraft over 10 years, Cathay Pacific discounts over 5 to 15 years and British Airways operates on a 12 to 20-year basis depending on the model and when it was acquired.

Companies include depreciation as a cost item in their profit and loss accounts. For the year to 31 March 1991, GPA made pre-tax profits of $281m after costs, including depreciation of $106m, were deducted from turnover of $1.89bn. In the year just past, analysts are predicting the cost of writing down the aircraft will have risen to $170m. Next year, BZW, GPA's joint broker, estimates a further hike to $210m.

One City analyst said: "If the company applied a shorter period the depreciation figure would rise at a steeper rate and eat into profits more severely.

"Nobody knows what the lifespan of an aircraft is. Most airlines take the view it is quite a lot shorter than 25 years."

A GPA spokesman said the company leased mainly new generation aircraft that are expected to have longer working lives. Airlines take a tougher approach "for tax reasons", he said, so that when they sell their aircraft they can show a bigger book profit. GPA could justify a 25-year writedown because as a bulk buyer it is able to purchase planes more cheaply.

"An airline buys a plane for $29m and depreciates it over 15 years. We buy the same plane for $24m and depreciate it over 25 years," he said.

Source: Independent on Sunday, 3 May 1992

DEPRECIATION BASED ON USAGE

It is not common in business to apply methods based on usage to assets which do not have a known traded value. But they are probably fairer methods for certain types of asset which have a life expectancy based on 'wear and tear'. The procedure for calculating the depreciation is quite straight forward. In the car example:

Depreciation/year

$$= (\text{loss in value/total usage}) \times \text{usage in year}$$

$$= \frac{(£8\,000 - £2\,500)}{100\,000} \times 30\,000$$

$$= £1\,650 \text{ in Year 1}$$

The difference between calculating depreciation on a time basis as opposed to a usage basis is that the cost is no longer a fixed cost but should be treated as a variable cost. In the time system the depreciation is fixed or constant irrespective of use, whereas in the usage system no charge would be made if the asset was not used.

ACCURATE DEPRECIATION PROVISIONS

Calculation of a fair depreciation provision is becoming increasingly important as businesses and industry in particular are becoming more capital intensive. When the fixed assets comprised only a few machines, errors in calculating the annual depreciation were not significant. Now that some assets, such as corporate computer systems, are valued at many hundreds of thousands of pounds, accuracy is very important in order to show true profits. Figure 6.3 (previous page) examines the depreciation policies of different airlines.

When commonly traded assets, such as private cars, are depreciated, it is possible to find the written down value from published information. In such cases, the known depreciation should always be substituted for the theoretical value. Theoretical calculations are needed for assets which are never traded, such as a very specialized piece of machinery, which have no value to anyone else but the user. This is called the Going Concern Concept.

ACTIVITY 6.2

Select a popular make of car which has been produced as the same model over the last four or five years (for example, Ford Escort). Select a common specification for this model (for example, manual gear change, engine size).

Research the present-day selling prices of this model for different ages. Do this by finding information in newspapers, car magazines and visits to second-hand car sales organizations.

When you have collected at least ten prices for each age category, or registration letter, calculate the average for each age group and plot this value on a graph against the car age.

Plot on the graph the theoretical value of each age group if the second-hand price was equal to a reducing balance of 10 per cent, 20 per cent and 30 per cent of the new price for each year.

Compare the actual loss in value of the car for each year against the theoretical curves.

What are your conclusions from your research?

Stock Valuation

The correct valuation of stock is important in calculating the profit earned by a trading or manufacturing business. This is because the value of stock sold to a customer is usually calculated by subtracting the end-of-period stock value from the value put into stock.

For example, assume that a business has purchased 100 televisions at £200 each for sale to the public at £300 each. Records might suggest that 80 televisions had been sold. Therefore, the gross profit earned can be calculated as follows:

Sales: 80 TVs at £300	£24 000
Cost of sales: 80 TVs at £200	£16 000
Gross profit	£ 8 000

The net profit is obtained by deducting all the operating costs from the gross profit.

However, what if a stock count was taken and only fifteen televisions were found as opposed to the theoretical value of twenty? What do you think the reasons for this discrepancy are? The first reason is pilferage, but there could be other reasons. Perhaps the sales manager has lent a set to a customer who returned a set for repair? Perhaps the person responsible for counting the stock made a mistake? But, whatever the reasons, this loss must be interpreted as a trading cost and consequently the gross profit is smaller, as shown by the following calculation:

Sales: 80 TVs at £300		£24 000
Stock at start of period:		
100 at £200	£20 000	
Stock at end of period:		
15 at £200	£ 3 000	
Stock consumed		£17 000
Gross profit		£ 7 000

By using the end-of-period stock value, a true measure of costs is achieved. Naturally, business-people will want to know how the loss in expected stock level occurred and how it can be corrected.

In the television sales example, every television would have a serial number and even though the buying price to the trader might change during the accounting period as a result of price changes by the manufacturer, the end stock value can still be correctly calculated by referring the television in stock to the invoice containing that television's serial number. But what if the items in stock had no serial number, and the end-of-period stock comprised an unknown combination of identical items which had been purchased at different prices?

This problem occurs with many commodities such as wood, coal, steel and even household goods such as furniture. There are three methods for valuing stock of this type:

- First In, First Out (FIFO)
- Last In, First Out (LIFO)
- Average Cost (AVCO)

a FIFO

The First In, First Out method assumes that all the identical stock is arranged in order of receipt, as in an orderly queue, and the 'oldest' stock is used up first – that is, stock is taken from the head of the imaginary queue. The items remaining in stock are the latest ones purchased. In times of rising prices, customers receive lower cost stock first, and the newer purchases tend to remain in stock. Remember, this is only an imaginary situation. In reality, all the stock is identical, all mixed up, and nobody is capable of telling which stock was purchased at which price. It is merely a system of valuation.

b LIFO

The Last In, First Out method assumes that all the stock is delivered to a pile and new deliveries are placed on top of the pile. Customers are given stock from the top of the pile. The items remaining in stock are the oldest ones purchased. In times of rising prices, customers are theoretically passed the latest costs quickly, and one would expect prices to reflect this or reported profits would fall.

c AVCO

No need to use our imagination here! All deliveries to stock are well and truly mixed into the old stock and the mean cost is worked out. A new mean cost is worked out each time there is a delivery.

Example

On 1 January a toy manufacturing business had no materials in stock. However, it soon purchased identical two-metre lengths of cedar wood for conversion into toy frames during January. The buying and usage transactions were as follows:

3 Jan: purchased 20 lengths at £5 per length
5 Jan: issued 12 lengths to production department
10 Jan: purchased 20 lengths at £6 per length
18 Jan: issued 12 lengths to production department

On 19 January the storekeeper confirmed that sixteen lengths of cedar wood remained in stock. There was no way of knowing when each strip of cedar wood had been purchased. What is the value of this stock?

FIFO method

The stock issued of twenty-four lengths leaves sixteen lengths at the latest price.

FIFO valuation is sixteen lengths at £6 = £96.00

LIFO method

The stock remaining comprises eight lengths at the £6 price and eight lengths at the £5 price. Remember, stock was issued from the top of the imaginary pile.

LIFO valuation is £5 × 8 plus £6 × 8 = £88.00

AVCO method

When the last stock was delivered, eight lengths at £5 (value £40) remained of the old stock. The new delivery added twenty lengths, making twenty-eight lengths and added £120 value, making a total value of £160.

The average value of items in stock after the last delivery is £160/28 = £5.71 per length.

AVCO valuation is sixteen lengths at £5.71 = £91.36.

Profit and Stock Valuation

If the cedar wood strips in the above example were not used to manufacture toys but were resold at a fixed £10 per strip, the different end of period stock valuations would lead to different reported profit for the period. This is shown in the table below.

Valuation method	*Sales value*	*Purchase costs*	*Closing stock*	*Cost of sales*	*Gross profit*
FIFO	£240	£220	£96.00	£124.00	£116.00
LIFO	£240	£220	£88.00	£132.00	£108.00
AVCO	£240	£220	£91.36	£128.64	£111.36

Notes:

Total sales are 24 strips at £10, and total purchases are £220.

The cost of sales is purchases less closing stock.

Gross profit is sales less cost of sales.

The table shows that the higher the valuation of the closing stocks the higher the reported profits. Similarly, the lower the stock value the lower the calculated profits.

KEY POINTS 6.2

- **Depreciation is not a cash cost**
- **There are different methods for calculating depreciation. The method chosen must be fair. Accountants tend to allocate depreciating assets to a number of appropriate fixed percentage reducing balance bands (for example, 10 per cent, 15 per cent)**
- **Different stock valuation methods lead to different reported profits. Higher valuations lead to higher reported profits**

Direct Costs and Overheads

So far in this chapter we have examined costs in general rather than as being allocatable to a specific product or service.

Although the sum of all the revenue costs must be set against the sales for the period to calculate the total profit for the business, it is important for the business to know what part of this total profit is being generated by specific products or services.

For example, a company which manufactures a range of computers needs to know what each model is contributing to the overall profit figure. Models which do not contribute much profit directly should be considered for replacement, unless the inclusion is justified as being part of an essential range of products. Sometimes, manufacturers will produce one or two products at a loss because the managers feel that customers want to have a full range of products to choose from. Such decisions can only be made when specific cost information is to hand.

One method for determining the product or service costs is to separate all the revenue costs into two types: direct costs and indirect costs.

DIRECT COSTS

A direct cost is one which can be allocated to a specified product or service *in total*. There is no argument. The cost being considered is totally the responsibility of that product. No other product has a claim to it!

Typical examples of direct costs are:

- Direct materials – materials used to build the product
- Direct labour – labour costs used to build the product
- Direct expenses – for example, licence fee to produce the product

INDIRECT COSTS

All costs which are not direct costs are indirect costs, more commonly called overheads. In some countries, such as the USA, the word used is 'burden'.

Often it is costly to work out the cost of small items, such as screws, and inappropriate to regard these as direct costs even though, by definition, they are. Consequently, many small, low-cost items are treated as overheads.

A typical overhead in a factory would be the cost of operating the production control department, which is engaged in scheduling and planning the production of all products. The cost of the staff doing this work needs to be shared, or apportioned, over all the products.

ACTIVITY 6.3

In a 'one-product' business, all the costs are direct costs of the product since they are all totally allocatable to the product or service. The usefulness of the separation of costs applies when more than one type of product or service is given.

Consider a service with which you are familiar. It could be a cafeteria supplying meals, a bus service, a doctor's surgery or a local engineering firm. Define one product type or service type which you have used lately. What were the direct costs of that service or product, and what were the overheads? Just put names down, not values.

Ask a colleague to check you answer. Did you leave anything out? Do you agree completely on the different classifications? The chances are that there are differences, and you should begin to realize that professional accountants do not always agree among themselves over the classification of some costs. For example, are packaging materials direct costs or overheads?

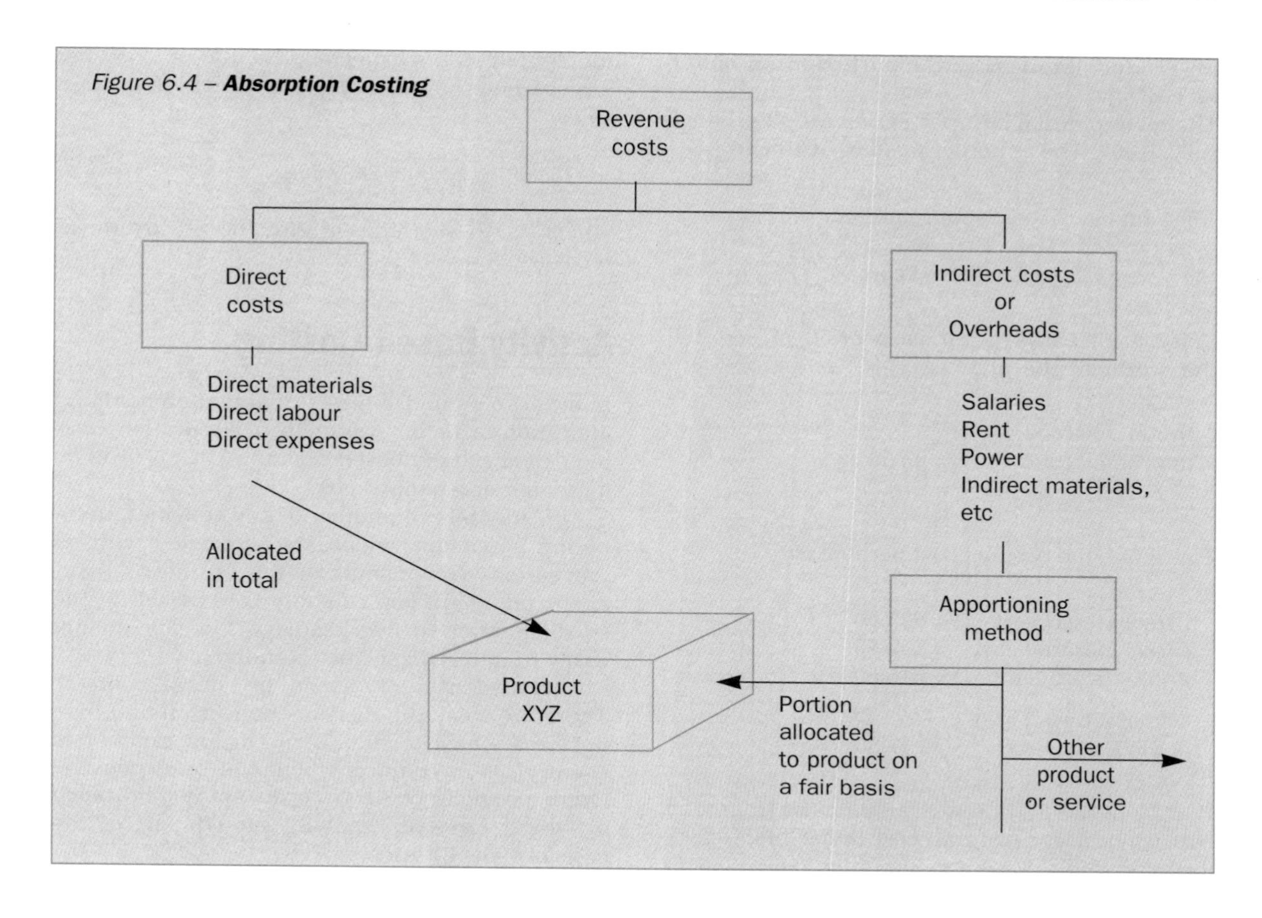

Figure 6.4 – **Absorption Costing**

Absorption Costing

Absorption costing is the most common method used for costing products and services. In this method, all direct costs are allocated to the product or service and the remaining overheads are apportioned and allocated to each product on a fair basis. It is the variety of 'fair' systems which give rise to a number of different estimates of the cost of the product or service. Figure 6.4 illustrates the method of absorption casting.

The following example shows how costs are allocated and also why different costs arise if the basis for apportionment changes.

Example

The manager of a carpentry business, which makes a range of domestic furniture, calculated that at the end of a period the total production overheads amounted to £500 000. During this period, the capacity of the manufacturing division was 200 000 man hours, this being the total time spent by all operators in making all the products. In addition, the business used 250 000kg of wood at £1 per kg (that is, £250 000 of wood during the same period).

One of the products, the Essex Chair, used 50 000 man hours in manufacturing 10 000 units during the period. Total direct material costs for the Essex Chair amounted to £75 000, and the direct labour cost was £5 per hour.

Calculate the manufacturing cost of the Essex Chair using an absorption costing method based on (a) operator capacity and (b) material throughput.

(a) Production overhead apportioned on operator capacity.

The total capacity of the business is 200 000 operator hours per period. The apportionment of overhead is:

Prodn. overhead apportionment
= £500 000/200 000 hrs
= £2.50/direct lab. hrs

Since each Essex Chair uses five hours of direct labour, the allocation of overhead is:

Prodn. overhead allocation = £2.50 × 5 = £12.50

Therefore, the product cost per unit is:

Direct labour cost	=	£25.00 (5 hrs at £5/hr)
Direct material cost	=	£ 7.50 (7.5kg at £1/kg)
Prodn. overhead	=	£12.50
Manufacturing cost of the Essex Chair	=	£45.00

(b) Production overhead apportioned on material cost

The total material cost per period for all products is £250 000. The apportionment of overhead is:

Prodn. overhead apportionment
= £500 000/£250 000
= £2 per £ material cost

Since each Essex Chair uses £7.50 of material, the overhead allocation is:

Prodn. overhead allocation/chair	= £7.50 × 2
	= £15

Therefore, the product cost per unit is:

Direct labour cost	= £25.00
Direct material cost	= £ 7.50
Prodn. overhead	= £15.00
Manufacturing cost of the Essex Chair	= £47.50

We can see that there is an increase in product cost when using material cost rather than operator cost as the basis for apportionment. On the other hand, other products will cost less using this basis, since the total overhead to be recovered remains constant.

Choosing the best and fairest basis for apportioning overheads is sometimes difficult. In general, because overheads are time based, in reflecting costs which vary with time (such as wages and rent) apportionment on a time basis (such as direct labour hours) seems the fairest method. However, some businesses which are highly material-orientated, in terms of high stocks, special storage and delivery systems, may use material weight or material cost as the basis for apportionment.

Calculating costs after the event, or at the end of a time period, are reasonably accurate compared with estimating costs before the event. Absorption costing requires knowledge of what the overheads are likely to be and what is the capacity of the business as regards a selected resource (such as direct labour hours). Both have to be estimated, and there is some danger that if capacity fails to reach the expected values, overheads will not be fully recovered over the time period.

For example, in costing the Essex Chair according to method (a), if the actual labour capacity turns out to be 175 000 hours rather than the 200 000 hours expected, the rate of £2.50 per direct labour hour is not going to be high enough since:

175 000 × £2.50 = £437 500

which is a shortage of £62 500 in overhead recovery.

Activity Based Costing

In order to minimize errors of apportionment and allocation, a recent variation of absorption costing called activity based costing (ABC) is used by a number of organizations.

ABC identifies a number of key activities, numbering about ten, which are associated with all the various components of the business's overheads (although one category is reserved for the small number of overhead costs which do not easily fit into any specific category).

A typical category could be 'client contact'. There are some products or services offered by a business which involve a significant number of client visits or contacts which can be expensive. Other products or services do not require such activities, however, so why should part of the costs of visits be added in?

When a new product or service is costed, a check is made on the number of key activities utilized and a proportion of the associated overhead is allocated. For example, if the product does not have any marketing effort associated with its supply, that product does not have any overhead associated with marketing.

ABC became necessary when one of a range of products had production changed from a labour intensive operation to a machine operation. This resulted in a significant drop in direct labour content, and thus any overhead apportionment based on direct labour capacity became grossly distorted. In ABC, the introduction of a machine manufacturing 'activity' would result in a significant overhead allocation to replace a manual manufacturing 'activity'.

Costing Conventions

Read the following Bloodhound Case Study. This case shows that although some costs are often regarded as overheads, leading to a system of apportionment and allocation, it is dangerous to presume that this is true all the time. Any cost which can be fairly allocated in total to a product or a service is, by definition, a direct cost. Direct costs are allocated totally to that product or service and are not shared out over other products.

CASE STUDY

The Bloodhound

In the 1960s, the UK government gave a contract to Ferranti, a large aerospace manufacturer, to produce a number of ground-to-air missiles called Bloodhounds. These missiles were primarily designed to defend military airfields.

Ferranti was not in a competitive market situation – that is, it could not charge the market price for the missiles. The price was agreed between the government and Ferranti after an examination of the methods of manufacture, an agreed production overhead rate, and an agreed profit margin. The overhead rate was calculated by adding up all the normal production overhead costs which included a significant design and development expense. These costs were apportioned on a production labour basis and allocated to the Bloodhound missile on the estimated direct labour hours for each unit produced.

Sometime after the missiles were produced and paid for, the government 'watch dogs' (The Public Accounts Committee) who examine significant expenses, found that Ferranti had produced the missiles at a lower cost than initially estimated and had made much higher profits than agreed by the government. The time taken to manufacture a missile had been less than quoted, and therefore the apportioned overhead should have been less. Consequently, the government forced Ferranti to repay very large sums to the Exchequer. This action very nearly caused the collapse of the firm.

Ferranti's explanation for the apparently large profits, which it disputed, was that the research and development (R&D) section had spent a great deal of time successfully reducing the time and materials of manufacture, and making the product much more reliable. In fact, the R&D had worked almost exclusively on the Bloodhound contract in order to achieve these results.

An investigation at a later date suggested that had Ferranti realized that the R&D section was a direct cost of the Bloodhound missile and not, as is usually the case, an overhead, the problems about overcharging could have been minimized. By making the R & D cost a direct cost, the overheads would have been significantly less, and the overhead apportionment per time unit would have been smaller.

In order to examine and illustrate this problem in more depth, let us make up some costs to show how these vary in an imaginary organization similar to Ferranti.

Missile direct material cost	£150 000 per unit
Expected missile labour cost	50 000 hours at £10 per hour
Overheads (ex. R&D)	£4 000 000 per year
R&D costs	£6 000 000 per year
Expected no. missiles completed per year	10
Expected total overhead (inc. R&D) per year	£10 000 000
Expected total direct labour per year	500 000 hours
Overhead apportionment rate	£10 000 000/ 500 000 = £20/direct labour hour

Therefore, the costs per missile using an absorption method with this overhead apportionment rate are:

Direct material per missile	£150 000	
Direct labour per missile	£500 000	(50 000 hrs at £10/hr)
Total direct cost	£650 000	
Overhead allocation £20/hr	£1 000 000	(50 000 hrs at £20/hr)
Total cost	£1 650 000	per missile

If the actual direct labour time dropped from 50 000 hours to 40 000 hours per missile, the adjusted cost per missile would be as follows (assuming a fixed agreed overhead apportionment of £20 per hour):

Direct material per missile	£150 000	
Direct labour per missile	£400 000	(40 000 hrs at £10/hr)
Prime cost	£550 000	
Overhead allocation £12/hr	£800 000	(40 000 hrs at £20/hr)
Total cost	£1 350 000	per missile

We can see why the government would request the organization to pay back £300 000 per missile, the difference between the initial estimated costs and the actual costs (£1 650 000 less £1 350 000). It is assumed that the R&D costs can be allocated evenly to each of the ten missiles manufactured per year.

However, if the organization had allocated the R&D cost as a direct cost of the missile rather than as an overhead, the following calculations would have resulted:

Expected total overhead (ex. R&D) per year	£4 000 000
Expected total direct labour hours per year	£500 000
Overhead apportionment rate	£4 000 000 /500 000 = £8 per hour
Direct material per missile	£ 150 000
Direct labour per missile (50 000 hrs at £10/hr)	£ 500 000
Direct R&D cost per missile	£ 600 000
Prime cost	£1 250 000
Overhead allocation £8/hr (50 000 hrs at £8/hr)	£ 400 000
Total cost	£1 650 000 per missile

exactly as before.

If the actual labour time dropped from 50 000 hours to 40000 hours per missile, the adjusted cost per missile would be as follows (assuming a fixed agreed overhead apportionment of £8 per hour):

Direct material per missile	£ 150 000
Direct labour per missile (40 000 hrs at £10/hr)	£ 400 000
Direct R&D cost/missile	£ 600 000
Prime Cost	£1 150 000
Overhead allocation £8/hr (40 000 hrs at £8/hr)	£ 320 000
Total cost	£1 470 000 per missile

In this case, although the organization would have complained that the quoted price of £1 650 000 per missile was valid commercially in spite of the reduction in hours, the pressure would have been to agree to £1 470 000, based on the agreed overhead apportionment rate, which represents a pay back of £180 000 per missile rather than the £300 000 using the other overhead rate. By regarding the direct R&D cost, incorrectly, as an overhead, it cost the organization an extra refund to the government of £120 000 per missile.

The interesting point is that the organization thought that it could make more profit by investing more in R&D, reducing the time of manufacture and yet charging the same price per missile. If such an organization had been aware that the government would 'claw back' costs if manufacturing times were less than expected, would the organization have bothered to reduce the times in the first place? This is always the problem with a monopoly firm. If it is already making a reasonable profit, how do you encourage it to reduce costs? Why would a state-run organization, where all costs are met by the state, want to increase its productivity? It is these issues which have led some countries to privatize state monopoly organizations.

Variable Costing

There is an alternative method of costing called variable costing. In this procedure, all costs are defined as either variable or fixed.

A variable cost is one which varies with the number of products produced. For example, if a business manufactured one type of exercise bicycle, the difference in total costs between making one hundred and making one hundred and one is the variable cost of an exercise bicycle, or sometimes called the marginal cost. The costs which stay the same whether the business makes one hundred or one hundred and one bicycles are called fixed costs.

Fixed costs do not stay fixed for ever – for example, a managing director's salary, which is fixed for one year, may increase the next. Nor do fixed costs remain constant for all production or output levels. The total cost of supervision salaries may stay fixed over the employment range 350–400 employees. If the number of employees increased to four hundred and fifty, it may be necessary to employ more supervisors, thus increasing the fixed costs of supervision.

Both variable costs and fixed costs can be either direct costs or overheads. It must not be assumed that all direct costs are variable costs and that all overheads are fixed costs (see Figure 6.5).

For example, the operating costs of a new refrigerated warehouse for storing one special type of product is both a direct cost of the product since all the costs are allocatable, and it is also a fixed cost irrespective of the number of products stored (over a reasonable range).

In another example, the cost of normal packing materials is an overhead, but clearly the cost varies with the level of production. To make matters even more complicated, many costs are part fixed and part variable, such as the cost of electricity where there is a 'standing charge' even if no electricity is used.

Fixed overheads are sometimes called period costs because most are costs which relate to a time period. Typical examples are rent, salaries, straight line depreciation and local taxes.

One of the prime purposes of variable costing

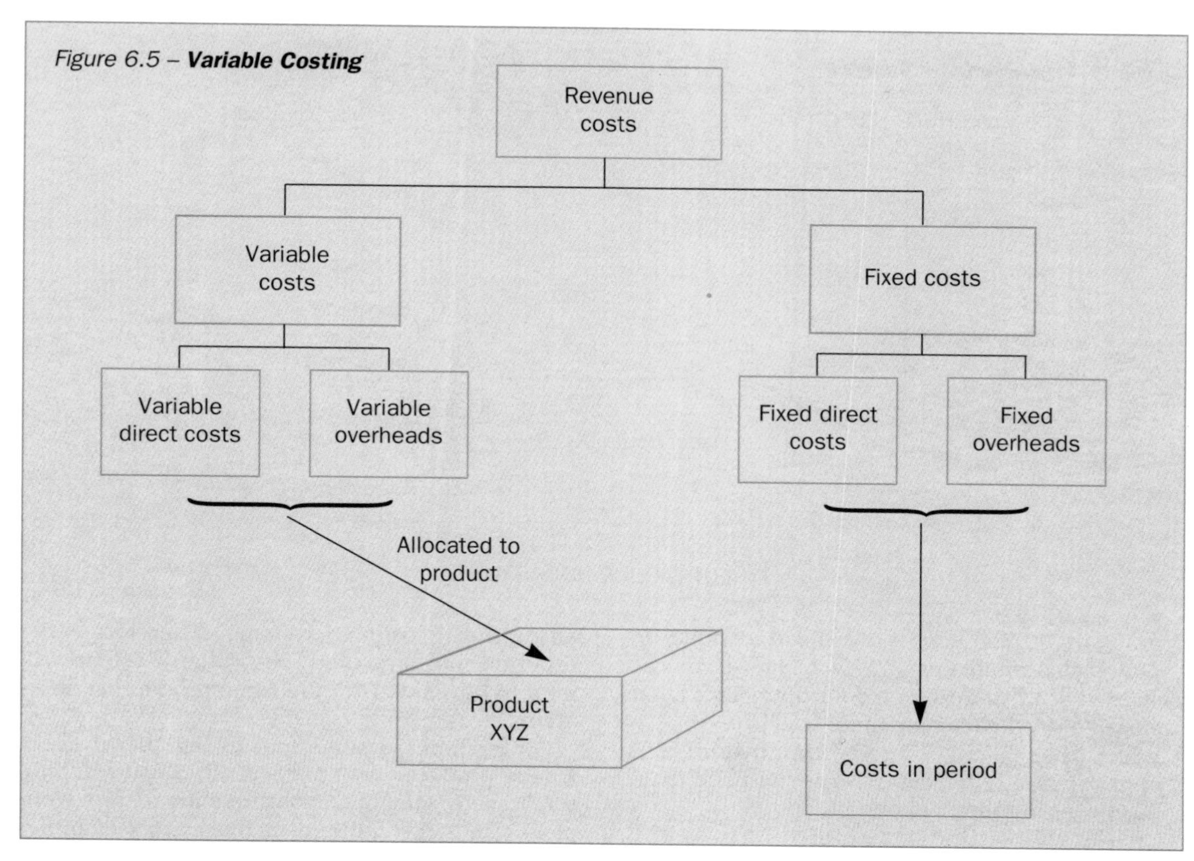

Figure 6.5 – ***Variable Costing***

is to show more clearly the relationship between volumes of output and changes in costs. This is developed more fully in Chapter Seven in the application of variable costing to profit planning situations.

Calculating Fixed and Variable Overheads

It is not easy to find the value of the variable component of the overheads, because of the complex way in which some individual overheads change with changes in output. To avoid the problem, there is a temptation to assume that all overheads are fixed over a reasonable output range. This assumption suggests that any variation in overhead is small and therefore can be ignored.

This may well be a correct assumption, but it has to be justified.

The only reasonable way of finding out how overheads vary with output is to measure the total overhead costs at different output levels over a constant working period.

The results of such an investigation into the overhead costs of a carpentry business which we looked at earlier are given in the table below. This shows the overheads obtained from the accountant. The total overhead for each of the eight periods is shown together with the output for the same period measured in hours of work of each direct operator. Hours of work is the only way of expressing output if more than one product or service is produced. The Essex Chair was only one product made from a range.

Period ref.	*Output in direct labour hours*	*Total overhead this period (£)*
1	162 000	397 000
2	175 000	445 000
3	134 000	385 000
4	199 000	499 000
5	157 000	398 000
6	203 000	498 000
7	145 000	372 000
8	164 000	418 000

The values shown in the table are plotted in Figure 6.6 (next page), and a line of 'best fit' (see Chapter Four) has been drawn through the points.

Although the line drawn in Figure 6.6 is only relevant over the range of outputs from approximately 134 000 labour hours to 200 000 labour hours, the following observations can be made:

- The increase in variable costs per direct labour hour can be found by calculating the slope or gradient of the cost line. This line shows a theoretical increase (Y) of £400 000 over a direct labour increase of 200 000 hours (X). The

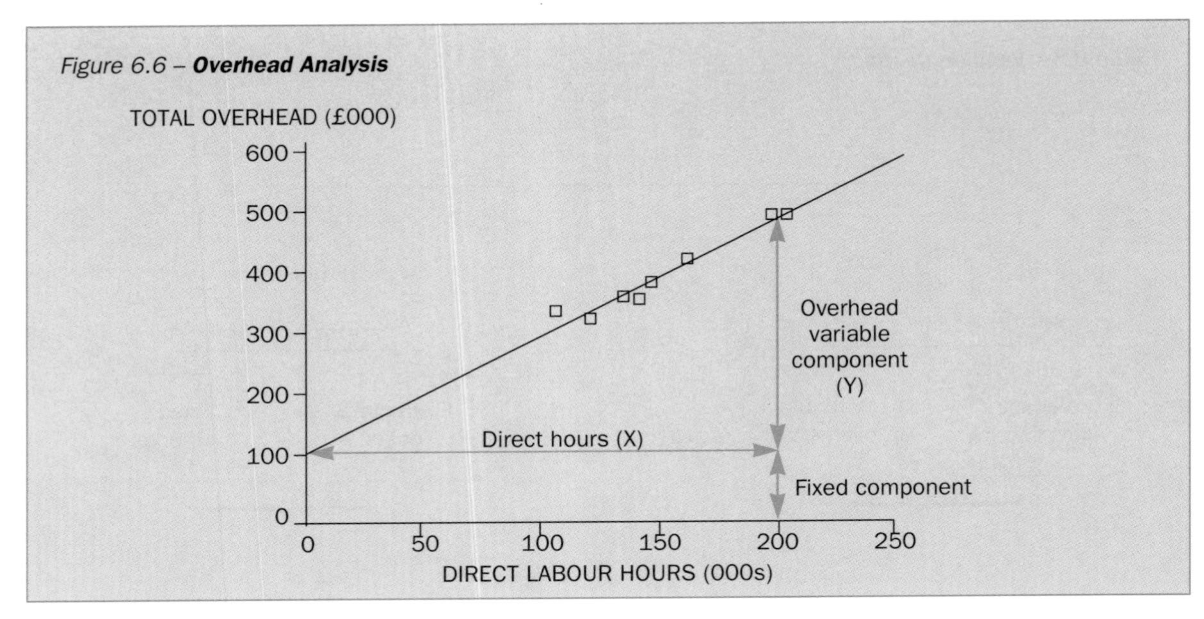

Figure 6.6 – ***Overhead Analysis***

gradient of the line is overhead divided by direct labour hours (or X/Y), which is easily calculated at £2 per direct labour hour. This is the variable overhead component
- When the output is zero, the overhead is approximately £100 000. This is the fixed overhead over the range of output plotted

We can now repeat the costing exercise for the Essex Chair, using the variable costing method:

Variable labour cost = direct labour cost per chair
= 5 hrs at £5/hr
= £25 per chair

Variable material cost = direct material cost per chair
= 7.5kg at £1/kg
= £7.50 per chair

Variable overhead cost = 5 hrs at £2/hr
= £10 per chair

Therefore:

Total variable cost of Essex Chair = £42.50

Stock Valuation

If a product is put into stock at the end of a period, the product is valued as the sum of the variable cash. It will not include any part of the fixed production costs which are totally included in the operating costs for the period. The absorption costing system does include a proportion of the fixed production costs in the stock valuation, and consequently, not all production costs are included in the total operating costs for the period. Hence, a variable costing system tends to report higher costs for a period than an absorption costing system. Therefore, the reported profit for an absorption system will tend to be smaller for the same production operations.

For example, assume that of the 10 000 Essex Chairs produced by the carpentry business, only 8 500 were sold and, consequently, 1 500 were placed in stock for sale in the next accounting period.

Under the absorption costing system using operator time as the basis for apportioning the overhead (which gave a production cost of £45 per chair), the cost value of an 'unexpired' Essex Chair put into stock and not set against revenue for the period is:

1 500 × £45 = £67 500

However, using a variable cost of £42.50 per chair, the value of the stock would be:

1 500 × £4 2.50 = £63 750

which is a reduction of £3 750. This has the effect of increasing the 'expired' costs for the period by a similar amount.

Advantages and Disadvantages

The big advantage of using variable costing is that it avoids making arbitrary decisions on how the fixed part of the overhead should be apportioned between products or services.

The disadvantage in using variable costing is that the true cost of a product or service can be disguised since the fixed overhead element is missing. Fixed overheads have to be paid even though they are not apportioned to the product or service.

Standard Costs

In the example above which illustrated the different costing methods for the Essex Chair, the following data was used:

Direct labour cost = 5 hours at £5 per hour = £25
Direct material cost = 7.5kg at £1 per kg = £7.50
Total direct cost per chair = £32.50

The question which must now be asked is: Where did these costs come from?

The chances are that all the costs, like the overhead costs examined previously, are the historical costs of past production. But what if these costs are the costs of an inefficient organization? What if the direct labour cost for producing an Essex Chair should be four hours at £4 per hour? In Chapter Five we examined the operations in a business and proposed that a production specification should be prepared for all products based on a 'scientific' approach using the best methods available. We called this approach work study.

Let us assume that an independent work study approach has been made on the production costs of the Essex Chair, with the following results (called the standards):

Standard direct labour time = 4 hours
Standard direct labour cost = £4.50 per hour
Standard direct material content = 6kg
Standard direct material cost = £0.75

These standards are different from the previously recorded values. The implications are that:

- Too much time has been allowed for production
- Cheaper labour could be used to achieve the same quality
- Less material should be used
- Cheaper material should be used to achieve the same quality

The resultant costs are:

Standard direct labour cost = 4 hours at £4.50 = £18
Standard material cost = 6kg at £0.75 = £4.50

Therefore:

Standard total direct cost = £22.50

Variances

The difference between a recorded cost and the standard cost is called a variance.

Cost variance = standard cost – actual cost

In our example above, the variances are:

Direct labour cost variance = £18 – £25 = –£7
Direct material cost variance = £4.50 – £7.50 = –£3
Direct cost variance = £22.50 – £32.50 = –£10

Negative cost variances are sometimes called Adverse (A) or Unfavourable variances (U), and positive variances are called Favourable variances (F).

The reason for calculating the variance is to allocate responsibility for its control to an individual. We could say to the person responsible for the direct labour variance: 'Why have you spent more time on making the chair than you should have done and why have you used more expensive labour than you should have done?'

There may be a perfectly valid answer to the question. Perhaps the person responsible had been

KEY POINTS 6.3

- **All costs can be separated into direct costs and indirect costs. Indirect costs are called 'overheads'**
- **Absorption costing apportions overheads on a fair basis and allocates these costs to a product or service**
- **Alternatively, costs can be separated into variable and fixed costs. In variable costing, stock valuations do not include fixed production overheads**
- **Standard costs should be derived by work study techniques and not from past performance**
- **Variances are only calculated if control of them can be achieved**

forced, because of delivery delays, to use a highly skilled and more expensive operator not accustomed to chair production. On the other hand, perhaps it was due to bad planning and supervision.

As can be seen from the above small example, a variance can be broken down into its component parts. The total direct cost variance of £10 (Adverse) is the sum of the £3(A) direct material variance plus the £7(A) direct labour variance.

One of the advantages of calculating variances is the ability to find problems before they become obvious. Examine the following variance results:

Total direct cost variance = £0
Direct material cost variance = £20(A) or –£20
Direct labour cost variance = £20(F) or +£20

In this example, the overspend in material costs is exactly balanced by the underspend in labour costs. Thus, the total direct cost is exactly what it should be and the variance is zero. If component variances are not calculated and the company is satisfied with total costs, it is missing an important problem: why are material costs so high, and will the variance increase?

EXAM PREPARATION

SHORT QUESTIONS

1 Explain the differences between FIFO, LIFO and AVCO stock valuation methods.

2 What is the difference between a variable cost and a direct cost?

3 (a) Differentiate between fixed and variable costs.
(b) How do you think Sunday trading might effect a large retailer's cost structure and profitability?

4 A machine costs £12 000 and is planned to last five years after which its estimated scrap value will be £3 000. What is its annual depreciation provision using the straight line method?

5 What is meant by an adverse variance?

6 On re-examination, an accountant thinks that the closing stock valuation should be increased by £25 000. What is the effect of this change on the previously calculated profit for the period?

7 How should a business calculate the standard labour cost for a product?

8 An accountant is unsure as to whether the new computer equipment, purchased for £100 000 with an estimated life of five years and zero residual value, should be depreciated at 35 per cent reducing balance per annum, or on the current straight line method. What affect would this change have on this year's profit?

9 (a) Differentiate between a revenue cost and a capital cost.
(b) A business has changed the building's heating system from oil fired to gas fired. Is this a capital or a revenue cost?

10 A business apportions overheads on the basis of direct labour hours. The estimated overheads for the current period are £2 000 000 and the expected capacity is 100 000 direct labour hours. Job A234 is estimated to have direct costs of £300 and to consume 15 direct labour hours. If 40 per cent is added to the factory cost to establish the selling price, what is the quoted price for A234?

DATA RESPONSE QUESTIONS

1 Bill Pilkinton, the Production Manager of Universal Wood Toys Ltd, was considering the purchase of a new wood forming machine costing about £50 000 and wondered how his department would be charged for using it. Bill knew that there were several different ways of calculating the depreciation cost and he wanted to make sure that his department would not be charged an unfair amount. His reputation at Universal was in some way based on his control of costs in his department, and he did not want to see an unfair rise in these costs, especially since they were outside his responsibility. He decided to seek some informal information from the accountant, George White.

'We know there is a sound case for purchasing the machine,' said George. 'Remind me about the life expectancy and the residual value.'

'I've never seen a second-hand machine on the market,' said Bill. 'So the residual value is the scrap value at about £500. As far as the life expectancy is concerned, I think we would expect 20 000 hours's use at approximately 2 000 hours use per year. Could be more, could be less. I would be surprised if we used it for more than ten years.'

While George was doing some rough calculations, Bill made a comment which had been worrying him for some time. 'By the way,' he added, 'if the firm pays for the machine up front, and then you charge my department for the privilege of using it, aren't you using us as a source of funds for other activities?'

Questions

(a) What do you think is the most appropriate way of charging depreciation in this case?
(b) Do you agree with Bill that depreciation is a source of funds?
(c) If, after five years, the cost of a new machine had doubled, do you think that Bill's depreciation charge should also increase?

2 For some time, the price of 2 × 2 timber purchased by Universal Wood Toys Ltd had been fairly constant at £1.50 per metre, and there was a reasonable quantity in store. According to the stock cards, one hundred metres were in stock, valued at £150.

That morning, Harry Symonds, the stores supervisor read in the papers that wood was increasing in cost by as much as 25 per cent, and possibly more for certain specifications. Harry rang up the accountant, George White, to see if they should revalue their existing wood stocks immediately.

'We are not a petrol station,' said George over the phone. 'Leave the stock cards alone, we will make the adjustment when the time arrives.'

Later that week, the new delivery of 2 ×2 arrived: one hundred metres at £2.00 per metre to join the fifty metres remaining in stock. Very soon after this, production demanded one hundred and twenty metres of 2 ×2, leaving a balance of thirty metres.

The next weekend saw the periodic stock count and evaluation. Harry Symonds viewed the stack of 2 ×2 with some consternation. As far as he could see, there were no means of knowing whether the wood was the old stock, the new stock or any combination of both!

'Well,' said Harry, 'will someone please tell me the value of this little pile.'

Questions

(a) Should George White have revalued existing stocks at the latest market prices when replacement costs went up? Why?
(b) Calculate the value of Harry's 'little pile' using LIFO, FIFO and AVCO methods. Which do you consider is the most appropriate method to use at Universal.

3 Gulls Ltd makes components for the motor industry. There are four departments, Milling (M), Manufacturing (N), Packing (P) and Administration (A). The following cost information is available:

	M	*N*	*P*	*A*
Number of workers	20	15	8	4
Wages per worker/hour	£4.50	£4	£3.75	£5
Materials per unit	50p	40p	20p	—
Capital used at cost	£120 000	£150 000	£140 000	£50 000
Working hours/week	40	40	40	40
Indirect overheads/week	£200	£250	£100	£40

On average 2 000 units are produced per week. Assume that there are fifty weeks per year. Gulls pay £18 000 rent per annum. A weekly budget for each department is required. Note that the costs of the Administration department (A) are to be allocated to the other three productive departments in accordance with direct labour costs. Ten per cent of the rent is to be charged to A and the rest allocated to the other departments in line with labout costs. Gulls's cost of capital is 15 per cent.

Questions

(a) Prepare a cost statement showing:
(i) A's total costs for an average week (3)
(ii) the required allocation of A's costs to the other three departments (2)
(iii) the weekly total costs of these three departments and of the firm in total . (5)

(b) Calculate (stating your assumptions):
(i) the average variable cost of a finished product (2)
(ii) the average total cost of a finished product. (2)

(c) Gulls Ltd has just been approached by Sharp Motors Ltd with a special order to buy 15 000 components at a total price of £82 500. Under what assumptions would you advise Gulls Ltd
(i) to accept the order (3)
(ii) to reject the order? (3) (Cambridge June 1989)

ESSAYS

1 Discuss the advantages and disadvantages of absorption costing over variable costing.

2 'Depreciation calculations are so inaccurate, they are best avoided altogether.' Discuss this proposition.

CHAPTER 7

Financial Planning

▷ ▷ **QUESTIONS FOR PREVIEW** ▷ ▷

1 *How can a business find out how well it is doing compared with others?*

2 *How can a business plan to supply the most profitable range of products or services?*

3 *How can a business find out if an investment in new resources is worthwhile?*

4 *How does a business prepare a budget?*

Information for Planning

ALL BUSINESSES have to make enough profit in order to continue in business, and therefore financial planning is extremely important. It sounds very plausible to state that a business operates to serve a customer or to provide a service to the public, or even to maintain people in work. However, without a sound financial plan resulting in sufficient funds to keep the business going, all these other objectives come to nothing. This also applies to public service organizations or similar which need to control costs in order to operate within allowed cash limits. The days of a sponsor, such as the government, agreeing to support a business which spends more money than it has been allowed are certainly numbered.

Steps in Financial Planning

Financial planning follows exactly the same steps as any other planning activity. These steps are:

a What is going on now?
This means an audit or an investigation of what is happening in the organization in terms of profitability, cash availability and investment.

b What should be going on?
If a business has previously made plans for the future, then it must be possible to find out what profit levels, cash flows and investment programmes should be taking place. These are the current objectives of the business.

c What will happen if we do not do anything about it?
We must now be able to predict, by forecasting trends, any differences or gaps which are likely to exist in the short and long term between plans and forecasts.

d Is this what we want to happen?
The gap found in step C may be quite small and we might be happy that our existing plans are adequate.

e What, if anything, must we do now to make our future plans happen?
If the gap between current plan and likely forecast is significant, the existing plan must be modified.

f How often must we check to make sure everything is going to plan?
If actual results of performance indicates rapid change, the frequency of measuring performance must increase to stop large gaps appearing. It would be foolish to wait once a year for financial results in a rapidly changing business environment.

g Do we have contingency plans available in case the worst happens?
It may be essential to have contingency plans 'up our sleeves' if any new plan needed as a result of step E takes time to implement. A plan to launch a new product cannot be implemented quickly. Therefore, a contingency plan to build a prototype new product might be authorized now, just in case a new product is required.

The questions posed in steps B, D and G imply that the managers of any business organization already have a good idea of where they want to go, and what they will do about it if something happens to challenge these plans.

There are owners who keep well away from any of the company's management activities. They turn up for periodic meetings with others who may also own a share of the business, but providing their regular dividend from profits is satisfactory, and provided that their future dividends appear equally satisfactory, they have very little need to be involved with any major decisions over the running of the business. If a business has shareholders, approximately 25 per cent of the shareholders could dictate the operations of the business since the other 75 per cent are usually not interested.

Only in well publicized events will the 'sleeping' majority of shareholders arouse themselves to activity, such as during the 'take over' of the business, the possible insolvency of the business, or the business being involved with any illegal activities and the consequent jailing of some of the directors. The main consideration for all owners is not the current state of performance of the business but the future plans, the ability of the business to generate profits and the likely growth in dividends.

There is an increasing number of owners who are only interested in the short-term profitability of the business. Perhaps they purchased shares in the business for £1 with a view to selling them within a year for £2. This represents a quite significant 'rate of interest'. Growth of this type is likely if the business is purchased by another company, or if there are expectations of such a 'buy out'. The Midland Bank shares rose from about 240p to 450p in less than one year on speculation that there was going to be an offer by another bank to buy Midland shares, coupled with a successful period of strong management and profitable growth.

Giant companies, such as ICI, are always apprehensive about movements to buy significant proportions of their shares. The fear being that a take over bid was being planned by people who thought that they could make better profits than the current directors. In most take overs the first action is to dismiss most of the existing directors, so there is an element of self-protection amongst the existing board. It is perhaps a coincidence that when companies get fearful of a take over, several cost-cutting and profit-generating exercises take place within a short time in order to improve short and long-term profits.

Although the absolute measure of profits is important, the more discerning shareholder, owner or senior manager of a business is also very interested in comparing the performance of the business with other competitive businesses, not just in one country, but in any country in the world.

Financial Ratio Analysis

Financial ratio analysis is a means of comparing financial statements to find trends in performance, and to compare this performance against competitors.

In many cases, a financial ratio can convey more information about the performance of an organization than an absolute value. Take for instance the following statement:

> An organization reports a profit before tax for the year of £325 416 which compares with last year's figure of £308 974. The capital invested in the business is £2 500 000 this year compared with £2 000 000 last year.

Obviously, this year's profit figure is higher than last year's, but can it be said that the organization is 'better'? What if inflation is running at 20 per cent per annum? What if a significant financial investment in new machinery had been introduced to halve production costs? What if all the competitors are reporting relatively higher figures?

If the profit was expressed as a ratio, such as:

$$\frac{\text{Profit}}{\text{Capital employed}}$$

then the values in the statement could be expressed as:

$$\text{ROCE (this year)} = \frac{£325\,416}{£2\,500\,000} = 0.13 \text{ (or 13\%)}$$

where ROCE is a common abbreviation standing for 'return on capital employed' and 'return' means 'profit'.

$$\text{ROCE (last year)} = \frac{£308\,974}{£2\,000\,000} = 15.4\%$$

The business does not appear to be operating as efficiently this year as last year, if the ROCE ratio is the important criterion.

Often, inflation can distort profits. For example, a business could report an increase in profits over the last twelve months of 8 per cent. But if inflation was 12 per cent over the same twelve months, what it really indicates is that the business has not even 'stood still'. It has in effect made a loss of 4 per cent.

If the profit is expressed as a ratio such as the ROCE, then inflation factors will not only distort the profit value but also the capital investment value. Consequently, when the values of profit and investment are part of the same ratio, the common factor of inflation will tend to be cancelled out from both numerator and denominator.

There are three prime reasons for generating ratios from the financial accounts:

- **a** Using ratios to compare the performance of a business with the norms in that industry, even though businesses are of different size – for example, comparing the ROCE of a small private petrol station with the ROCE of all other petrol station businesses
- **b** Using ratios to show changes within the business over a short, medium or long term – for example, the ROCE of a private petrol station owner for each month over the last six months
- **c** Comparing the planned ratios with the reported ratios in order to calculate the differences for control purposes – for example, comparing the actual ROCE with the planned ROCE in the latest budget

Calculating a ratio is very much like taking the temperature of something (for example, a human body, a cup of tea or a swimming pool). The resultant temperature by itself does not tell us very much unless we compare it with another temperature. For the same three reasons we could ask:

- **a** How does the temperature of this human body compare with that of a healthy body? If it is different, is the patient ill?
- **b** The temperature of a cup of tea is taken every ten seconds. Does the change in temperature give an indication of when the tea might be cool enough to drink?
- **c** The swimming pool owner planned for the heating of the pool to give a water temperature of 26 degrees during the winter months. Has this been achieved?

In a business there are two levels of financial information available: internal information and external information. If you are a senior member of a business, you would have full access to all the internal financial accounts. These accounts would contain details of all the costs, the value of all assets and all the sales of the different services and products. This is called internal information.

If you did not work for the business, you would only be able to find out the financial information which the business is obliged to give by law, or by gleaning information from newspaper reports. All companies have to present information annually, but much of the detail is missing and very little information on cost is given. Businesses are reluctant to disclose any more information than they have to, for fear of giving help to competitors. This is called external information.

External Financial Ratios

External ratios are those which can be calculated from published accounts, and from information available to the public because the shares of the business are sold on the open market.

These ratios are concerned with profitability, financial structure and liquidity. Liquidity is a measure of the cash available to the business. No business likes to have cash 'sitting around' and not working, so most cash would usually be invested in either working capital or short-term investments. Liquidity measures the total cash which could be generated in the short term.

PROFITABILITY RATIOS

$$\textbf{Return on capital employed} = \frac{\text{profits before tax}}{\text{capital employed}}$$

This is an important ratio, and one which has been considered before.

The capital employed is the owners's equity (capital and reserves) plus loans taken over a long period (i.e. greater than one year). The value of this ratio, commonly abbreviated to ROCE, needs to be appropriate to the risks taken in the business. Risky businesses need to have a greater ROCE than more stable ones since investors will need to compensate for any losses by higher returns over their portfolio of investments. Serious investors will not place all of their investments in one risky business; they will spread the risk over several businesses. The word 'portfolio' describes a collection of different investments.

$$\textbf{Margin on sales} = \frac{\text{profits before tax}}{\text{annual sales}}$$

This ratio indicates the average percentage profit per £ of sales, or turnover.

$$\textbf{Gross profit margin} = \frac{\text{gross profit}}{\text{annual sales}}$$

This shows the ratio of the gross profit to the turnover. Gross profit is sales value less the direct costs of production of the product or service before other overheads (such as administration costs) are considered. The gross profit margin is more commonly used by trading businesses and food supply businesses. In a trading business the gross profit is simply the selling price less the buying price.

FINANCIAL STRUCTURE RATIOS

Capital gearing $= \dfrac{\text{long-term loan capital}}{\text{owners's equity}}$

The long-term loan is now called 'creditors of more than one year' in published accounts. It represents the amount of cash which has been borrowed over a long period at agreed interest rates and agreed repayment dates.

Equity is the name given to the owners's total investment in a business, both in terms of initial cash and retained profits.

A highly geared business might have a ratio as high as 1:1, although most lenders would like to see a maximum of 0.5:1. This last ratio means that a lender will put into the business 50p for every £1 put in by the owners. Lenders will only lend this money on security of some specified asset (for example, land) which they will sell if the debt or interest is not paid.

In times of recession and high interest rates, highly geared businesses are at a disadvantage; but in times of high profits, a highly geared business makes much more profit on borrowed money than it pays in interest charges to the subsequent benefit of the owners.

Lowly geared businesses have no worries about paying high interest charges, and this gives them quite a lot of flexibility in what they do. Highly geared businesses have usually little flexibility since a significant part of their profits must be paid to lenders of loan capital.

Interest cover $= \dfrac{\text{profits before interest charges}}{\text{interest charges}}$

This ratio supports the gearing ratio to give a measure of how easily a business can cover its interest charges. A ratio of less than 10:1 coupled with high gearing would cause some concern to prospective investors. It would show that the business is not only heavily in debt but that also it is possibly not generating sufficient profits to pay the interest charges on these debts.

Earnings per share (EPS) $= \dfrac{\text{profits after tax}}{\text{number of shares issued}}$

The earnings per share gives a measure of the net profits which could be distributed to the shareholders, although it is not likely that all profits after tax would be distributed.

Price earnings ratio (PER) $= \dfrac{\text{price paid for a share}}{\text{earnings per share}}$

The price paid for a share is the average price of the share over a specified time period. Thus, if the price of a share is £2.00 and the earnings per share are reported at 20p, the price earnings ratio is 10. To put it another way, it would theoretically take ten years of similar earnings to repay the price of a share.

Financial advisers independently suggest a PER value based on the risks associated with the business. If such specialists suggested that the PER should be 8, then in this example the share price should be £1.60 if the EPS remained the same. In this case, the financial adviser would probably recommend to his client to sell the shares since £2 is a good price for something which may only be worth £1.60.

Dividend per share $= \dfrac{\text{total dividend paid}}{\text{total number of shares issued}}$

This is a straightforward ratio, provided that all the shares have the same issue price.

Dividend yield $= \dfrac{\text{dividend per share}}{\text{issue price of the share}}$

If the issue price of a share is 25p (the most common face value), and the dividend per share is reported at 5p, the dividend yield is 0.20 or 20 per cent.

LIQUIDITY RATIOS

Current ratio $= \dfrac{\text{current assets}}{\text{current liabilities}}$

This ratio compares the short-term assets of a business (such as debtors, stock, cash) with the short-term liabilities (such as creditors, tax payments – commonly called 'creditors of less than one year'). There is no intention that the business should suddenly sell all its stocks and call in all its debts to pay its creditors. The ratio is a measure of the business's ability to respond to changes in activity by having sufficient working capital (current assets minus current liabilities). This ratio should normally have a value of 2, but lower values are acceptable for very stable organizations.

Acid test or liquidity ratio $= \dfrac{\text{current assets} - \text{stock}}{\text{current liabilities}}$

This ratio is a test of the business's short-term ability to pay its debts. By excluding stocks which are difficult to value in a business 'under pressure', this ratio measures the amount of cash which could be obtained within a month or so (providing all the debtors pay up) to pay all the short-term bills. This ratio would be expected to be 1:1 – that is, there is sufficient cash available in the short term to pay the short-term debts of the business. However, larger, profitable businesses can exist with a liquidity of less than 1, because of confidence held by the current creditors.

Debtors turnover = $\frac{\text{annual credit sales}}{\text{debtors at end of year}}$

The debtors turnover indicates how promptly debtors pay up. Dividing fifty-two weeks by the debtors ratio gives the average time a debtor takes to pay a bill. For example, a ratio of 8:1 gives a payment time of 52/8, which is 6.5 weeks.

Stock turnover = $\frac{\text{annual sales}}{\text{stock at year end}}$

The stock turnover ratio is not an exact measurement because the stock should be compared with sales at stock valuation (for finished goods stock) rather than at selling prices. However, the ratio does give an indication of how well the investment in stock is working or not. Dividing fifty-two by the stock ratio gives an indication of the average time stock is dormant. For example, a ratio of 4:1 means a dormant stock time of 52/4, or thirteen weeks.

Creditors turnover = $\frac{\text{annual purchases on credit}}{\text{creditors at year end}}$

On the basis that creditors totally represent materials purchased but not yet paid for, this ratio gives an indication of how quickly or not the business pays its debts. Dividing fifty-two weeks by this turnover gives the average time in weeks. Most businesses try to collect money (debtors ratio) faster than they pay out (creditors turnover). However, since one person's creditor is another person's debtor, it is usually only the big firms which can arrange this. Small firms do not have the 'clout' to force large customers to pay up promptly.

ACTIVITY 7.1

Using the report and accounts in Appendix A, or any other set of similar accounts, calculate the external ratios as illustrated above.

Did you have any difficulty in finding the appropriate information in the accounts? Do some of the ratios appear strange or non-existent?

One of the problems which exists in many published accounts which make ratio analysis difficult, is the inclusion of group or consolidated accounts. These accounts summarize the accounts for all individual companies in a group, rather than showing the accounts for one company. Consequently, loans made from one company in a group to another company are not easy to identify and can distort ratios such as the gearing ratio. Is this statement applicable to the AGFA accounts in Appendix A?

Internal Structured Ratios

If you are able to access the detailed financial information within a business, it is more useful to 'structure' the ratios rather than to calculate ratios in a random fashion.

Firstly, a structured approach to calculating ratios is more efficient. A structured approach is similar to a fault-finding chart which is often supplied with more complex pieces of machinery. The manufacturers suggest a sequence of checks to locate the problem area quickly. Keen motorists tend to follow a structured approach to diagnosing why a car will not start. A random approach could lead to hours of frustration before the realization that the problem is . . . no petrol!

The second reason for a structured approach is that a pattern of abnormal measurements could indicate an underlying problem. Perhaps high material cost ratios and high work in progress ratios indicate poor storage management? There is some medical evidence that certain diseases cause slight changes in skin temperature over the body. It has been suggested that it is possible to diagnose certain diseases by measuring temperature patterns. This analogy can be continued into business. Certain patterns of financial ratios tend to suggest specific problems. Investors in business would be prepared to pay well for information suggesting that a business, apparently quite healthy at the moment, was likely to fail in the short term because this was indicated by a pattern of ratios. Many financial specialists, who sell advice to investors, work on this type of financial analysis.

Organizations such as the Centre for Interfirm Comparison (CFIC) can supply sets of structured ratios for a wide range of industries. The CFIC operates by collecting all the confidential internal financial reports from its members and publishing the results of its analysis in ratio format. Each participating member knows what its results are and can compare them with the other businesses in its group. However, individual companies cannot find out which financial ratios belong to which of its competitors.

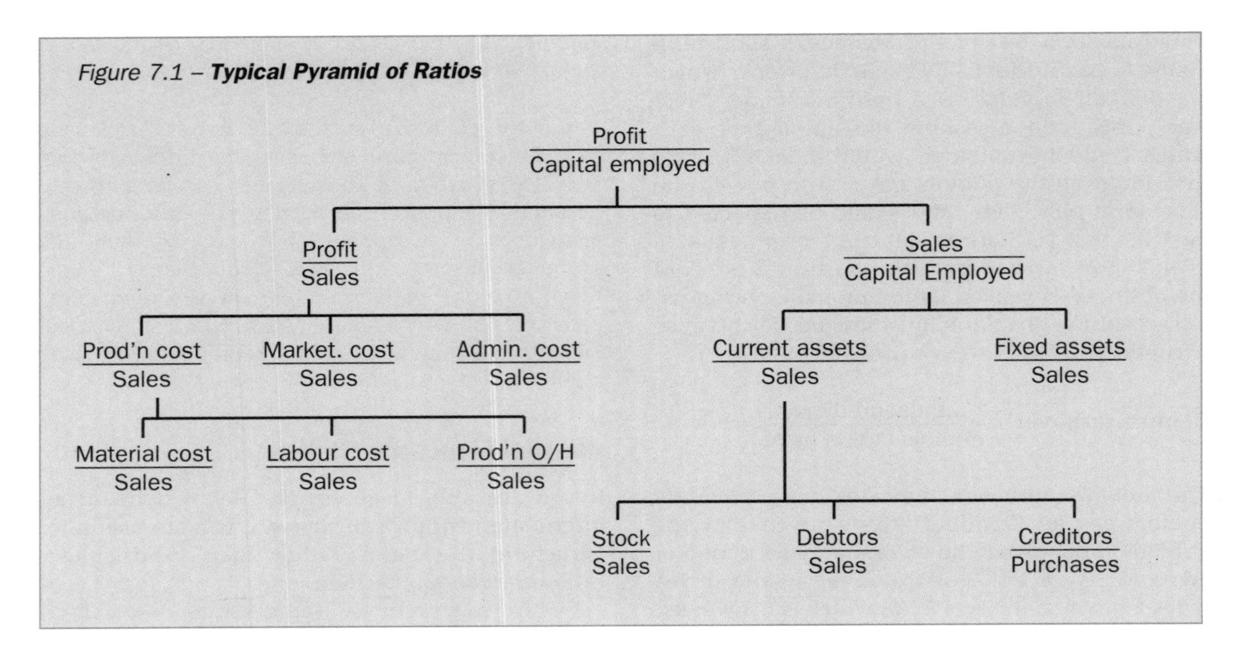

Figure 7.1 – ***Typical Pyramid of Ratios***

The Pyramid of Ratios

The pyramid approach to financial ratio analysis is based on a key ratio which is divided into two major components, each of which is split into further dependent components. There is not always a direct mathematical link for a split. In some cases a component ratio is suggested since it has 'an affect' on the major ratio.

The best way of describing a typical pyramid structure is by means of a chart. In the specific example shown in Figure 7.1, most of the values are ratios that involve sales. This does not always have to be the case. The components of the ratio are chosen in order to convey information.

In Figure 7.1, the key ratio of return on capital employed (ROCE) is subdivided into two ratio streams: profitability ratios and asset ratios.

It is not always necessary to draw up a pyramid. The ratios of different organizations or the

Figure 7.2 – ***Profit and Loss Account: Good Packaging Ltd, December 1989/90 (£000)***

	1989	*1990*
Total sales	1376	1945
Opening stock	63	75
Purchases	534	760
Wages	143	242
Factory overheads	333	420
Total costs	1073	1497
less Closing stock	75	122
Production costs	998	1375
Gross profit	378	570
Less admin. costs	162	181
Less marketing costs	68	103
Net Profit before interest	148	286
Interest on loan	12	12
Net profit after interest	136	274

Figure 7.3 – ***Balance Sheet: Good Packaging Ltd, December 1989/90 (£000)***

	1989	*1990*
Fixed assets (a)	1200	1320
Current assets		
Stock	75	122
Debtors	265	470
Cash	18	0
Total current assets (b)	358	592
Current liabilities		
Creditors	85	216
Overdraft	0	70
Tax due	71	82
Dividend due	50	50
Total current liabilities (c)	206	418
Net working capital (d) = (b) – (c)	152	174
Total assets (a) + (d)	1352	1494
Financed by:		
Ordinary shares	1250	1250
12 per cent loan	100	100
Reserves	2	144
Capital employed	1352	1494

same organization over a period of time can be laid out in a tabulated format.

Example

The Good Packaging Company Ltd manufactures flat cardboard boxes which are assembled by their customers. The company purchases cardboard sheet which is fed into automatic cutting machines. Good Packaging does not hold any finished goods in stock. Production is immediately delivered to local customers.

Figures 7.2 and 7.3 show a summary set of accounts for the last two successive years. The problem is to analyse these accounts using a structured technique.

In Figure 7.4, the company is reporting a high increase in profitability coupled with an increase in margins on sales (profit ratios).

The financial ratios show a very low gearing and high interest cover, which are good signs for increasing long-term loans. With the company returning 18.3 per cent on capital employed, loans of less than 14 per cent will give good 'leverage' – that is, earning more than interest charges on borrowed money.

The functional and production ratios are reasonably constant. The increase in wages ratio should be investigated but is perhaps due to increasing overtime.

Asset utilization shows encouraging extra sales without significant increases in fixed or current assets. There are, however, worrying points about the debtors and creditors turnover. Creditors are having to wait on average fourteen weeks for their money. This could give rise to bad supplier problems. Debt collection also seems to be slipping with decreasing debtors turnover.

The liquidity ratio has decreased to 1.12 but is still good. The current ratio, however, is falling and is now less than 1.5. This figure is too low and injection of extra working capital is required soon. This can be done by increasing borrowings.

It is suggested that an extra loan of £250 000 should be considered to finance the company's expansion.

Ratios as Plans

So far we have regarded ratios solely as aids to analysing past information. However, there is an important application of ratios in budgeting, since specific ratios may be the objectives of a year's performance, rather than absolute values – for example, setting a return on capital employed, or setting a profit on sales turnover.

Care has to be taken to ensure that the business is not distorted in order to satisfy the ratio. If the profit in a year is £1 000 and the capital employed is £20 000, it might be very tempting to

Figure 7.4 – ***Ratio Analysis of Good Packaging Ltd Accounts***

Ratio type	Ratio name	Year 1	Year 2
Financial	Gearing	0.08:1	0.07:1
	Interest cover	7.3 times	23.8 times
	Current ratio	1.73	1.42
	Liquidity ratio	1.37	1.12
Profitability	Profit/Capital %	10	18.3
	Profit/Sales %	10	14.1
	Sales/Capital %	100	130
	Gross profit/Sales %	27.5	29.3
Functional	Prodn. costs/Sales %	72	71
	Admin. costs/Sales %	11.7	9.3
	Market. costs/Sales %	5	5
Production	Wages/Sales %	10.4	12.4
	Materials/Sales %	37.9	36.6
	Prodn. o'head/Sales %	24.2	21.6
Asset utilization	Fixed assets/Sales %	87	67.8
	Current assets/Sales %	26	30.4
Stock turnover	Sales/Stock	18.3 times	15.9 times
Debtors turnover	Sales/Debtors	5.2 times	4.1 times
Creditors turnover	Purchases/Creditors	6.3 times	3.5 times

KEY POINTS 7.1

- **Financial ratios are used to compare current performance with plans and potentials**
- **Profit by itself is not good enough. Profit needs to be compared with what the best could be**
- **A structured approach to ratio analysis is more efficient than an unstructured one**

pay back £10 000 of the capital to the owners, just before the end of the year, in order to achieve the target of 10 per cent return! This is called 'window dressing'.

A ratio is a control device. It cannot by itself diagnose problems; it simply indicates that a problem could exist if the value of the ratio is significantly different from that expected. The expected value could be one based upon the previous year's performance within the same business, the best of the competition or the planned (budgeted) performance.

Contribution

Variable costing is a form of costing and mention of it was made in Chapter Six. The benefits of using variable costs as opposed to absorption costing methods for products or services are that the variation of costs with volumes of sales can be more easily seen. With an absorption costing system, the overheads need to be re-calculated for different activity levels because some overheads are fixed and some are variable. A variable costing system is only concerned with costs which vary with activity levels. This is very useful in helping to plan future activities.

The difference between the selling price of an item and the variable cost of the item is called the contribution.

Contribution = selling price − variable cost

The contribution from selling one unit of a product is multiplied by the total product sales in a period to give the contribution for that product. The contribution from all product sales in a period is called the total contribution. The only costs remaining are the fixed costs, and therefore total contribution less fixed costs equals the profit:

Profit = total contribution − fixed cost

Example

The Hardwear Carpet Co makes and sells three ranges of carpeting. The selling prices, volume of expected sales and variable costs are shown in Figure 7.5. The fixed costs of the business are £950 000.

The total contribution from the sales of all carpets is:

Total contribution	£1 180 000
less Fixed costs	£950 000
Profit	£230 000

The fixed costs comprise those overheads which do not vary with output. Some of the fixed costs are controllable or programmed, such as advertising costs which are planned to be at a certain level. Other fixed costs are less controllable, such as rent and salaries.

The question now is: Does the expected profit equal or exceed the profit required to satisfy the business objectives? If it does not, the profit must

Figure 7.5 – ***Carpet Contributions***

Type	*Selling price £/sq.m*	*Variable cost £/sq.m*	*Contrib. /sq.m £*	*Expected sales sq.m*	*Contrib. /product £*
Gold	12	7	5	50 000	250 000
Silver	10	6	4	120 000	480 000
Bronze	8	5	3	150 000	450 000

be improved, and the business managers must address those factors which can improve profits in both the short and long term.

Profit Planning

In absolute terms, profit improvements can only be achieved by encouraging more cash to come into the business and trying to stop cash going out of the business. Areas for 'attack' include:

- Reducing fixed costs
- Increasing sales volumes
- Increasing selling prices
- Reducing product variable costs
- Introducing an extra new product if capacity is available
- Replacing a product with a new one with higher contribution

We will now look at these opportunities for increasing profit in turn.

a Reducing fixed costs
Reducing fixed costs in the short term usually means making staff redundant. In the longer term a business may look for cost savings by moving premises from a high rent area to a low rent area. Many London based businesses have moved from Central London to the provinces in order to save on rent and other costs.

b Increasing sales volumes
Increasing sales in the short term cannot take place without increasing the fixed costs of either promotional activities or sales staff. Alternatively it can be achieved by reducing prices. In the longer term improvements in quality management could lead to higher sales without significant increases in fixed costs. Knowledge of each product's price/demand relationship is important.

c Increasing selling prices
In monopoly businesses, an increase in the selling price may not have too great an effect on sales, but in a competitive market, increases have to be carefully introduced. It is quite possible that the increase in contribution per unit rises faster than a decrease in sales quantity.

Take, for example, a business selling instant coffee. Daily sales are 10 000 jars at a price of £2 per jar, giving a contribution of £1 per jar, or £10 000 per day. This does not give sufficient profit, so it has been decided to increase the selling price to £2.20, which results in a fall in sales to 9 000 jars per day. But since variable costs remain the same the contribution is now £1.20 per unit, or £10 800 a day. This represents a profit increase of 8 per cent, since there is possibly no increase in fixed costs. However, if sales fell to 8 000 jars per day at the new price, the profit would decrease to £9 600.

We can see from this example that knowledge of the price/demand relationship provides extremely valuable information. This relationship between price and demand is fully covered in *The Business Environment* book in this series.

d Reducing variable costs
Variable costs can be reduced in the medium term by decreasing the labour content of a product or service through improved techniques of working and reducing material costs. Perhaps cheaper materials of the same quality are available, or perhaps with better design, less materials are required? Variable overheads are often related to energy costs. Careful control of energy can result in significant savings, as can control of telephone calls.

The application of 'scientific' study to the optimum design of product and production specifications was covered in Chapter Six.

e New products
Introducing a new product to utilize available capacity, or replacing an existing product, is a major decision activity for most businesses. There is a temptation when business activity is low for a company to diversify into another market area purely to generate cash and profits. Such a procedure is dangerous since the business does not have the skill or experience to operate in a new market without significant investment in market and marketing research.

One of the most important techniques for keeping existing products under observation, and also for testing the viability of new products, is the break even chart, which is limited to businesses which only supply one product type. Break even analysis is a simplified version of a technique called linear programming which can be applied to businesses which supply more than one product. Linear programming is a complex mathematical technique which requires a computer to carry out the calculations, and is beyond the scope of this book.

Break Even Charts

The break even point (BEP) for a single product is that sales volume which generates sufficient contribution to cover the fixed costs.

Normally, this calculation can only apply to a one-product business since the fixed costs cannot be apportioned to more than one product.

The break even point can be calculated using simple equations, but more understanding of the sensitivity of the relationships between costs, sales and volumes of production are achieved using a graphical display. The following problem in calculating profit and break even points is done manually and shown pictorially.

One result of the break even analysis is the calculation of the margin of safety, which is defined as the volume of trading above that level which is the break even level. The result is expressed as a percentage above the break even volume.

For example, if a business is trading at an output of 500 units per period when the break even output is 400 units, then:

$$\text{Margin of safety} = \frac{500 - 400}{500} = 0.2 \text{ or } 20\%$$

That is, output could fall by 20 per cent before a loss-making situation developed.

Example

Consider the case of George Sanders Ltd, manufacturers of boiled sweets.

At the moment, the company is manually intensive and fixed costs are £50 000 per year. The variable cost of production is 60p per kilo, and the selling price to wholesalers is £1 per kilo.

The owners of George Sanders Ltd are considering the purchase of an automatic production process which will increase the fixed costs to £90 000 per year, but reduce the variable cost of production to 40p per kilo. The selling prices will stay the same.

(a) What is the difference in the break even quantities between the manual and automatic systems?

(b) What is the profit and margin of safety at a sales level of 180 000kg per year?

By definition, the break even point occurs when the profit equals zero:

BEP = sales – costs = 0

or BEP = sales – variable costs – fixed costs = 0

or BEP = contribution – fixed cost = 0
ie, when contribution = fixed costs

The total contribution from one product is the number of sales multiplied by the contribution from that product:

Contribution = sales quantity × contribution/product

Therefore:

$$\text{Sales quantity at the BEP} = \frac{\text{fixed costs}}{\text{contribution/product}}$$

Figure 7.6 shows the results of the calculations for the George Sanders problem. The results for the manual option were derived as follows:

Contribution/product = selling price – variable cost
= £1 – £0.60
= £0.40

Break even quantity = fixed costs/contribution per kilo
= £50 000/£0.4
= 125 000kg

At a current output level of 180 000kg/year, the margin of safety is:

$$\text{Margin of safety} = \frac{180\,000 - 125\,000}{180\,000} = \frac{55\,000}{180\,000} = 0.31 \text{ or } 31\%$$

Figure 7.6 – **Break Even Results: George Sanders Ltd**

	Manual	Automatic
Selling price/kg	£1.00	£1.00
Variable cost/kg	£0.60	£0.40
Contribution/kg	£0.40	£0.60
Fixed cost/yr	£50 000	£90 000
Break even kg	125 000 kg	150 000 kg
Margin of safety	44%	20%
Profit at 180 000 kg	£22 000	£18 000

There are two types of break even graph. The conventional break even graph showing total costs and total sales is shown in Figure 7.7. The profit/volume graph shown in Figure 7.8 allows the profit to be read from the scale.

CONSTRUCTING BREAK EVEN GRAPHS

The break even chart (Figure 7.7) is constructed by first drawing the horizontal axis to represent the output (kg) of boiled sweets, and a vertical axis to represent costs and sales values (£). The scale of the horizontal axis is 0–250 000kg, and the vertical axis £0–300 000.

The total cost equals the variable cost plus the fixed cost. Calculate the total cost when the output is a convenient number, say 100 000kg. This is £60 000 variable and £50 000 fixed, giving a total cost of £110 000.

Draw a straight line containing the mark of £50 000 on the vertical axis, the fixed cost amount, and connect this point to the point representing 100 000kg output and £110 000 cost. This is the cost line for the manual system.

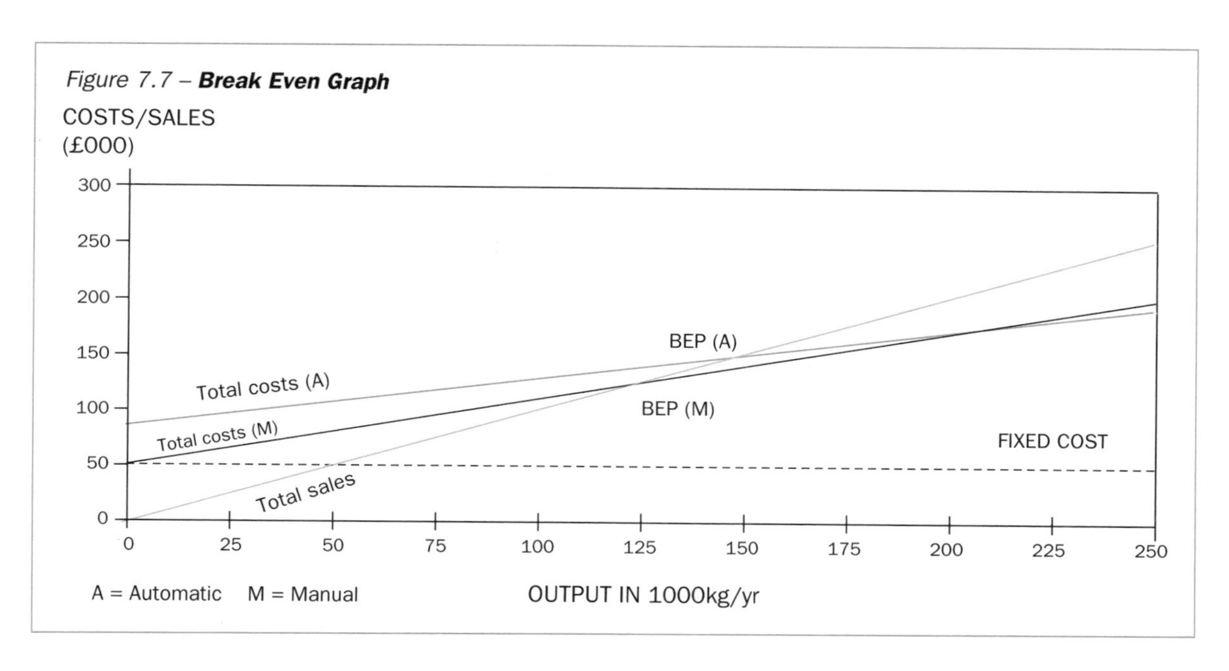

Figure 7.7 – ***Break Even Graph***

At an output of 100 000kg the sales value is £100 000. Draw a straight line containing the point 100 000kg and £100 000 to the origin. This is the sales line. Where the cost line and sales line intersect is the break even point, and should be equal to 125 000kg. This is how Figure 7.7 was drawn.

The profit at any output can be measured from the break even graph by the separation of the sales and cost lines (a negative separation below the break even point). This is inconvenient, and it is much more useful to construct a profit/volume graph as shown in Figure 7.8.

The horizontal scale of Figure 7.8 is the same as the break even graph, but the vertical scale now represents the profit. The profit for the manual system is easily shown by drawing a straight line beginning at the value of total costs at zero output (£50 000) and through the break even quantity (125 000) already shown in Figure 7.7. The profit at any output rate can then be read from the profit/volume graph.

Calculate the values for the automatic system to confirm that the graphs shown are correct.

USING BREAK EVEN GRAPHS

Comparison between the manual and automatic processes can be seen clearly in Figures 7.7 and 7.8. The higher fixed cost of the automatic process, probably due to high depreciation costs,

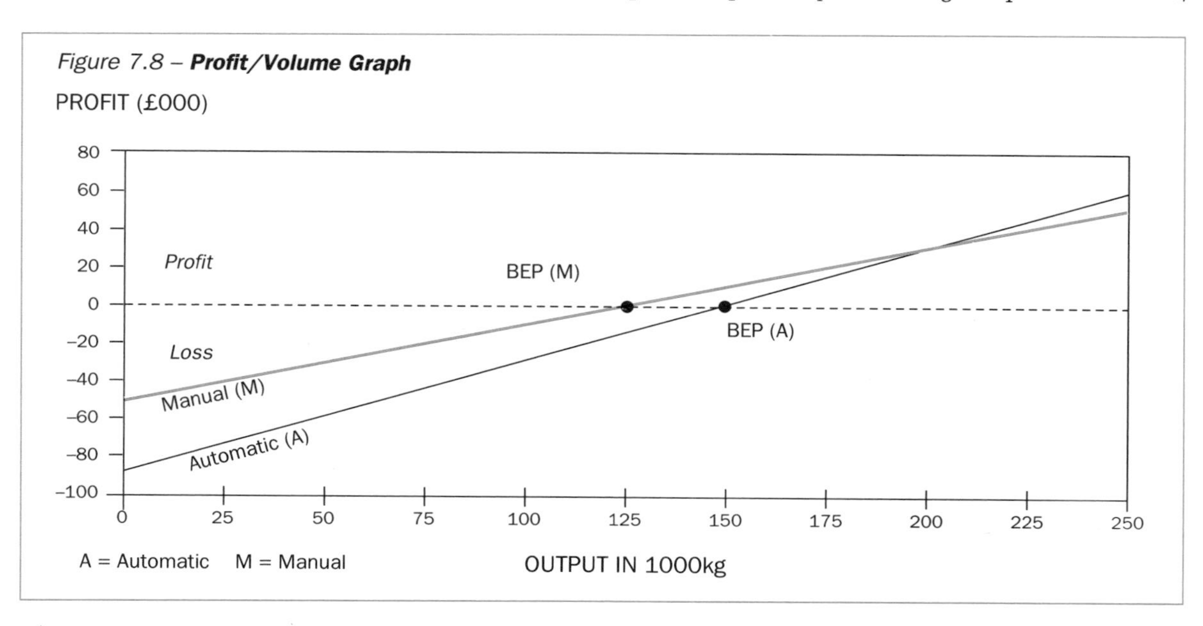

Figure 7.8 – ***Profit/Volume Graph***

and the lower variable cost do not give a clear advantage over the manual system until an output of 200 000kg has been reached.

The break even point has been increased from 125 000kg to 150 000kg by moving from a manual to automatic plant. It would appear that this transfer will only be justified if sales increase to at least 250 000kg in the short term. Above this level, profits from the automatic plant are increasing quickly compared with the manual system.

ACTIVITY 7.2

Repeat the calculations for the George Sanders Ltd problem, but only consider the automatic production system, and use a number of different selling prices (such as 80p, £1.20 and £1.50). Plot all the results on one break even graph and one profit/volume graph.

What conclusions can you draw from your results?

A profit of £20 000 is required, so plot this as a horizontal line on the profit/volume graph. What minimum sales quantities would be required to achieve this profit for the different selling prices?

Pareto Analysis

It is useful sometimes to view all products in terms of their net contributions. This can best be achieved by constructing a table showing the cumulative percentage contribution generated by all products, listed in decreasing order of net total contribution. This type of graph is called a Pareto graph, named after an Italian mathematician.

Example

A company produces five different types of garden seat. The Apple (A) range, the Beech (B) range, the Cedar (C) range, the Dark Oak (D) range and the Elm (E) range. Each product represents 20 per cent of the entire product range. The total contributions per year generated by these products and the percentage each contributes to the total is shown in Figure 7.9. Figure 7.10 shows the products arrayed in order of decreasing contribution.

Figure 7.9 – ***Product Contributions***

Product	*Contribution £*	*% Contrib.*
A	20 000	10
B	160 000	80
C	10 000	5
D	4 000	2
E	6 000	3
Total	200 000	100

Figure 7.11 (next page) shows that 20 per cent of the company's product range generates 80 per cent of the total net contribution. This result is very common and does not apply only to contribu-

Figure 7.10 – ***Order of Decreasing Contribution***

Product	*% Range*	*Cum. % range*	*% Contribution*	*Cum. cont. %*
B	20	20	80	80
A	20	40	10	90
C	20	60	5	95
E	20	80	3	98
D	20	100	2	100

KEY POINTS 7.2

- **Contribution is sales value less variable cost**
- **Break even graphs can be constructed for one-product businesses to show sensitivity of profit to increases in costs**
- **A Pareto analysis of current product range will show that there is usually a major dependence on a small proportion of the total number of products or services offered to the customer**
- **Contribution analysis identifies how profits can be improved by treating all fixed costs separately**

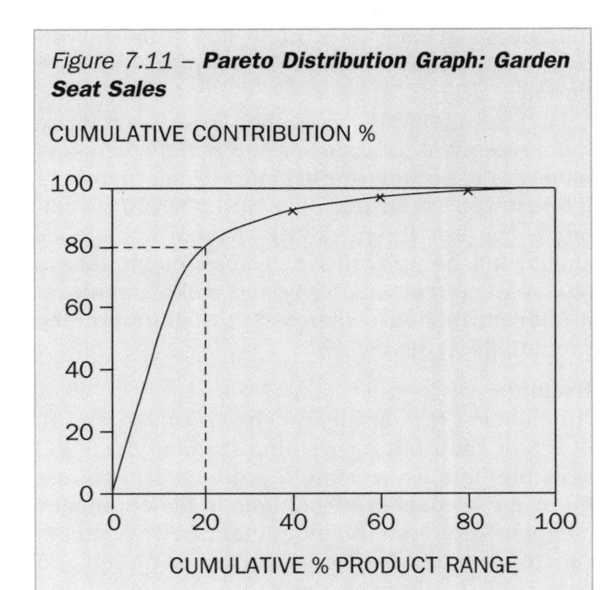

Figure 7.11 – ***Pareto Distribution Graph: Garden Seat Sales***

tions. Sometimes the Pareto distribution is called an 80/20 distribution since this ratio appears so often – that is, 20 per cent of the input is responsible for 80 per cent of the output. 20 per cent of the payers of income tax pay 80 per cent of the tax collected, for example.

In this example, product B is very important to the company. In any budgeting exercise, the plans for the Beach range need to be considered very carefully. If any product has to be dropped, then the Dark Oak (D) should be the first one to be examined.

Long-Term Financial Planning

Many think that planning is restricted to a period of one year, and certainly one-year budgets are the most common. However, a one-year budget is only part of a longer-term plan, and there are important issues within the longer-term plan which must be considered in the shorter term. For example, an investment in a new product or a new piece of machinery may not show any benefits for some time, perhaps years. But there are significant outgoings which must be considered in the short term. These cash flows will certainly affect the short-term budget.

Longer-term plans are called corporate plans and the corresponding short-term investment plans are called capital budgets. Therefore, a business has two short-term budgets: a 'revenue' budget relating to planned sales and costs in that period, and a 'capital' budget associated with capital investments in the same period.

CASE STUDY

Return on Investment

An organization is considering the purchase of a new computer-controlled production machine which has an installed cost of £250 000. The time for manufacturing a standard product will be reduced significantly, and although such savings are likely to reduce over the investment life time of six years, the pessimistic forecast for increased profits is as follows:

Year	*Savings (£)*
1	100 000
2	90 000
3	80 000
4	60 000
5	50 000
6	20 000

The machine will become obsolete, with little or no scrap value, at the end of the sixth year. The savings indicated above are assumed to be timed for the end of the year shown.

The director of production, Mike Press, has been told by the chief executive that only investments returning at least 15 per cent (termed the 'hurdle rate') will be considered by the board.

Mike Press looked at the figures again and did some quick arithmetic:

Total savings	£400 000
Investment	£250 000
Net saving	£150 000 = £25 000 per year
Average return/yr	25 000/250 000 = 10 per cent

Sadly, Mike shook his head. There was no way that the board would approve this idea.

Average Annual Rate of Return

The calculation which Mike Press performed in the Case Study above is a reasonably common sense approach and is called the average annual annual rate of return (AARR). However, this method does not take into account the time value of money, and is not a useful technique for evaluating investments.

Consider the following propositions for investing in either Project A or B:

Project A: initial investment £10 000
Returns: £100 in Year 1 and £12 000 in Year 5

Project B: initial investment £10 000
Returns: £12 000 in Year 1 and £100 in Year 5

Both of these projects will give the same AARR, but there is little doubt that most people would ignore Project A because the £12 000 paid out in the first year of Project B could be invested to give a significant increase in return over the five-year period.

Since the AARR method cannot distinguish between two investments like Project A and Project B, which are clearly quite different, it is useless as a means of investment appraisal.

Payback

A very popular method for evaluating an investment is to calculate how quickly the investment is 'paid back'. A business may have a criterion which states that no investment can take place unless it 'pays back' within two years, say.

Payback is a very conservative approach to investment. The method is essentially aimed at protecting the initial investment, which in times of uncertainty is a very natural thing to do.

Payback is a very easy technique to use. In the previous Case Study, the initial investment of £250 000 is 'paid back' within three years. Any return on the investment after this period is seen as profit. However, as we have discussed above, this does not take the time value of money into account.

In spite of these reservations, the payback method possibly remains the most common for evaluating a potential investment. Simplicity of calculation coupled with uncertainty are the most likely reasons for using this empirical approach. Payback is used extensively by organizations for products and equipment which cost less than £1 000 and which probably become obsolete fairly quickly (for example, a modification to a machine for manufacturing a product more efficiently).

The payback criteria can be used to establish a minimum payback time, or to locate the investment opportunity with the fastest payback period.

Payback methods are applied incorrectly when the investment is large and the time value of money is important (for example, think about the interest you could get on a £10 000 000 investment in just three days!). Payback methods should not be applied when investments take a few years to reach maturity and make significant profit contributions, whereas in the short term the profitability is almost zero.

Example
An engineer has designed two versions (A and B) of a new fixture for a welding system which will save the time for welding a product. The criteria for using the payback technique in the engineer's company are that no unauthorized investment can proceed unless it costs less than £1 000 and pays back within twelve months.

Product A costs £900 to purchase and saves manufacturing costs at the rate of £100 per month. The payback in one year is £1 200.

Product B costs £970 to purchase and saves manufacturing costs at the rate of £75 per month in Year 1 and £150 in Year 2. The payback in one year is £900.

Clearly both designs pass the criterion regarding cost of less than £1 000, but Product B fails to pay back in twelve months or less, irrespective of the savings made in the second year.

The Bank Statement Approach

Let us examine the previous Case Study problem on the basis that the company has £250 000 to invest. Should it let the money ride in a bank deposit account earning interest, or should it invest in the new machine tool? A reasonable criterion for the decision would be to choose that investment with the higher terminal value (i.e. most cash in the bank at the end of the investment period).

Assuming that the deposit account earns interest at the rate of 15 per cent per annum, then the compounding interest investment would be that shown in Figure 7.12. Compounding means that the interest earned in one year is not withdrawn, but increases the investment.

Figure 7.12 shows that the closing bank balance at the end of six years would be £578 300. However, if the company purchased the machine tool and invested the savings in the same deposit account at 15 per cent per annum, it would have the residual balance shown in Figure 7.13, remembering that the savings are deposited at the *end* of each year. The amount in the bank at the end of six years would be £637 100.

Figure 7.12 – ***Investment at 15% Compounding***

Year ending	*Year start balance (£000)*	*Interest earned at 15% (£000)*	*Year-end balance (£000)*
1	250.0	37.5	287.5
2	287.5	43.1	330.6
3	330.6	49.5	380.2
4	380.2	57.0	437.3
5	437.3	65.6	502.8
6	502.8	75.4	578.3

Figure 7.13 – ***Investment at 15% on Machine Savings***

Year ending	*Year start balance (£000)*	*Interest at 15% (£000)*	*Savings from machine (£000)*	*Residual balance (£000)*
1	00.0	00.0	100.0	100.0
2	100.0	15.0	90.0	205.0
3	205.0	30.8	80.0	315.8
4	315.8	47.4	60.0	423.1
5	423.1	63.5	50.0	536.6
6	536.6	80.5	20.0	637.1

There would be more cash in the bank if the company invested in the machine and banked the savings, than if it let the money remain in the deposit account earning interest at 15 per cent per annum. The difference in favour of the machine investment is:

£637 100 – £578 300 = £58 800

Clearly, the machine returns a greater percentage than the 15 per cent offered by the deposit account and, in the Case Study, Mike Press should not be dismayed. The exact return given by the machine could be discovered if the company had time to locate the theoretical bank deposit rate which equated both investments. This rate is called either the true rate of return, the true yield or the internal rate of return.

It would be depressing indeed if this type of bank statement analysis had to be undertaken each time the value of an investment was considered. Fortunately, there is a much simpler approach using the concept of discounting, which will give the exact same answer.

Discounting and Net Present Value

If you had £100 to invest now, and you found a rate of return of 20 per cent per annum, the sum of money due to you at the end of the first year would be £120. In two years's time, if you let the interest remain invested, the sum due to you would increase to £144, and so on. This is a simple compound interest calculation:

$$100 \times 1.2 \times 1.2 = 144$$

This can be expressed mathematically as:

$$\text{Value after two years} = 100(1.2)^2$$

Theoretically, although you may argue against this from a cash availability point of view, you are indifferent as to whether you have £100 now or £144 in two years's time. That is, £100 now has the same value as £144 in two years's time; £144 receivable in two years's time has a present value of £100.

Any sum of money due to be received in the future can be equated to a present value, providing that we know the investment rate over the time period. The formula for calculating the present value is as follows:

$$\text{PV of £x} = \text{£x} \times \text{discount factor}$$

$$\text{Discount factor} = \frac{1}{(1 + r)^n}$$

where:

r = discount rate (e.g. 20% = 0.2)
n = no. of years to be discounted

Example
Jill is due to receive £35 000 from her late aunt's will in ten years's time. Jill knows that if she had any money now she could invest it at 10 per cent if she wished. How much money do you think Jill should be prepared to accept as an alternative gift from her aunts's estate now rather than wait another ten years? In other words, what is the present value of £35 000 receivable in ten years's time?

$$\text{PV of £35 000} = 35\,000 \times \text{discount factor} = \frac{35\,000}{(1.1)^{10}} = \frac{35\,000}{2.593} = \text{£13 500}$$

Jill is theoretically indifferent between receiving £13 500 now or waiting ten years for £35 000. £13 500 is the present value of £35 000 receivable in ten years's time when the investment rate is 10 per cent.

Consequently, any sum of money receivable or payable in the future can be discounted to a present value. There are companies which are in the business of advancing sums of money on inheritances. However, such firms have to make a profit themselves and, in the case of Jill, the sum advanced would be less than £13 500 to allow for their 'cut'.

A Discount House is part of the banking system which will give money in exchange for a secured payment due in the future. For example, say you were the chief accountant of an organization which had recently sold an expensive product, such as a power station, to an overseas country for £100 000 000 and this sum was guaranteed to be paid in six months's time. You would probably be able to sell this 'bill' to a discount house for its present value, which depends on the current investment rates applicable to six-month investments, the risks involved and the normal commission due to the discount house. You would probably receive about £95 000 000 for the 'bill'. You get this money now, and the discount house gets £100 000 000 in six months's time, which is equivalent to an average 10 per cent per annum interest rate.

Appendix C at the back of this book contains a table showing the discount factor for different discount rates and various time periods. Multiply the future sum by the appropriate discount factor to find the present value.

We can now apply the present value principle to the Case Study presented at the start of this section, where the discount rate is 15 per cent. Figure 7.14 shows the present value calculations.

*Figure 7.14 – **Present Value Calculations***

Year ending	*Cash saving (£)*	*Discount factor*	*Present value (£)*
1	100 000	.8696	86 960
2	90 000	.7561	68 050
3	80 000	.6575	52 600
4	60 000	.5717	34 300
5	50 000	.4971	24 860
6	20 000	.4323	8 650
		Total	275 420

The net present value is:

Total present value	£275 420
less Initial investment	£250 000
Net present value	£25 420

Imagine that in one hand you hold the present value of the future savings (£275 420) and in the other hand you hold the investment of £250 000 that you are about to make. Clearly you are £25 420 better off now.

If you invested this current 'profit' at the 15 per cent rate for six years, you would have a terminal value of :

$$£25\,420 \times (1.15)^6 = £58\,800$$

The same value as shown by the bank statement approach.

THE INTERNAL RATE OF RETURN

The internal rate of return (IRR), or sometimes called the true yield, is the investment return of a project.

If the present value of the cash flows of an investment are exactly equal to the initial 'simple' investment (a 'simple' investment is one involving one initial payment only), this means that the extra returned funds over and above the initial investment are equal to the interest charges on the borrowed investment.

For example, say a company borrows £10 000 at 12 per cent to invest in a project which returns cash over a known number of years. If these cash flows, when discounted at 12 per cent, gives a present value of £10 000, then the project must be giving the company a return of 12 per cent. The net present value (NPV) in this case is zero.

Consequently, if the company is able to determine the discount rate which gives a NPV of zero, then this discount rate is the true return of the project. This special discount rate can be determined by a trial and error method, or usually by a simple computer program.

ACTIVITY 7.3

Find the internal rate of return of the previous Case Study by a trial and error method. We have found that the net present value is equal to £25 420 when the cash flows are discounted at 15 per cent. Use higher discount rates until the NPV equals zero.

THE PROFITABILITY INDEX

It is sometimes useful to rank competitive projects in terms of the net present value as a percentage of the initial investment. Obviously, this only makes sense if the investment is a 'simple' one – that is, one with a single initial payment.

$$\text{Profitability index} = \frac{\text{NPV} \times 100\%}{\text{initial investment}}$$

FACTORS INFLUENCING THE USE OF THE PRESENT VALUE METHOD

These include the following:

- The calculations are based only on *cash flows* and do not include *depreciation* charges, or

KEY POINTS 7.3

- **The present value method using discounting techniques is the only accurate method for analysing investments. Other methods do not include the effect of time on the value of money**
- **Payback is a common investment criterion because it is simple to use and is applicable in times of high risk**
- **The average annual rate of return (AARR) has no value as a means of evaluating investments**

interest charges relating to the initial investment

- Taxes on increased profits and any allowances given on the initial investment must be included. This requires a knowledge of tax levels and tax payment dates
- If inflation has a significant effect on longer-term interest rates, then the estimated future cash flows must be similarly adjusted. Thus, if current interest rates contain a factor due to current inflation, then the expected future cash flows *must* reflect the inflation trends. Future cash values must not be made in terms of today's values. For example, if the present interest rate of 10 per cent includes a factor of 4 per cent due to current inflation, then future cash flows must be increased by 4 per cent per annum to reflect this factor

Budgeting

Budgeting means the preparation of financial accounts, usually over the next twelve months, which reflect the results of planned activities needed to achieve long-term objectives. The twelve-month accounts can be broken down into months for closer control.

Ratio analysis techniques will enable planners to measure performance over the budget period and make corrections as necessary. Standard costing and variance analysis are essential aids to allocating responsibility for differences between planned performance and reported performance.

Contribution analysis will enable planners to select the best mix of products, services and activities to reach desired long-term objectives.

Investment analysis will help planners to decide the essential investments needed in new resources to support long-term activities.

Zero Base Budgets

If there is a need for significant changes in plans, and past performance is not a reliable aid, then a zero based approach is often applicable. Zero base budgeting means starting from a blank sheet of paper and building up a system of sales and associated costs rather than allowing last years's figure to be a guide.

For example, an advertising department had a budget last year of £150 000 and, allowing for 'natural increases' and inflation, requires a budget of £180 000 for the coming period. This process is called extrapolation. The zero base approach would be to allow nothing initially, and gradually build up a budget to meet necessities in order of priority.

Zero base budgeting is a time consuming activity and requires the full attention of a large number of senior managers. Extrapolating last years's budget, called extended budgeting, is very simple and cheap. However, many businesses find that a new approach to budgeting, involving the skills and knowledge of many staff working at all levels in a business, is required. Staff can identify their own ideas in the final budget, and this is often a good motivator for success.

The Cash Budget

When the product or service mix has been decided, and all the programmed costs and other operating expenses have been considered, a trial profit and loss account is constructed. This has all the detail necessary to relate departmental activities and costs, and the final profit figure is compared with the needs of the long-term plan.

If the long-term plan requires a profit of £1 000 000 for the coming period and the budgeted profit is £900 000, the budget is rejected since the plan for £1 000 000 should be the *minimum* necessary to meet future needs. The budget is sent back for revision.

When the budget for activities and resultant profit has been agreed, a detailed cash budget is prepared to ensure that money is available at all stages to fund activities, and to pay the fixed costs as they arise (for example, salaries, rent, interest on loans, tax, dividends to shareholders).

The preparation of the cash budget is extremely important, particularly when a business is growing or when trading conditions are uncertain. In both of these situations the business, especially manufacturing businesses, need to pay out for materials and wages well in advance of receiving the cash from customers when the goods or services are sold.

Normally the business's bank will lend money by means of an overdraft (see Chapter Four). Overdraft facilities need to be discussed in advance and there is no guarantee that they will be given. A great deal depends on the lender's interpretation of the business's current and budgeted accounts, probably by using many of the ratios given earlier in this chapter. An essential document required by a bank will be a predicted cash flow analysis which shows the business's predicted cash surplus or deficiency each month over the next twelve months. The deficiency has to be covered by a bank overdraft.

The following example shows the construction of a cash flow analysis from the planned budget for the twelve-month period starting in six months's time. Predictions about the start of the new budget period usually have to be made at least six months in advance. These figures would be obtained from staff who are monitoring and controlling the budget for the current period.

Example – cash flow budget

Harewood Construction Hire is in the plant hire business. It hires out equipment to construction firms who are building new roads and other relatively large construction projects. In order to maintain an efficient pool of vehicles, Harewood has to replace its vehicles fairly regularly. Two other factors have an effect on Harewood's business. Firstly, the business can be highly seasonal. Sometimes in the middle of the winter months little construction work is taking place because of weather conditions. Secondly, many of Harewood's customers are not very good at paying their debts promptly.

The Harewood accountants have prepared the following summary of the planned activities for the year beginning January 1993. Although budgeted activities result in a satisfactory profit, the cash flow implications have to be considered and a monthly cash flow analysis is now required for the first six months of the year.

All hirings are on credit and debtors take on average three months to pay their bills. The expected hirings for the last three months of 1992 are:

October	£120 000
November	£120 000
December	£ 90 000

The expected hirings for the first three months of 1993 are:

January	£100 000
February	£ 60 000
March	£130 000

Harewood's expenses for wages, salaries, materials and all other normal administration and marketing costs are paid in the month they arise. The budgeted costs of these activities are:

January	£80 000
February	£70 000
March	£80 000
April	£80 000
May	£80 000
June	£80 000

Harewood will be selling, by auction, old plant in February and expects to receive £80 000. New plant costing £130 000 is planned for March.

Harewood has a tax bill of £70 000 to pay in February, and a dividend of £40 000 has been promised for payment in June to the shareholders. The predicted cash account at the beginning of January is £10 000 in credit.

The cash analysis is shown in Figure 7.15. This indicates that overdraft facilities are required to cover cash deficiencies in March and May. A request for £80 000 to cover this deficiency is requested from the bank.

If the bank will not allow the overdraft, Harewood must either seek funds from another source (but this usually means a long-term loan) or reconsider its plans to purchase new plant. This is basically the reason for the overdraft request. The alternatives are to lease the new plant and not purchase, or to hire the plant on a temporary basis. Many of the alternatives chosen can be analysed using discounted cash flow investment methods.

ACTIVITY 7.4

Approach a local high street bank and ask if you could have a copy of one of their publications designed to help people start their own business. Not only do these publications contain a lot of valuable advice and suggestions, but they normally have a blank cash flow form included. Perhaps the bank you visit issues these forms separately? Most banks are very helpful when responding to specific requests like this.

Study this form, the results of the above exercise and Figure 7.15 carefully before attempting the cash flow questions in the Exam Preparation section.

Figure 7.15 – ***Monthly Cash Analysis for Harewood***

Month	*January*	*February*	*March*	*April*	*May*	*June*
Sales income	120 000	120 000	90 000	100 000	60 000	130 000
Plant sales		80 000				
Cash IN	120 000	200 000	90 000	100 000	60 000	130 000
Expenses	80 000	70 000	80 000	80 000	80 000	80 000
Plant purchases			130 000			
Tax & dividends		70 000			40 000	
Cash OUT	80 000	140 000	210 000	80 000	120 000	80 000
Cash IN – OUT	40 000	60 000	(120 000)	20 000	(60 000)	50 000
Cash at month start	10 000	50 000	110 000	(10 000)	10 000	(50 000)
Cash at month end	50 000	110 000	(10 000)	10 000	(50 000)	0

Notes:

1 Cash at the start of month equals cash at end of previous month

2 Numbers in brackets signify negative values

KEY POINTS 7.4

- **Budgets are financial plans to minimize the risk of not reaching planned objectives**
- **Short-term budgets are formed to reach longer-term budgets**
- **Profit objectives have to be achieved within agreed cash flow plans**
- **Extended budgeting is cheap but often not efficient**
- **Successful budgets require ratio analysis, contribution analysis, investment planning and staff involvement**

EXAM PREPARATION

SHORT QUESTIONS

1 Explain the term 'discounted cash flow' as used in accounting terminology.

2 Show how the following accountancy ratios are calculated:
(a) Dividend yield
(b) Gearing
(c) Return on capital employed.

3 What are liquidity ratios?

4 (a) What is the definition of contribution?
(b) A product has a variable cost of £10, a selling price of £16, and allocated fixed costs of £48 000 per year. What is the break even sales quantity?

5 What does a Pareto graph relating to product contribution show?

6 Define the Net Present Value and the Internal Rate of Return.

7 Why is 'payback' a popular method of investment appraisal?

8 A manufacturing company has the following financial details: debtors £10 000; trade creditors £7 000; cash £11 000; stock £7 000. Calculate the current and acid test ratios.

9 What is the difference between zero base budgeting and extended budgeting?

10 If the planned output from a factory is 25 000kg of product and the break even output is 20 000kg, what is the margin of safety?

DATA RESPONSE QUESTIONS

1 **(a)** Using the information given below, produce a cash budget for the seven months to 31 December 1990, showing clearly the bank balance at the end of each month.

PAYMENTS	£'000						
	Jun	Jul	Aug	Sep	Oct	Nov	Dec
Business purchase	2100						
Rent	5	5	5	5	5	5	5
Electricity			20			20	
Advertising	40			40			
Wages	120	140	160	180	200	200	200
Raw materials	—	280	480	540	600	600	600
Other expenses	40	40	40	40	40	40	40

RECEIPTS	£'000						
	Jun	Jul	Aug	Sep	Oct	Nov	Dec
Capital at start	2190						
Debtors (one month)	—	420	490	560	630	700	700
(two months)	—	—	180	210	240	270	300

[20]

(b) Give your suggestions for dealing with any deficits that may arise. [20]

(c) If the company exercises its option to buy its premises in June 1991 at a price of £700 000, give your advice for financing the deal together with reasons for your choice. [10]

(Cambridge May 1990)

2 The summarized accounts of Wilkinson Norman Ltd, a manufacturer of portable radios.

Wilkinson Norman Ltd 1988

Sales		1 455.00
Gross profit		620.00
Selling and administration expenses		225.00
Depreciation		15.00
Interest payable		20.00
Net profit		360.00
Balance sheet		
Net fixed assets		320.00
Current assets		
Stock	390.00	
Debtors	275.00	
Bank	15.00	
	680.00	
Less: *Current liabilities*		
Trade creditors	290.00	390.00
		710.00
Share capital	125.00	
Reserves	425.00	
Loans	160.00	
		710.00

(a) Calculate one ratio to illustrate each of the following and state briefly its importance to the firm:
(i) the liquidity of the business
(ii) how the directors have looked after the shareholders's interests.

(b) Suggest policies in the area of stock (inventory) control which would be necessary to ensure a satisfactory cash flow for a firm.

(JMB April 1991)

3 ABC Ltd had the following cost information for the year ending 31 December 1988:

Sales for the year	20 000 units
Direct costs per unit:	
Materials	£100
Labour	£150
Fixed costs	£1 000 000
Selling price per unit	£500

The following changes were expected from 1 January 1989:

Sales to increase by 10%
Material costs to increase by 25%
Labour costs to increase by 33.3%
Selling price to fall by 10%

(a) Produce a break-even chart to show the break-even quantity in 1988. *(9 marks)*

(b) Calculate the break-even quantity for 1989. *(7 marks)*

(c) Calculate the estimated change in profit between 1988 and 1989. *(9 marks)*

(d) Outline the advantages to a firm of the use of break-even analysis. *(5 marks)*

(AEB November 1989)

4 A company manufactures four products. The labour cost is £4 per hour, and material costs £10 per kg. The selling prices, sales, overheads and costs are given below.

Product	*1*	2	3	*4*
Sales price (£)	5	7	12	20
Sales/month (units)	600	450	125	90
Labour time (mins)	3	4	5	6
Material (kg)	0.1	0.2	0.3	0.4
Unit variable overhead (£)	1.2	1.8	2.3	2.5

Using the information in the table, calculate the proportion of contribution generated by each product.

ESSAYS

1 Discuss the limitations of financial ratios as management aids. Given these limitations, why are they still considered desirable? (AEB November 1990)

2 Explain the concept of break even analysis. To what extent is the concept useful in the making of business decisions? (AEB June 1991)

3 What do you think are the reasons why many small organizations ignore discounted cash flow as a method of project appraisal, and use payback instead?

CHAPTER 8

Computers in Business

▷ ▷ QUESTIONS FOR PREVIEW ▷ ▷

1 *What is a database?*

2 *What is a spreadsheet?*

3 *What is electronic mail?*

4 *What does CAD/CAM mean?*

TODAY THERE are not many businesses which do not use a computer for one reason or another. Possibly the most common use for a computer is as a word processor. This makes it possible for any person to type a letter of high professional quality, and it enables a trained typist to produce reports at a high rate. Computerized accountancy systems are quite common, and many businesses can produce detailed accounts and send out bills using fairly basic programs. However, it is perhaps fair to say that in many businesses which use computers, the computer is not being used to its true potential. A common reason is inadequate computer training amongst managers or owners of the business.

The Four Cs of Computers

It is easy to remember the main functions of a computer which make it an important part of many business systems. These functions are the four Cs:

- A computer COLLECTS and stores data, information and instructions
- A computer CALCULATES and generates information from data
- A computer CONTROLS processes and machines by giving instructions
- A computer COMMUNICATES data and information to other machines

A computer is also part of an Information Technology (IT) system. IT is a common name to describe the three main components of a modern business computer system. These components are:

- The computer and any associated machines, which are basically boxes containing electronic equipment and usually called 'hardware'
- The instructions in the form of electronic signals (voltages) which are used to program the computer to perform different jobs. These electronic signals and the instructions to generate these signals by pressing keys on a keyboard or pressing a switch are called 'software'
- The communications links, such as electric cables, optic fibres, lasers and radio waves, which allow computers in any part of the world to 'talk' to each other

Many scientists and engineers work in developing these components independently from the IT system. Hardware designers often work independently from software designers, and communications engineers may be employed in industries where the product is not computers but human voice transmission. The high rate of independent development of these three components of the IT system has in turn led to a very high rate of development of computer systems.

The Computer Program

A computer program ('program' is always spelt the American way) is a set of instructions written in a manner that can be understood by the computer. These instructions can, for example, teach the computer to sort numbers or to telephone the fire service if a smoke detector is alerted. The program is 'fed' into the computer using a keyboard or a disk on which the signals corresponding to the keyboard entries have been stored. Some programs are in the computer all the time for common jobs such as copying disks or turning on the printer. Other programs are removed from the computer when not needed to free valuable working space.

For example, we can give the computer a set of disks in order to do the business accounts. The computer reads the disks and is able to process the accounts. When the accounts have been processed, we can remove the program simply by loading in another program.

A big incentive to business users of modern computer systems is that costs have fallen while performance has increased. The modern computer costs less and does more than comparable versions of only a few years earlier.

Why a Computer?

The four Cs of a computer system can also be performed by a human being. So why use a computer? The reasons are:

- The computer works at least a million times faster than a human being
- The computer does not make mistakes
- The computer does not get bored
- The computer is more accurate

So, if a computer is so clever, why can it not run a business all by itself?

Certainly the day is fast approaching when a computer system will completely replace some types of manufacturing system. In fact, this has already occurred in some areas.

In Japan, for example, there is a prototype factory unit comprising a building containing computer-controlled machines. Machines automatically select material from a store, cut it to shape, assemble different machined items to make a component, and place these components in a packing case. When the packing case is full, it is sent out of the building, and a new cycle commences. The big difference between this factory and a normal factory is that:

- Production continues for six days (twenty-four-hour days) continuously
- There are no windows and no lighting systems, since the machines generate what little light they use for 'picking up' items, using robotic arms and fingers
- There is no environmental heating since the machines generate their own heat to keep themselves at the ideal working temperature

During the seventh, non-production day, maintenance engineers service the machine tools.

In the UK, a major computer supplier has a demonstration facility showing a designer working on a computer-controlled 'drawing board', specifying the shape of a metal component. When the designer is satisfied, the drawing is automatically sent by wires to a computer-controlled machine tool which selects material from stock and proceeds to produce the item exactly as drawn. The finished item is sent back to the designer a few minutes after it was drawn.

Finally, in financial control, computers are commonly used to generate complete sets of financial reports immediately upon request. These reports used to take trained accountants many days to produce. With this degree of up-to-date information, managers and owners can make important short-term decisions in periods of crisis, and plan longer-term activities. The business centre of an organization will begin to look more and more like the command centre of a battleship, with all current financial and operational information being instantly available, as well as the current state of all resources.

What a Computer Cannot Do

Although, theoretically, a computer system can replace many business functions, there are four main activities which will retain human participation:

- Directing a business to seek future objectives
- Negotiating agreements between parties
- Designing new products or services
- Selling products or services

All these activities require innovative imagination, and this is not a service offered by a machine. Directors must have the vision to seek new horizons; negotiators must have empathy in understanding other people's point of view; designers must have the imagination to turn marketers's dreams into reality; and a salesperson must be able to understand the customer's needs and gain his or her confidence.

The Computer as a Collector

The first C of a computer is its ability to collect and store vast amounts of data in a very small space. Rather like human beings, computers store data in different places, depending on the degree of importance.

If the word 'cat' was put in front of your eyes now, an image of a cat might fill some part of your imagination. If you were asked to image this cat walking under a tree, your imagination is now working quite well. All this activity is taking place in the 'forward' part of your brain – that part which is concerned with current matters.

The computer has a similar current storage area which is called Random Access Memory (RAM) and different computer manufacturers would tell you how much RAM their machine has. The more RAM the bigger the capacity of the machine to do fast, current work. A typical commercial personal computer may be described as having 640KB RAM. The letter K means 'a thousand' and the letter B means 'a byte' which is a measurement of electronic storage. One byte can store a number (such as '156') or a common word.

We can now get rid of the cat (if you can!) and talk about another animal. We shall give you some clues as to the animal we have in our mind. Clues are called 'addresses' in computer language. This animal is quite well known to you, but it does not yet have a place in the 'forward' part of your brain. It is stored in the 'back' area of your brain and needs to be pulled forward; but first it has to be located. Feel the tension building up? This animal roars and the male has a large mane. It lives in Africa. Hopefully we have generated enough addresses for you to pull forward the name and image of a lion, which now occupies part of your 'forward' brain. It certainly was not there before unless you read the end of this paragraph before the start.

Computers, like humans, have fast back up stores which contain large amounts of information which can be 'accessed' (meaning 'looked at') very quickly. These storage devices are called 'hard disks'. They are rather like LP records of various sizes which store information. In fact, although disks look like LPs, they operate like circular pieces of magnetic tape where the track is laid out as a large number of concentric rings. The pick-up head can move very quickly over any part of the disk, and locate well addressed data within milliseconds. There are one thousand milliseconds in a second. In large computers, disks can be stacked and data can be read from either side. In a small personal computer, the hard disk is built into the machine and hermetically sealed to prevent dust and moisture from affecting the surface. Small personal computers would have a hard disk capacity of 30MB, where the letter 'M' means a million. This fast back up store has approximately fifty times the capacity of the RAM of a personal computer.

Finally, if you cannot remember a piece of data, either because it is not in your brain or because your own addressing system is not functioning well, you will need to consult your notes or reference books. This can be a lengthy process, and not one recommended for quick answers. A computer uses the same type of facility, but the data is stored on tape which has to be accessed sequentially, although at fast speeds, or on replacement packs of disks where the data can be accessed randomly. This is an important distinction between storage on tape or disk, but one which can be easily imagined. If you wanted to hear a particular track on a LP record you could, theoretically, put the stylus down on the exact spot quite quickly. On the other hand, if you were accessing a tape you would have to run through the tape until you reached the piece you needed. The time of access between the two systems would be quite different. Tape is used commercially for storing rarely used data because it is a cheap medium.

Databases

Data can be recorded by any system in one of two ways. The first is as a file, and the second is as a database. This is explained by means of an example. Figure 8.1 shows the fictitious addresses of four people who are customers of Great Pies Ltd. Figure 8.2 shows a list of customers who last purchased pies on Monday 12 September 1991.

Figure 8.1 – ***Great Pies Ltd: Customer Addresses***

A L Price
14 West Gardens
Aldershot
Hants

P J Clarke
The Grange
Harston
Leeds

H K Graham
125 Station Road
Tonbridge
Kent

A D Franks
14 Phillips Crescent
Westgate
Leeds

Figure 8.2 – ***Great Pies Ltd: Sales for Monday 12 September 1991***

A D Franks	12 dozen cherry pies	£36.00
P J Clarke	30 dozen apple pies	£64.00
A L Price	20 dozen cherry pies	£60.00
H K Graham	6 dozen pear pies	£15.00

The data shown in Figures 8.1 and 8.2 can be typed into a computer in two files. The first file is a list of addresses, and the second file is a list of sales. The computer would allow the operator to select any file entry quite quickly, even if the list ran to 1 000 names and addresses, and perhaps 100 sales transactions. The computer would also enable the operator to print out any file address

Figure 8.3 – ***Database of Great Pies Ltd Customers***

Customer	*Address*	*Key town*	*Last order date*	*Sales value (£)*	*Pie type*	*Amount (dozens)*
Price, A L	14 West Gardens	Aldershot	12.9.91	60	cherry	20
Graham, H K	125 Station Road	Tonbridge	12.9.91	15	pear	6
Clarke, P J	The Grange, Harston	Leeds	12.9.91	64	apple	30
Franks, A D	14 Phillips Crescent, Westgate	Leeds	12.9.91	36	cherry	12

or file sale transaction very quickly. However, the computer would not, with the information in this format, allow an operator to ask it to print out the names and addresses of all customers who live in Leeds and who spent more than £30 on 12 September 1991. A database, on the other hand, would contain the same fictitious data in a different format, as shown in Figure 8.3.

The database shown in Figure 8.3 is a logical structure – the actual physical way in which it is stored in the computer is as a pattern of convenient electronic signals. Each line in the database is called a record. Each column in the database is called a field. Usually, one field is termed the key field which gives order to the database. In Figure 8.3 the key field is the customer's name.

The database can now be interrogated by a statement, such as:

Print out the names and addresses of all customers who satisfy the following conditions:

- The town is Leeds
- The date of the last purchase is 12.9.91
- The amount of purchase is greater or equal to £30

These conditions will result in the names and addresses of Clarke and Franks being printed in a way which can also be exactly stated. For example, the printing could be on a letter or a label, or at appropriate places in a letter. You have probably seen a letter from a mail order business or book club which has obviously been sent to thousands of other people, but which includes personal references to each recipient in terms of first name and where they live.

Database Management

The aim of all database operators is to enter data once only. There should be no need to type in a customer's address more than once whatever the number of transactions between the business and the customer. Naturally some sort of reference will be needed, but this can be quickly coded and entered.

A database management system is a way of cross-referencing between different databases. For example, the database entries relating to the customer's address would be on a separate database together with any other information of importance, such as how long the customer has been a customer. Another database lists the sales and production records for a time period. Yet another database has entries for each customer's account: how much is owing, when the last bill was paid and so on. The database manager program carries out the essential cross-referencing, to produce results exactly as shown in Figure 8.3 but using a range of separate databases.

ACTIVITY 8.1

Choose twelve of your own books. List for each book the following information:

- The title (do not include the word 'the' or 'a' or 'an')
- The author (only the first author if more than one)
- The publisher (only the first if more than one)
- The date of publication
- The printer
- The published price, if known. If not known, put zero (0)
- The number of pages
- The ISBN reference number

You should be able to find all this information printed in the book.

If you are able to type this information into a computer database, please do so.

Answer the following questions (in computer language this would be called generating a report) by specifying a condition(s) in each field:

(a) How many books do you own which have been published within the last three years?

(b) What is the name of the author who has written the book with the most pages?

KEY POINTS 8.1

- **A database is data represented by rows called records, and by columns called fields**
- **It should only be necessary to enter data once into the business computer database system**
- **A database manager is a program to control the interactions between separate databases**

(c) List the book titles in order of decreasing price.

(d) List the names of the printers and the ISBN numbers for all books with less than one hundred pages.

If you have a computer and you are familiar with a database program, you should be able to answer most of these questions. If you are answering the questions manually, you will realize why a computer is an essential piece of library equipment.

The Computer as a Calculator

Computers can add and subtract at the speed of light! Calculations are performed in many parts of a business, from design calculations to financial reports to market research analyses. Production departments are constantly updating plans, personnel departments are working out wages and salaries, and the transport manager is trying to find the most economical way of loading a van.

Spreadsheets

There are many specialized programs that can be purchased to perform different calculations, but one of the most common and flexible is called a spreadsheet. A spreadsheet program presents a blank table on to the computer visual display unit (VDU). This table has rows and columns which are numbered and lettered. A typical spreadsheet may have up to two hundred and fifty-five columns starting A, B, C, and going on to BF, BG, BH, BI and so on. A typical number of rows is 10 000.

It is obvious that only a part of the spreadsheet can be shown on the computer VDU at any one time, and this is usually about twenty rows by eight columns. Each column is wide enough to take up to ten characters, but this can be changed if required. Each row and column intersection is called a cell, or an element, and a word, number or calculation formula can be entered into each one.

For example, the cell referenced D6, which is the element at the intersection of column D with row 6, can have placed in it:

- A word such as 'sales'
- A number such as '14 000'
- A formula such as 'A4*E2/B3', which means: multiply the contents of cell A4 by the contents of cell E2 and divide the answer by the contents of cell B3. Put the answer into cell D6. Note that in computer language the symbol * means multiplication. This is to make sure that the normal cross sign is not confused with a column or a variable referenced 'X'

The most important feature of a spreadsheet is that if changes are made to any numbers, and these numbers are processed by means of formulae, the resultant answers automatically change as the new number is entered.

For example, in the formula example above, a formula was entered into cell D6. This formula is:

A4*E2/B3

If A4 contains the number 1 000, E2 contains the number 4 and B3 contains the number 10, then the result

1000*4/10 = 400

would appear in cell D6 (see Figure 8.4, next page).

However, if the number in cell A4 was changed to 1 200, the result in cell D6 would immediately change to the new result:

1200*4/10 = 480

If any cell in a formula was not a number, but a word (called 'text') or a formula, the spreadsheet program would signal that an error has been made.

Spreadsheets are extremely useful for planning when some data is uncertain. Perhaps in a financial

Figure 8.4 – ***A Spreadsheet Layout***

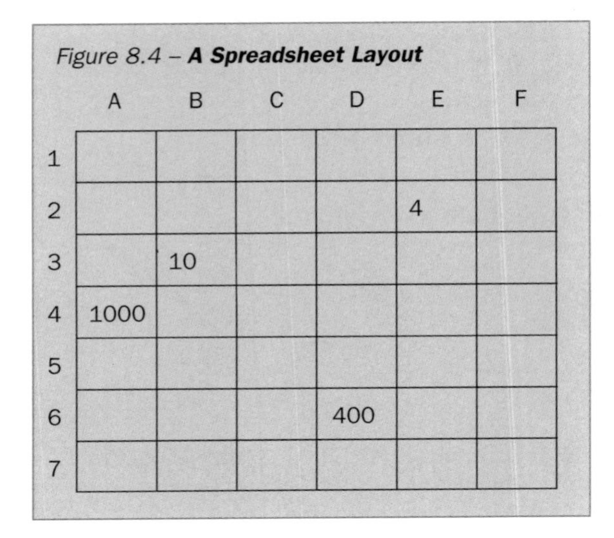

	A	B	C	D	E	F
1						
2					4	
3		10				
4	1000					
5						
6				400		
7						

budget the sales figure for January is uncertain. It might be 1 000 units or 1 200 units. Providing the entries are connected by formulae, a change on a spreadsheet from 1 000 to 1 200 would immediately show a different budget, saving a great deal of recalculation time.

This procedure is termed either 'What if'ing . . .', meaning 'What if we changed cell . . .' or 'sensitivity testing', meaning that we are uncertain of the real input and would like to know how sensitive the result is to changes in values of this input. If the result is very sensitive to the input, then we need to know the input more exactly. On the other hand, if the result does not change much over the input range, a good guess is sufficiently accurate. Sensitivity testing of this type is a powerful facility.

Figure 8.5 contains a spreadsheet showing a budget for a business for the periods January to June. The numbers entered directly from the keyboard are the sales (row 6), the production cost/unit (row 10) and the administrative and marketing costs (rows 12 and 13). All the other numbers are the result of formulae.

Figure 8.6 shows the result of changing the January entry for sales units from 1 000 to 1 200. All the formula connected cells have changed automatically.

Spreadsheets can also be used to produce graphs and diagrams. A vertical bar chart showing the sales figures from Figure 8.5 is shown in Figure 8.7.

Spreadsheets can be used by designers to carry out complex calculations with a very high degree of accuracy. There is virtually no limit on the type of calculations that can be performed, and on the way in which the results are presented on the VDU or printed.

Accountancy Packages

Since a great deal of accounting preparation and reports are in row and column format, the financial reporting aspects of business are well suited to spreadsheet applications. However, a more efficient method for preparing and analysing accounts would be to use a program designed for this purpose. There are many of these packages available. A popular package for the smaller business is called Sage Sterling and a page from this package is shown in Figure 8.8 (on page 149).

Computer-based accounting systems can provide the managers of the business with instant

Figure 8.5 – ***A Budget on a Spreadsheet***

	A	B	C	D	E	F	G
1	Budget for 1993						
2							
3							
4	Month	January	February	March	April	May	June
5							
6	Sales (units)	1000	1200	1400	1400	1500	1600
7	Price/unit	1.2	1.2	1.3	1.4	1.4	1.5
8	Revenue	1200	1440	1820	1960	2100	2400
9							
10	Prodn.cost/unit	0.65	0.65	0.7	0.72	0.74	0.73
11	Tot. Prodn.Cost	780	936	1274	1411	1554	1752
12	Admin Costs	234	235	235	300	300	302
13	Market.Cost	120	120	120	140	140	150
14	Total cost	1134	1291	1629	1851	1994	2204
15							
16	Profit	66	149	191	109	106	196
17	Cum. Profit	66	215	406	515	621	817

Figure 8.6 – ***'What If'ing' on a Spreadsheet***

	A	B	C	D	E	F	G
1	Budget for 1993						
2							
3							
4	Month	January	February	March	April	May	June
5							
6	Sales (units)	1100	1320	1540	1540	1650	1760
7	Price/unit	1.2	1.2	1.3	1.4	1.4	1.5
8	Revenue	1320	1584	2002	2156	2310	2640
9							
10	Prodn.cost/unit	0.65	0.65	0.7	0.72	0.74	0.73
11	Tot. Prodn.Cost	858	1030	1401	1552	1709	1927
12	Admin Costs	234	235	235	300	300	302
13	Market.Cost	120	120	120	140	140	150
14	Total cost	1212	1385	1756	1992	2149	2379
15							
16	Profit	108	199	246	164	161	261
17	Cum. Profit	108	307	553	717	877	1138
18							
19	WHAT IF?....Resulting profits if sales per month increase by 10%						

information on the financial affairs of the business and removes the 'hard slog' of preparing tax returns, stock evaluations and a host of equally time-consuming activities. The computer does these jobs accurately and quickly.

The real value of instant accounts, as opposed to the once-a-year variety, is that the state of the business can be quickly understood and corrections

Figure 8.7 – ***A Bar Chart from a Spreadsheet***

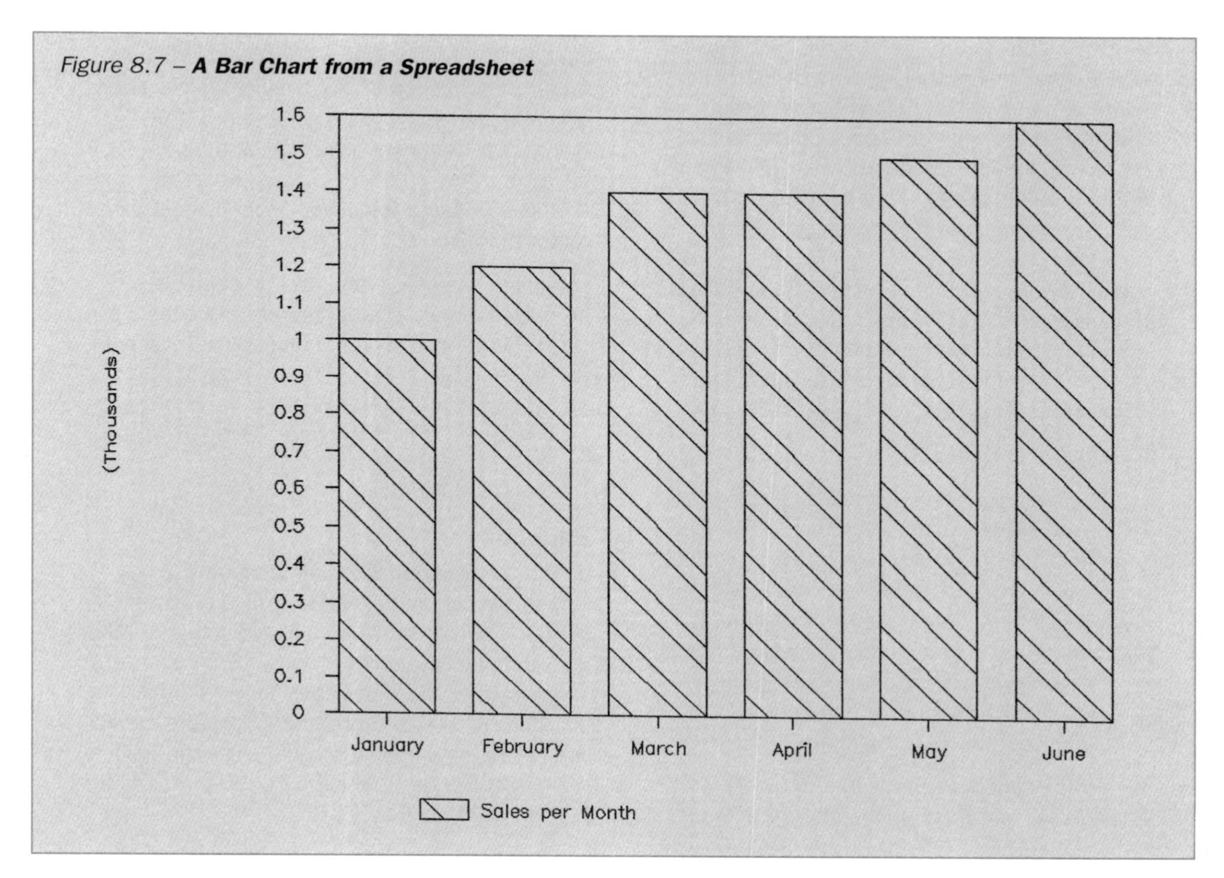

CASE STUDY

Accountancy Crosses Europe

British accountants may still have a bowler-hatted image but these days they are more interested in software than hardware as the latest hi-tech computer solutions are increasingly used to solve traditional financial problems.

One company which has been on the crest of this wave of interest in accountancy software has been the Kettering-based Pegasus Group – which supplies business software packages covering stock-control, invoicing and ledger entries, amongst a wide range of other accounting techniques.

Today, following a boom in software sales throughout the 80s, the company has built a turnover of around £13 million and leads a highly competitive UK market in micro-computerised software packages for use on companies' personal computers.

Europe venture

Now Pegasus is embarking on a new European venture, so strong is the company's belief that the future rests with the development of pan-European products. Pegasus Managing Director, Martin Ruda, explains: 'The computer services industry in general, and accountancy services in particular, have become much more sophisticated markets in recent years. This is leading to a rationalisation in the UK, which is spreading to Europe, resulting in a smaller number of larger companies offering business software.

Continuing techniques

'Although accountancy practices vary from country to country across Europe, it is clear that there is a core of common techniques, which make pan-European feasible. There are, in fact, clear benefits in "internationalising" core systems, so that we can offer packages which work equally well in, say, France as in the UK – and just require national adaptations to suit individual countries' requirements.'

With this in mind, Pegasus has formed a partnership with the French software company Saari to develop pan-European products.

Fifty-fifty split

Some Pegasus staff have moved to France as a result, and the two companies have agreed to a 50-50 split in the costs of developing new pan-European products.

European Business Development Manager, Jim Stone, takes up the story. He says: 'We chose to base the project at Saari's Paris offices for purely practical reasons. They had more space available for a start – but, perhaps more importantly, they are in a central position within easy striking distance of other key countries.'

The main aim of the joint venture, adds Jim, is to 'utilise the knowledge, expertise and resources accumulated by two companies which are market leaders in their own countries.'

Most of the differences encountered by Jim and his team have resulted from variations in accounting practices from country to country, rather than from changing product specifications or testing requirements. He explains: 'The French, for example, include three different payment dates on their invoices, while the Portuguese use a system of "negative debits" rather than credits.

Language has also presented an obstacle to producing a multilingual program, because file headings have to accommodate different length words.

Source: Single Market News, Spring 1992. Reproduced with the permission of the Controller of Her Majesty's Stationery Office.

QUESTIONS

1. What have been the main problems in transferring an English language program using British accountancy techniques to other European countries?
2. What does the statement 'they are more interested in software than hardware' mean?
3. Do you think Pegasus could enter the French market without forming a 50/50 partnership with a French business?

Figure 8.8 – ***Accounting Page: Sage Sterling***

Nominal Ledger Reports - Trial Balance.

Date : 280688
Page : 1

Ref.	Accounts Name	Debit	Credit
0038	Debtor's Control		374.78
0065	Creditors Control	231.03	
0069	Tax Control		9.58
0088	Cash	98.50	
0089	Bank		1181.25
1010	Product A Sales		65.22
1020	Product B Sales		174.10
2020	Product B Purchases	174.10	
4020	Rent	700.00	
4021	Rates	600.00	
4040	Stationery	1.30	
		1804.93	1804.93

Esc : Menu -> : Fast Forward Any other key : Continue

KEY POINTS 8.2

- **A spreadsheet is a large table of columns and rows, which contain cells**
- **Each cell in a spreadsheet contains text, a number or a formula**
- **Spreadsheets are used for 'What if'ing?' and sensitivity testing**

introduced. When the economic environment is changing fast, it is important that the financial affairs of the business are closely controlled.

Project management programs allow managers to draw and analyse networks to determine the best planned sequence of activities, and to control this plan when operations start. Network analysis techniques were examined in Chapter Five.

The Computer as a Controller

When a computer is used as part of a control system it is sometimes called a microprocessor. Many modern cameras have a small computer installed in order to adjust aperture size, focus and shutter speed automatically. The settings are probably more accurately made than if an average photographer were to do it.

Computers control large machines in production departments. By typing a set of instructions into a keyboard, the computer will send signals to motors to move 'arms' in a certain direction for a specific distance, to grab with its 'fingers' a piece of material, and to place the material within clamps where another machine, similarly computer-controlled, welds one material to another. At every instant in the process, the computer is constantly finding out where it is and comparing this with where it should be. Minute corrections are made continuously. Such computer systems are a common part of a car production line where robots have replaced human beings.

Security systems in large, important buildings are often computer-controlled, working in conjunction with pressure switches under carpets, switches on windows and doors, movement and smoke detectors, and infra-red sensitive devices. Such a large number of devices could easily fail individually and cause false signals, but guided by the computer program, the following imaginary sequence could happen:

> Window 46 has opened. Check pressure pad under window is working OK. It is. Pressure pad under window has been activated. Motion detector aimed at window space has been activated. Intruder alert sequence activated. Telephone automatic message to Police HQ, and wait for acknowledgement code. Repeat until acknowledged. Wait four minutes, during which time record sequence of motion detectors activated. After four minutes, sound main alarm bells and illuminate all rooms. Activate video cameras in all rooms which have had motion detector triggered. Continue until master code has been entered into control panel.

Such a sequence of activities can be programmed with a reliability that could only be equalled by a large number of security guards.

Computer control is common in the chemical process industry where large volumes of chemicals of varying degrees of toxicity are manufactured and mixed with other chemicals. Plant controllers who have the responsibility of adjusting valves, turning on heaters and controlling pumps to make the process happen used to have a team of men to carry out the functions according to a set plan. Nowadays these functions are computer-controlled in response to the process plan and the current state of the plant.

For example, if it is important to mix the contents of Tank 23 at a temperature of 85°C with the contents of Tank 45 at a similar temperature in the initially empty Tank 54, the computer will not start operations until the temperatures have been reached. The computer will be adjusting the heating for both tanks and continuously checking for leakages, pressure changes and any other malfunction so that safety levels are maintained.

In many chemical process plants, the operators can open or close valves on tanks some distance away by touching the computer VDU in the control room. The VDU will show a diagrammatic representation of the chemical process, with each valve shown with two tabs, each the size of a typewriter key. One tab has OPEN written on it, the other CLOSE. Touching the VDU at the OPEN tab point will be sensed by the computer and the corresponding valve in the plant will start to open. The VDU will show how open or closed the valve is, and will also indicate the rate of flow through the valve as measured by a flowmeter.

It only needs your imagination to think of any manually controlled system which could be replaced by a computer system. The accuracy, precision, speed and reliability of a computer system can seldom be bettered, at a cost which is acceptable if quantities of production are high. Specialized designs and applications will always be costly since the high salaries of designers and operators can only be spread over a few products.

ACTIVITY 8.2

Define a manual system with which you are familiar. Write down how this system could be improved if computer control was incorporated. To give you a few ideas, computers activate switches in response to signals from devices and these switches can operate motors, play recordings, ring bells, turn on taps and shut doors.

In what ways has the manual system been improved? Is the computer system very expensive? Has the reliability of the system improved?

Computers as Communicators

Computers can 'talk' and 'listen' to other computers and devices. We have already seen how computers in the control of systems 'listen' to signals from pressure switches, but in this section we will consider more complex messages and instructions such as books and drawings.

Word Processors

A word processor is a program which enables a keyboard operator to write text on to a computer VDU. This text is at the same time filed – that is, converted into electronic signals and temporarily stored. In addition to text, graphics can also be designed and stored in the same way. In the simplest example, the text is a letter and when it is finished to the operator's satisfaction in terms of layout, spelling accuracy and meaning, it is printed. The letter is posted in the normal way.

However, we can go one step further. If the receiver of the letter has a computer, it is possible to send the stored version of the text via telephone wires from one computer to the other. The letter is then shown on the receiving VDU exactly as on the originator's VDU. The computer at each end of the system checks what has been sent, what has been received and translates the signals

Figure 8.9 – ***The Development of Teletext***

Information for everybody, on TV

DATA BROADCASTING conjures up images of space satellites beaming information halfway across the world. However, one of the biggest data broadcasting services in Britain makes use of the conventional rooftop television aerial.

The data is mixed with the signal that carries television programmes from the transmitter to the home.

A television signal is composed of 625 lines, but only 575 of them are used for the picture. The unused lines are known as the vertical blanking interval, and some of the spare lines are used for the teletext service, which provides text and graphic information on items such as the news, weather and sport.

Teletext is essentially a public service, and anybody can use it by buying a television or video-recorder equipped with a decoder.

Some of the teletext lines, however, are also used for commercial data broadcasting services, which are designed for business users.

An organisation sends its information to a data broadcasting company, where it is processed before being transmitted with the normal television signal. During processing, the data is scrambled or encrypted so that it can be seen only by authorised users with special decoders.

The decoded information may be displayed on a computer screen or television set.

Some services are for 'closed user groups'. For example, a head office may wish to send information to its regional offices.

Marks & Spencer uses the system to send price information to all its stores. Other services may be used for multiple display purposes, such as information kiosks in shops. Data can also be sent to individual decoders.

Private teletext was made possible by the 1985 Cable and Satellite Act, which allowed television companies to run subscription services. It was also helped by the deregulation of the stock market.

'Suddenly, many companies thought, "How do we get all this data to our clients?"' says Lawson Brown, the head of broadcasting services at BBC Enterprises, the BBC's commercial arm.

BBC Enterprises launched its service, known as Datacast, in 1986. Today Datacast's annual turnover is £2 million and its services include Market Eye, which carries stock exchange and financial information, and Cardcast, which provides stores with information about stolen credit cards. Another client is Post Office New Media, which produces information for the display screens at many post offices. Coral, the bookmaking company, also uses Datacast to send racing results and odds to its betting shops.

In 1985, Oracle, the ITV teletext company, allocated one of its teletext lines to data broadcasting and awarded the commercial licence to Aircall Teletext, now known as DBI.

Private teletext services received a boost with the 1990 Broadcasting Act, which obliged the Independent Television Commission to take some of the public service teletext lines and sell them to commercial companies.

Possible markets include home shopping, home banking, and point-of-information and point-of-sale kiosks, which provide consumers with up-to-date information on a company's products or services – what market analysts call 'uninterrupted browsing'.

Data broadcasting can also be used to help people with special needs, such as the blind. This summer will see the launch of a 'digital newspaper', a service that will enable blind and partially sighted people to hear a newspaper by using a computer.

The project is being developed by the Royal National Institute for the Blind, Intelligent Research, a London company, and Aptech, a Newcastle upon Tyne company that develops hardware for the disabled.

When the system is in operation, the newspaper will be converted into teletext data and broadcast at night. The data will then be stored on the computer hard disc.

David Levy, the marketing manager of Intelligent Research, says: "The service will be wonderful for blind people because it means they can wake up to find the morning newspaper on their desk. It will also be possible for users to store interesting items on disc and search for specific stories or items simply by typing a name on the computer."

Source: Times, 16 April 1992, George Cole. © Times Newspapers Ltd. 1992

into a VDU presentation. The receiving computer can process the letter in any way it requires and can print it out on its own printer. This process is called electronic mail.

Word processing is not just for typing letters. Businesses use word processors to produce individual quotations from standard 'chunks' of text. A quotation is an offer to produce a product or service for a customer at an agreed price. When the service offered is quite large, such as the installation of a new internal telephone system for a business, the cost can be high. There is often a need to give the customer some degree of confidence in the specification and quality of the installation.

One type of transmission of data is teletext. Figure 8.9 (previous page) contains an article on the development of teletext.

For the most part the text is fairly standard and can be copied from stored text generated previously. However, each customer likes to think that the quotation was specially written, and even the standard text needs to have the customer's name included periodically. The word processor can do this easily. You have probably seen or been sent 'junk mail' which includes your name at various relevant points in a letter. The letter you receive is probably one of a million sent out, each one 'individualized' in the same way.

Data Banks

A data bank is a database which has been designed at high cost and is accessible to computer operators for a fee, unless it is part of a government facility or organization (such as the police). The databank can be installed in any large computer system anywhere in the world. In fact, some owners of databanks will negotiate storage fees for their information and if it is particularly high in one country, will move the databank abroad.

A typical database could be a list of all the legal cases reported in a country, together with a resumé of the case, the opinions expressed and the judgements given. If a law firm agreed to become members of the data bank list of customers, it would be able to contact the data bank for any information it required. An example could be a request of the listings and judgements given for all cases heard in the last five years involving ships colliding with harbours as a result of strike action by tugmen. Any lawyer involved in a similar case would find this information extremely valuable. Each customer would be given a password to prevent unrestricted access.

The cost of receiving this information would be the cost of a local telephone call plus a time fee worked out by the data bank computer on an agreed basis.

For lawyers this would not be cheap. The lawyer's computer would be able to copy the information and print it on its own printer. The cost would be printed at the same time, and the bill would shortly follow.

Networks

Computers which are linked together in order to share facilities, such as printers, are called computer networks. This enables all the computers in a

Figure 8.10 – ***Telecottaging***

Electronic boost for Country life

THE INCREASING affordability of fax machines, modems and other high-tech equipment has been a great boost to small businesses. But while the developments mean that proximity to urban centres is no longer essential, those in remote parts of the country tend to lack the support services that their metropolitan counterparts take for granted.

The advent of the 'telecottage' is changing this, by supplying electronic office services and up-to-date information.

As well as stocking sophisticated machinery, the telecottage is a low-cost training centre, teaching local people to use technology. Entrepreneurs can do the work themselves, using on-site computers or their own at home, or they can pay telecottage workers, usually home-based, to do it.

The telecottage concept is based on a Swedish idea and has been developed in the UK during the past two years to stimulate rural economies by supplying services to commerce and communities.

A Devon telecottage, for example, has a skills register, useful when a local architect wanted to contact others to share expensive equipment.

In Warwickshire, business owners needing expert advice can meet enterprise agency staff by appointment at the Stoneleigh telecottage, and can hire an office for meetings with clients. A crèche is shortly to open for children of women using the cottage.

Simon Berry, the manager, emphasises his telecottage's role as a meeting-place and business club. 'There has been a tremendous response since our informmal opening last October. We want to keep it a social place where people can come in and make themselves a cup of coffee.'

Wales, with about a dozen telecentres, plans to launch 'Telecottages Wales', a promotion drive to businesses, this autumn. Antur Tanat Cain Telebureau, at Llangedwyn, in Clwyd, emphasises quality controls. It has won contracts from ICL (scanning), the Government (word processing) and a local authority (training in desktop publishing).

Telecottage backers include local authorities, the Rural Development Commission, and such companies as British Telecom.

Source: Independent, 2 March 1992

business to talk to each other quite easily because they will be sharing the same programs. The operator of any computer can communicate with the operators of other computers in the network, and can pass personal messages or files of data to be used on spreadsheets or databases, for example.

'Telecottaging' is the name given to the setting up of a small network in a private home that links to a larger commercial network. Figure 8.10 contains an article about telecottaging.

Computer Aided Design (CAD)

Computer aided design is the name given to a specialized program which enables designers to draw images on a VDU to represent the shape of machined parts, or the design of an electrical circuit, or the complete design of a building. The designer normally uses an electronic 'pencil' and a touch sensitive VDU or 'drawing board'. The keyboard of the computer will enable the designer to specify dimensions, to call up other computerized drawings for inclusion in the current drawing (such as the shape of a bolt) and to save or change what has been produced. Any line 'drawn' and represented on the drawing board can be straightened, erased, extended or curved. If the design is a plastic bottle, the program will automatically display the volume contained within the shape.

Computer Assisted Manufacture (CAM)

Specialized CAD programs will communicate with certain machines and will send a finished design to the computer that has been incorporated into the machine. The machine will proceed to manufacture the part automatically from materials previously loaded into the machine or from an automatic service system. Such machines are extremely expensive with high fixed costs.

Many computer manufacturing systems will control material stocks, prepare production plans and cost manufacturing processes automatically. Management reports are prepared regularly in detail and summary format which are then printed for management attention.

Check-Out Tills

Many national retail organizations are now equipped with computerized tills at the check-out point. These tills are linked to a local centralized point which sends up-to-date information to the head office as frequently as requested.

This means that the sales value of all stores can be presented at any time and the sales increase or decrease can be calculated. Sudden increases in the sales of any item, perhaps as a result of a local promotional activity, can be quickly noticed. If necessary, a lorry filled with suitable merchandise can be instantly re-directed to the store to make sure that there is no 'stock out'.

In addition to the constant analysis of all sales and corresponding profits, stores can also measure the number of items returned for a variety of reasons. This information would be quickly passed back to the manufacturer who may need to locate other defective stock before it reaches the customer. In special circumstances, the manufacturer may need to recall all the products supplied to all customers over a time period, and obviously the faster this can be done, the cheaper and more effective the recall will be.

In surpassing human efficiency, there seems to be no limit to the number of applications of the computer.

The Systems Analyst

In the computer's role as Collector, Calculator, Controller and Communicator, there is usually a combination of skills required in order to provide an efficient working system – that is, a system which is reliable and as easy to use as possible. These skills are those of the operator at all levels in the business, from process worker to chief executive, who all have the skills needed to carry out their responsibilities, and the skill of a person who knows the performance, limitations and resource requirements of the computer. It is this person – called a systems analyst – who will work with the user to provide an appropriate system.

The systems analyst will initially carry out a feasibility study to check that the concept of computerizing an activity or operation is acceptable and can be implemented at a realistic cost. The feasibility study will involve many hours of collecting information concerning the current methods. Answers must be provided to such questions as:

- What is the purpose of the current activity?
- How is it done?
- Who does it? When? Where? How often?
- How else could it be done?
- How much will it cost?

The answers to these questions may well suggest that a computer cannot help: the current method is easily the best there is. However, if a computer-based method looks encouraging and it is decided to accept the feasibility study, a more detailed investigation will be undertaken. The results of this investigation will lead to a formal proposal which will list the costs of the recommended system in detail, and the savings or benefits expected. This information would be used to evaluate the investment decision.

If the proposal involves a great deal of money,

the systems analyst may need to make a prototype of the new system so that it can be tested in a real environment. This is expensive but essential, particularly if the treatment the system will get in real life cannot be simulated in the design department.

When the final authorization is given to proceed, the systems analyst will supervise the installation of both hardware and software, and the commissioning of the system. Operators will need to be trained to use the system efficiently and this will be a major cost. The systems analyst relinquishes control of the project only when it has been 'run in' successfully and achieves the objectives set for it.

KEY POINTS 8.3

- **A word processor enables text and diagrams to be stored electronically**
- **Electronic mail is the name given to the transmission of word processor output from one computer to another**
- **Designers can use computers to make better and quicker designs which can be transmitted to machines directly for production. This is called CAD/CAM**
- **Systems analysts are experts in designing computer systems which give users what they want at the right price**
- **Training users to understand the full potential of computers is essential**

EXAM PREPARATION

SHORT QUESTIONS

1 What is the difference between hardware and software?

2 How might the introduction of new technology create jobs?

3 Why do you think the price of computers has fallen so rapidly in recent years?

4 What is a spreadsheet and how does it work?

5 Suggest two uses of spreadsheets in a large retail organization.

6 What are the likely improvements in a company's decision-making processes with the introduction of information technology?

7 What is meant by the term 'telecottaging'?

8 What is the difference between a mainframe and a personal computer?

9 What is meant by the word 'programming'?

10 Define the differences between CAD and CAM.

ESSAYS

1 Following 'computer aided design' and 'computer aided manufacture', a new phenomenon has been identified which particularly affects small businesses, called 'computer aided bankruptcy'. How might such bankruptcy occur, and why are small firms particularly at risk? (AEB June 1989)

2 Why might information technology reduce the effectiveness of communications within an organization? (AEB November 1989)

Appendix A

COMPANY ACCOUNTS

AGFA-GEVAERT LIMITED and Subsidiary Company

CONSOLIDATED PROFIT AND LOSS ACCOUNT

FOR THE YEAR ENDED 31ST DECEMBER 1991

	Notes	1991 £000's	1991 £000's	1990 £000's	1990 £000's
TURNOVER	1		173 759		196 873
COST OF SALES			135 893		154 641
GROSS PROFIT			37 866		42 232
Distribution Costs		24 257		26 562	
Administrative Expenses		13 381		9 578	
			37 638		36 140
OPERATING PROFIT	2		228		6 092
Interest Receivable	5		643		250
			871		6 342
Interest Payable	6		3 656		5 331
(LOSS)/PROFIT BEFORE TAXATION			(2 785)		1 011
TAXATION	7		(1 758)		890
(LOSS)/PROFIT FOR THE FINANCIAL YEAR			(1 027)		121
BALANCE BROUGHT FORWARD			33 447		33 326
BALANCE CARRIED FORWARD			32 420		33 447

CONSOLIDATED BALANCE SHEET

AS AT 31ST DECEMBER 1991

	Notes	1991 £000's	1991 £000's	1990 £000's	1990 £000's
FIXED ASSETS					
Tangible Assets	8		6 824		6 321
CURRENT ASSETS					
Stocks	10	23 257		26 275	
Debtors	11	40 853		45 557	
Cash at Bank and in Hand		11 422		10 034	
		75 532		81 866	
CREDITORS: Amounts Falling Due Within One Year	12	45 257		50 799	
NET CURRENT ASSETS			30 275		31 067
TOTAL ASSETS LESS CURRENT LIABILITIES			37 099		37 388
CREDITORS: Amounts Falling Due After More Than One Year	13		—		4
PROVISIONS FOR LIABILITIES AND CHARGES	14		1 971		1 229
			35 128		36 155
Financed by:–					
CAPITAL AND RESERVES					
Called Up Share Capital	15		2 000		2 000
Share Premium Account			708		708
Profit and Loss Account			32 420		33 447
			35 128		36 155

AGFA-GEVAERT LIMITED
BALANCE SHEET AS AT 31ST DECEMBER 1991

	Notes	1991 £000's	1991 £000's	1990 £000's	1990 £000's
FIXED ASSETS					
Tangible Assets	8		**6 824**		6 321
Investment	9		**607**		607
CURRENT ASSETS					
Stocks	10	**23 257**		26 275	
Debtors	11	**40 853**		45 557	
Cash at Bank and in Hand		**11 422**		10 034	
		75 532		81 866	
CREDITORS: Amounts Falling Due Within One Year	12	**45 864**		51 406	
NET CURRENT ASSETS			**29 668**		30 460
TOTAL ASSETS LESS CURRENT LIABILITIES			**37 099**		37 388
CREDITORS: Amounts Falling Due After More Than One Year	13		—		4
PROVISIONS FOR LIABILITIES AND CHARGES	14		**1 971**		1 229
			35 128		36 155
Financed by: **CAPITAL AND RESERVES**					
Called Up Share Capital	15		**2 000**		2 000
Share Premium Account			**708**		708
Profit and Loss Account			**32 420**		33 447
			35 128		36 155

These Financial Statements were approved by the Board of Directors on 28th January 1992.

G. AHRENS
DIRECTOR

A. M. DAY
DIRECTOR

AGFA-GEVAERT LIMITED and Subsidiary Company
CASH FLOW STATEMENT
FOR THE YEAR ENDED 31ST DECEMBER 1991

	Notes	1991 £000's	1991 £000's	1990 £000's	1990 £000's
NET CASH INFLOW FROM OPERATING ACTIVITIES	21		**6 847**		4 832
RETURNS ON INVESTMENTS AND SERVICING OF FINANCE					
Interest Received		**661**		554	
Interest Paid		**(4 550)**		(3 290)	
NET CASH OUTFLOW FROM RETURNS ON INVESTMENTS AND SERVICING OF FINANCE			**(3,889)**		(2 736)
TAXATION					
Corporation Tax Paid		**(7)**		(2 530)	
Corporation Tax Repaid		**125**		—	
			118		(2 530)
INVESTING ACTIVITIES					
Payments to Acquire Tangible Fixed Assets		**(2 685)**		(1 562)	
Receipts from Sales of Tangible Fixed Assets		**997**		1 145	
			(1 688)		(417)
INCREASE/(DECREASE) IN CASH AND CASH EQUIVALENTS	22		**1 388**		(851)

AGFA-GEVAERT LIMITED and Subsidiary Company

NOTES TO THE FINANCIAL STATEMENTS

FOR THE YEAR ENDED 31ST DECEMBER 1991

1. ACCOUNTING POLICIES

a) **Basis of Financial Statements**
The financial statements are drawn up under the historical cost convention of accounting and in accordance with applicable accounting standards.

b) **Basis of Consolidation**
The group financial statements include the financial statements of the Company and its subsidiary. The profit and loss account of the holding company is identical to the consolidated profit and loss account.

c) **Finance Leases**
Assets held under finance leases are treated as fixed assets and recorded in the balance sheet at their fair value along with an obligation to pay future rentals. Finance charges are allocated on a straight line basis over the lease term.

d) **Operating Leases**
Rentals under operating leases are written off over the lease term.

e) **Depreciation**

(i) FREEHOLD BUILDINGS
The cost of freehold properties (excluding site value cost estimated by the Directors where not seperately identifiable) is being depreciated by equal annual instalments from date of acquisition either over 50 years, or over the remaining useful life if less.

(ii) LEASEHOLD IMPROVEMENTS
The cost of major improvements to leasehold properties is capitalised and written off over 5 years. Minor leasehold improvements are written off as incurred.

(iii) OTHER FIXED ASSETS
These are written off over their expected useful lives as follows:-

Plant and Machinery	3 – 5 years
Showroom Equipment	3 – 4 years
Assets Under Finance Leases	Over the Lease term

f) **Stocks**

(i) FINISHED GOODS AND GOODS FOR RESALE AND SPARES
Stock is valued at the lower of average cost and net realisable value.

(ii) EQUIPMENT ON HIRE
Equipment on hire to customers is being written off over its estimated life of three years.

g) **Foreign Currencies**
Assets and liabilities in foreign currency are translated at the rates ruling at the year end. Transactions in foreign currencies are recorded at the rate ruling at the date of the transaction.

h) **Deferred Taxation**
Provision is made for deferred taxation using the liability method on all material timing differences, where it is probable that a liability will arise in the foreseeable future.

i) **Turnover**
Turnover comprises the invoiced value of goods sold and services provided net of Value Added Tax and discounts.

AGFA-GEVAERT LIMITED and Subsidiary Company

NOTES TO THE FINANCIAL STATEMENTS

FOR THE YEAR ENDED 31ST DECEMBER 1991 (continued)

2. OPERATING PROFIT is after charging/(crediting):

	1991 £000's	1990 £000's
Directors' Remuneration (Note 3)	**171**	159
Auditors' Remuneration	**28**	65
Depreciation and Amortisation		
– Owned Assets	**1 137**	968
– Assets under Finance Leases	**9**	98
Hire of Plant and Machinery – Operating Leases	**2 050**	2 250
Hire of Other Assets – Operating Leases	**1 429**	1 534
Exceptional Items		
– Major Bad Debt	**3 137**	—
– Movement in Provision for Bad Debt	**(1 310)**	1 500
– Stock written off on Closure of Operation	—	835
Amounts Written Off Equipment on Hire to Customers (Net)	**1 762**	261

3. DIRECTORS' REMUNERATION

	1991 £000's	1990 £000's
a) Executive Remuneration and Benefits	**157**	146
Pension Contributions	**14**	13
	171	159
b) Emoluments (excluding Pension Contributions)		
Chairman	**NIL**	NIL
Highest Paid Director	**96**	91
Scale of Emoluments of Other Directors (excluding Pension Contributions)		
£NIL – £50 000	**3**	3
£50 001 – £55 000	—	1
£60 001 – £65 000	**1**	—

4. STAFF COSTS

	1991 £000's	1990 £000's
a) Wages and Salaries	18 329	18 579
Employer's National Insurance Contributions	1 525	1 567
Other Pension Costs	1 268	1 145
	21 122	21 291
b) The average weekly number of employees during the year was made up as follows:		
Technical	366	400
Selling and Distribution	506	559
Office and Management	97	102
	969	1 061

5. INTEREST RECEIVABLE

	1991 £000's	1990 £000's
Bank Deposits	625	141
Other	18	109
	643	250

6. INTEREST PAYABLE

	1991 £000's	1990 £000's
Bank Loans and Overdrafts	143	579
Group Company	3 510	4 740
Finance Changes on Lease Agreements wholly repayable within five years	3	12
	3 656	5 331

AGFA-GEVAERT LIMITED and Subsidiary Company

NOTES TO THE FINANCIAL STATEMENTS

FOR THE YEAR ENDED 31ST DECEMBER 1991 (continued)

7. TAXATION

	1991 £000's	1990 £000's
Corporation Tax on results of the year at 33.25% (1990 – 34.25%)	**(802)**	925
Adjustment in respect of prior years	**(956)**	(35)
	(1 758)	890

8. TANGIBLE ASSETS

Group and Company

	Freehold land and Buildings £000's	Plant and Machinery £000's	**Total £000's**
Cost			
Balance at 1st January 1991	5 123	7 297	**12 420**
Additions	—	2 685	**2 685**
Disposals	—	(1 705)	**(1 705)**
Balance at 31st December 1991	5 123	8 277	**13 400**
Depreciation			
Balance as at 1st January 1991	981	5 118	**6 099**
Charge for the year	92	1 054	**1 146**
Disposals	—	(669)	**(669)**
Balance at 31st December 1991	1 073	5 503	**6 576**
Net Book Value			
31st December 1991	4 050	2 774	**6 824**
31st December 1990	4 142	2 179	**6 321**

Freehold Land and Buildings include estimated site cost of £452 000 (1990 – £452 000).
The Net Book Value of Plant and Machinery of £2 774 000 (1990 – £2 179 000) includes an amount of £3 000 (1990 – £13 000) in respect of assets held under finance leases.

9. INVESTMENT

Shares in Group Undertaking

The following subsidiary, which did not trade during the year, is wholly owned and registered in England: Compugraphic (UK) Limited.

		1991 £000's	1990 £000's
Cost:	Ordinary £1 shares and Deferred £1 shares	**1 480**	1 480
Less:	Reduction to Equity Value brought forward	**(873)**	(873)
		607	607

10. STOCKS

	1991 £000's	1990 £000's
Group and Company		
Finished Goods, Spares and Goods for Resale	**21 504**	23 786
Equipment on Hire	**1 753**	2 489
	23 257	26 275

11. DEBTORS

	1991 £000's	1990 £000's
Group and Company		
Trade Debtors	**37 672**	44 219
Amounts owed by Group Undertakings	**824**	71
Other Debtors	**80**	91
Corporation Tax Repayable	**729**	—
Prepayments and Accrued Income	**1 548**	1 176
	40 853	45 557

The total trade debtors include an amount of £1 502 000 (1990 – £3 093 000) which falls due after more than one year.

AGFA-GEVAERT LIMITED and Subsidiary Company

NOTES TO THE FINANCIAL STATEMENTS

FOR THE YEAR ENDED 31ST DECEMBER 1991 (continued)

12. CREDITORS

Amounts Falling Due Within One Year

	1991 £000's	1990 £000's
a) Group		
Trade Creditors	**3 106**	3 125
Amounts owed to Group Undertakings	**33 985**	38 640
Corporation Tax	—	911
Social Security and Other Taxes	**2 126**	1 754
Accruals	**6 036**	6 360
Net Obligation under Finance Leases	**4**	9
	45 257	50 799
b) Company		
Trade Creditors	**3 106**	3 125
Amounts owed to Group Undertakings	**34 592**	39 247
Corporation Tax	—	911
Social Security and Other Taxes	**2 126**	1 754
Accruals	**6 036**	6 360
Net Obligation under Finance Leases	**4**	9
	45 864	51 406

13. CREDITORS

Amounts Falling Due After More than One Year

	1991 £000's	1990 £000's
Group and Company		
Net Obligation under Finance Leases	—	4

14. PROVISIONS FOR LIABILITIES AND CHARGES

Freehold

Group and Company	Reorganisation Costs £000's	Prepaid Processing £000's	Total £000's
Balance at 1st January 1991	858	371	**1 229**
Transfers from profit and loss account	2 356	590	**2 946**
Utilised in year	(1 548)	(656)	**(2 204)**
Balance at 31st December 1991	**1 666**	**305**	**1 971**

15. CALLED-UP SHARE CAPITAL

	1991 £000's	1990 £000's
Authorised, allotted, issued and fully paid share capital 2 000 000 Ordinary Shares of £1 each	**2 000**	2 000

16. CAPITAL COMMITMENTS

	1991 £000's	1990 £000's
Approved but not Contracted for	**300**	275

17. LEASE COMMITMENTS

a) **Operating Leases**

At 31st December 1991 the Group was committed to make annual payments under non-cancellable operating leases in 1992 as set out below:

	1991		1990	
Operating Leases which expire:**£000s**	**Land and Buildings £000's**	**Other £000's**	Land and Buildings £000's	Other £000's
In 1992	**0**	**58**	165	137
Between 1993 and 1996 inclusive	**661**	**1 577**	698	1 034
After 1996	**699**	—	642	—
	1 360	**1 635**	1 505	1 171

The leases of land and buildings are subject to rent reviews.

b) **Finance Leases**

At 31st December 1991 the Group's total net obligations under finance leases was as set out below:

	1991 £000's	1990 £000's
In 1992	**4**	13
Between 1993 and 1996 inclusive	—	4
	4	17
Less: Finance Charge	**(1)**	(4)
	3	13

AGFA-GEVAERT LIMITED and Subsidiary Company

NOTES TO THE FINANCIAL STATEMENTS

FOR THE YEAR ENDED 31ST DECEMBER 1991 (continued)

18. CONTINGENT LIABILITIES

There were no contingent liabilities at 31st December 1991 or 1990.

19. PENSION COMMITMENTS

The Group operates a defined benefits pension scheme for its employees, providing benefits based upon final pensionable earnings. The assets of the scheme are held separately from those of group companies and are invested in a segregated fund administered by Investment Managers. Under the terms of the trust deed the scheme is administered by the trustees, who delegate routine administration to a pensions administrator.

Employer's contribution to the scheme are charged to the profit and loss account so as to spread the cost of pensions over employees' working lives. The contributions are determined by independent qualified actuaries on the basis of triennial valuations using the accrued benefits method. The most recent valuation of the present scheme was carried out as at 6th April 1991. For the purpose of the valuation the actuaries assumed that the rate of return on new money invested will be 8.5% per annum, dividends will grow at 4% per annum, the Retail Price Index will grow by 5.5% per annum and that salary increases will average 6.5% per annum.

The pension charge for the year is shown in Note 4 to the Financial Statements. The valuation as at 6th April 1991 showed that the market value of the scheme was estimated to be £21 470 721. The acturial value of the scheme's assets represented in excess of 100% of the benefits that had accrued to members at that date.

Employer's and employees' contributions are 10.27% and 5.33% respectively.

20. PARENT UNDERTAKINGS

The immediate parent undertaking is Agfa-Gevaert N.V., incorporated in Belgium and the ultimate parent undertaking is Bayer A.G. incorporated in the Federal Republic of Germany.

NOTES TO THE CASH FLOW STATEMENT

FOR THE YEAR ENDED 31ST DECEMBER 1991

21. RECONCILIATION OF OPERATING PROFIT TO NET CASH INFLOW FROM OPERATING ACTIVITIES

	1991	1990
	£000's	£000's
Operating Profit	**228**	6 092
Depreciation Charges	**1 146**	1 066
Provisions	**2 205**	332
Loss/(Profit) on Disposal of Fixed Assets	**39**	(4)
Decrease in Stocks	**3 018**	5 240
Decrease in Debtors	**6 168**	9 179
Increase/(Decrease) in Creditors	**914**	(4 021)
Amounts repaid to Group Undertakings	**(5 408)**	(12 920)
Net Cash Inflow from Continuing Operating Activities	**8 310**	4 964
Net Cash Outflow in respect of Discontinued Activities and Reorganisation Costs	**(1 463)**	(132)
Net Cash Inflow from Operating Activities	**6 847**	4 832

22. ANALYSIS OF CHANGES IN CASH AND CASH EQUIVALENTS DURING THE YEAR

	1991	1990
	£000's	£000's
Balance at 1st January 1991	**10 034**	10 885
Net Cash Inflow/(Outflow)	**1 388**	(851)
Balance at 31st December 1991	**11 422**	10 034

Source: published by kind permission of Agfa-Gevaert Ltd

Appendix B

AREAS IN THE TAIL OF THE NORMAL DISTRIBUTION
(expressed as a proportion of the total area)

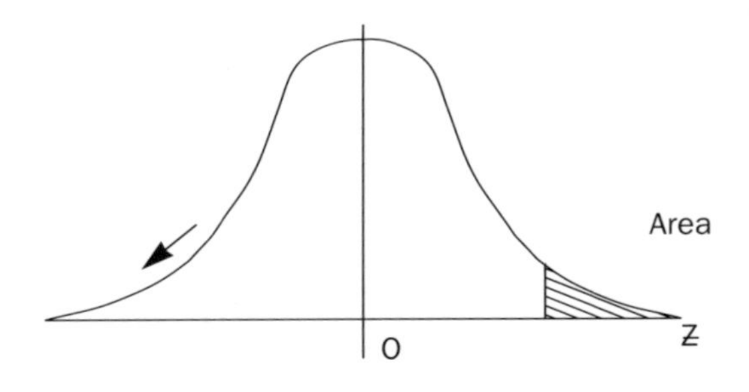

z	.00	.01	.02	.03	.04	.05	.06	.07	.08	.09
0.0	.5000	.4960	.4920	.4880	.4840	.4801	.4761	.4721	.4681	.4641
0.1	.4602	.4562	.4522	.4483	.4443	.4404	.4364	.4325	.4286	.4247
0.2	.4207	.4186	.4129	.4090	.4052	.4013	.3974	.3936	.3897	.3859
0.3	.3821	.3783	.3745	.3707	.3669	.3632	.3594	.3557	.3520	.3483
0.4	.3446	.3409	.3372	.3336	.3300	.3264	.3228	.3192	.3156	.3121
0.5	.3085	.3050	.3015	.2981	.2946	.2912	.2877	.2843	.2810	.2776
0.6	.2743	.2709	.2676	.2643	.2611	.2578	.2546	.2514	.2483	.2451
0.7	.2420	.2389	.2358	.2327	.2296	.2266	.2236	.2206	.2177	.2148
0.8	.2119	.2090	.2061	.2033	.2005	.1977	.1949	.1922	.1894	.1867
0.9	.1841	.1814	.1788	.1762	.1736	.1711	.1685	.1660	.1635	.1611
1.0	.1587	.1562	.1539	.1515	.1492	.1469	.1446	.1423	.1401	.1379
1.1	.1357	.1335	.1314	.1292	.1271	.1251	.1230	.1210	.1190	.1170
1.2	.1151	.1131	.1112	.1093	.1075	.1056	.1038	.1020	.1003	.0985
1.3	.0968	.0951	.0934	.0918	.0901	.0885	.0869	.0853	.0838	.0823
1.4	.0808	.0793	.0778	.0764	.0749	.0735	.0721	.0708	.0694	.0681
1.5	.0668	.0655	.0643	.0630	.0618	.0606	.0594	.0582	.0571	.0559
1.6	.0548	.0537	.0526	.0516	.0505	.0495	.0485	.0475	.0465	.0455
1.7	.0446	.0436	.0427	.0418	.0409	.0401	.0392	.0384	.0375	.0367
1.8	.0359	.0351	.0344	.0336	.0329	.0322	.0314	.0307	.0301	.0294
1.9	.0287	.0281	.0274	.0268	.0262	.0256	.0250	.0244	.0239	.0233
2.0	.0228	.0222	.0217	.0212	.0207	.0202	.0197	.0192	.0188	.0183
2.1	.0179	.0174	.0170	.0166	.0162	.0158	.0154	.0150	.0146	.0143
2.2	.0139	.0136	.0132	.0129	.0125	.0122	.0119	.0116	.0113	.0110
2.3	.0107	.0104	.0102	.0099	.0096	.0094	.0091	.0089	.0087	.0084
2.4	.0082	.0080	.0078	.0075	.0073	.0071	.0069	.0068	.0066	.0064
2.5	.0062	.0060	.0059	.0057	.0055	.0054	.0052	.0051	.0049	.0048
2.6	.0047	.0045	.0044	.0043	.0041	.0040	.0039	.0038	.0037	.0036
2.7	.0035	.0034	.0033	.0032	.0031	.0030	.0029	.0028	.0027	.0026
2.8	.0026	.0025	.0024	.0023	.0023	.0022	.0021	.0021	.0020	.0019
2.9	.0019	.0018	.0018	.0017	.0016	.0016	.0015	.0015	.0014	.0014
3.0	.0013	.0013	.0013	.0012	.0012	.0011	.0011	.0011	.0010	.0010

Appendix C

PRESENT VALUE TABLE

Table of discount factors to calculate the present value of future money

	Discount rate %							
No. years	2.5	5	7.5	10	12.5	15	17.5	20
1	0.976	0.952	0.930	0.909	0.889	0.870	0.851	0.833
2	0.952	0.907	0.865	0.826	0.790	0.756	0.724	0.694
3	0.929	0.864	0.805	0.751	0.702	0.658	0.616	0.579
4	0.906	0.823	0.749	0.683	0.624	0.572	0.525	0.482
5	0.884	0.784	0.697	0.621	0.555	0.497	0.446	0.402
6	0.862	0.746	0.648	0.564	0.493	0.432	0.380	0.335
7	0.841	0.711	0.603	0.513	0.438	0.376	0.323	0.279
8	0.821	0.677	0.561	0.467	0.390	0.327	0.275	0.233
9	0.801	0.645	0.522	0.424	0.346	0.284	0.234	0.194
10	0.781	0.614	0.485	0.386	0.308	0.247	0.199	0.162
11	0.762	0.585	0.451	0.350	0.274	0.215	0.170	0.135
12	0.744	0.557	0.420	0.319	0.243	0.187	0.144	0.112
13	0.725	0.530	0.391	0.290	0.216	0.163	0.123	0.093
14	0.708	0.505	0.363	0.263	0.192	0.141	0.105	0.078
15	0.690	0.481	0.338	0.239	0.171	0.123	0.089	0.065
16	0.674	0.458	0.314	0.218	0.152	0.107	0.076	0.054
17	0.657	0.436	0.292	0.198	0.135	0.093	0.064	0.045
18	0.641	0.416	0.272	0.180	0.120	0.081	0.055	0.038
19	0.626	0.396	0.253	0.164	0.107	0.070	0.047	0.031
20	0.610	0.377	0.235	0.149	0.095	0.061	0.040	0.026

Example

Present value of £5 000 receivable in 12 years's time when discount rate is 17.5 per cent is:

£5 000 × 0.144 = £720

Dictionary

absorption costing a system of product costing which assigns materials and labour, and overhead costs to units of product manufactured.

account, 1. a ledger record in which is entered details of all financial transactions relating to an individual supplier, or customer, or particular asset or liability, or type of expense or receipt.

2. a bank or building society's record of its dealings with a particular customer which itemizes the customer's business with the bank such as deposits of cash and cheques and withdrawals of funds.

accounting ratio a means of placing a firm's accounting results in context by expressing the figures as ratios or percentages of other figures in order to appraise their 'bigness' or 'smallness'.

accrual an expense which is outstanding at the end of a trading period and which needs to be included in the accounting results for the period.

activity chart or **process chart** a means of recording all the work tasks performed by a person and/or machine at a 'work station'.

activity sampling a means of recording all the work tasks performed by a person and/or machine at certain times.

allocation the breakdown of costs (and revenues) between different products, functions or company departments where it is possible to attribute costs (and revenues) directly to the departments where the cost (revenue) arises.

annual report and accounts a yearly report by the directors of company to the shareholders. It includes a copy of the company's balance sheet and a summary profit and loss account for the current and immediately-prior year, along with other information which directors are required by law to disclose to shareholders.

assembly line a method of organizing machinery and labour, where the parts of a product pass directly from one operation to another until the final product is produced.

asset an item or property which is owned by a business or individual and which has a money value.

authorized or **registered share capital** the maximum amount of share capital which a company can issue at any time.

average or **mean** a method of representing the middle of a set of numbers by a single number, ie, the sum of the set of numbers divided by the quantity of numbers in the set.

average cost the unit cost of a product (total cost divided by number of units produced).

bad debt an accounting term for money owed to a company by customers or borrowers which is highly unlikely to be paid.

balance sheet an accounting statement of a firm's assets and liabilities on the last day of a trading period.

bank loan or **bank advance** the advance of a specified sum of money to an individual or business (the borrower) by a commercial bank, savings bank, etc (the lender).

batch production a method of organizing production whereby a number of identical components or products are passed through one or more production operations or processes as a 'batch'.

board of directors the group responsible to the shareholders for running a company.

brainstorming a technique for generating ideas in which members of a group express ideas as they think of them. The object is to compile a list of ideas which can subsequently be considered and evaluated in greater depth.

break even the rate of output and sales at which a supplier generates just enough revenue to cover his fixed and variable costs, earning neither a profit nor a loss.

budgetary control a system for controlling costs and revenues by comparing actual results with budget estimates and then taking corrective action where necessary.

byte a group of eight bits (zeros/ones) used to represent a single number or letter in a computer. The capacity of a computer is often measured in terms of thousands of bytes (K), for example 640K; or millions of bytes, for example 20 megabytes.

capital, 1. the funds invested in a business in order to acquire the assets which the business needs to trade. Capital can consist of share capital subscribed by shareholders or loan capital provided by lenders.

2. goods such as plant, machinery and equipment which are used to produce other goods and services.

capital employed the total funds invested in a business made up of shareholders's funds and long-term loan capital.

capital expenditure expenditure on the acquisition or improvement of fixed assets.

capital good a good purchased by a business for use in producing other goods or services (eg, factory building).

cash account an account which records all of a company's cash incomings and outgoings.

chief executive the person who has overall responsibility for the management of a firm.

collateral security an asset which a borrower is required to deposit with, or pledge to, a lender as a condition of obtaining a loan, which can be sold off if the loan is not repaid.

computer an electronic/electromechanical device which accepts alphabetical and numerical data in a predefined form, stores and processes this data according to the instructions contained in a computer program, and presents the analysed data in an organized form.

computer program a set of instructions set out in a clear and logical sequence which tells a processor within a computer how to perform a particular task.

consolidated accounts the aggregate accounts of a group of companies.

contribution the difference between sales revenue and variable costs. If total contributions are just large enough to cover fixed costs then the producer breaks even; if contributions are less than fixed costs the producer makes a loss; while if contributions exceed fixed costs then the producer makes a profit.

corporation a company that is publicly registered, so that it acquires a legal identity separate from that of its owners, and so can stay in existence despite the death of any of its owners.

corporation tax a direct tax levied by the government on the profits accruing to businesses.

cost the expenditure upon resources incurred by a firm in producing and selling its output.

cost-based pricing pricing methods which determine the price of a product on the basis of its production, distribution and marketing costs.

cost centre a group of machines, a factory department or some other organizational subunit of a firm under the control of a manager, for which costs can be ascertained and used for purposes of cost control.

CPU (Central Processing Unit) the 'brain' of a computer which stores and processes data.

creditors (accounts payable) the money owed to individuals or firms because they have supplied goods, services or raw materials for which they have not yet been paid (trade creditors), or because they have made loans.

current assets assets such as stocks, money owed by debtors, and cash, which are held for a short period.

current liabilities all obligations to pay out cash at some date in the near future, including amounts which a firm owes to trade creditors and bank loans/overdrafts.

current ratio or **acid test ratio** an accounting measure of a firm's ability to pay its short-term liabilities out of its current assets.

data processing the organization and processing of information in a business.

debentures a means of financing companies through fixed-interest loans secured against company assets.

debt an amount of money owed by one person, company, etc to another.

debtors the money owed by individuals or firms because they have bought goods, services or raw materials for which they have not yet paid (trade debtors), or because they have borrowed money.

debtors ratio, average collection period or **debtor days ratio** an accounting measure of a firm's average collection period for debts, which expresses the amount owed by firm's debtors as a ratio of its average daily sales.

decision tree an aid to decision-making in uncertain conditions, that sets out alternative courses of action and the financial consequences of each alternative, and assigns probabilities to the likelihood of future events occurring.

depreciation, 1. the fall in the value of an asset during the course of its working life.

2. a decrease in the exchange rate of a currency against other currencies under a floating exchange rate system, reflecting a fall in market demand for that currency combined with a rise in market demand for other countries's currencies.

direct cost the sum of the materials cost and the labour cost directly linked to a product.

direct labour, 1. that part of the labour force in a firm which is directly concerned with the manufacture of a good or the provision of a service.

2. workers employed directly by local or central government to perform tasks rather than such tasks being contracted out to private-sector companies.

director an official of a company elected by the shareholders at the company's annual general meeting and charged with certain powers and responsibilities to run the company on behalf of the shareholders.

discount, 1. a deduction from the published list price of a product by a supplier to a customer.

2. the purchase of a bond, treasury bill or bill of exchange for less than its nominal value.

3. the sale of new stocks and shares at a reduced price. In the UK this involves the issue of a new share at a price below its nominal value.

discounted cash flow a method used in investment appraisal to evaluate the desirability of an investment project.

dividend a payment made by a company to its shareholders for providing share capital.

dividend cover a measure of the extent to which a firm's earnings cover dividend paid.

dividend yield the dividend paid by a company for a given accounting period expressed as a percentage of the current market price per share.

earnings yield earnings per ordinary share of a company for a given accounting period, expressed as a percentage of the current market price per share.

economic order quantity a method used in stock control which seeks to determine the optimum order quantity for a particular item.

economies of scale the reduction in the unit (average) costs of producing and distributing a product as the size of the firm's operations is increased.

equity ordinary shareholders's funds.

financial accounting accounting activities directed towards the preparation of annual profit and loss accounts and balance sheets in order to report to shareholders on their company's overall (profit) performance.

financial management the process of obtaining funds to finance a firm and advising on the use of these funds, which involves analysing the flow of funds through the firm.

financial year the period from 1 April to 31 March of the following year used for corporation tax purposes.

first in, first out (FIFO) a method of stock valuation which assumes that goods are withdrawn from stock in the order in which they are received, so that the cost of goods sold is based on the cost of the oldest stock, while the value of closing stock is based on the prices of the most recent purchases.

fixed assets assets such as buildings and machinery that are bought for long-term use in a firm rather than for resale.

fixed costs any costs that do not vary with the level of output.

flow chart a graphic representation of a sequence of operations.

franchise the granting by one company to another company (exclusive franchise) or a number of companies (non-exclusive franchise) of the right/s to supply its products.

gearing the proportion of fixed-interest loan capital to share capital employed in financing a company.

going concern accounting principle which suggets that all financial reports be prepared to reflect the business's expected continuation as a going concern which will trade in the future.

goodwill if another firm wishes to acquire this firm, goodwill represents the premium which the buyer must be prepared to pay for the firm over and above its asset value, because of the firm's trade contacts, reputation, established brand names, management expertise and general 'know-how'.

gross profit the difference between sales revenue and the cost of sales before the deduction of selling, distribution, administration and other costs in the profit and loss account.

hardware the electrical circuits and electromechanical devices that make up a computer system.

holding company a company that controls another company or companies.

indirect labour that part of the labour force in a firm which is not directly concerned with the manufacture of a good or the provision of a service. Indirect labour cost depends on the amount of remuneration paid to all those factory employees who are not directly engaged in making products but who provide support services (for example, supervision and clerical work).

indirect materials any raw materials which, while they are not incorporated in a product, are nonetheless consumed in the production process (for example, lubricants and moulds for metal castings). The cost of such indirect materials is usually counted as part of production overheads.

interest the charge made for borrowing money in the form of a loan.

interest rate the particular amount of interest which a borrower is required to pay to a lender for borrowing a particular sum of money to finance spending on consumption and the purchase of capital assets.

inventory the stocks of finished goods, work in progress and raw materials held by businesses.

inventory control see **stock control.**

invoice a document sent by a supplier to a customer that itemizes the products supplied to the customer, their prices, and the total amount of money owed by the customer for these products.

issued share capital the amount of its authorized share capital that a company has issued to shareholders in order to raise capital.

last-in, first-out (LIFO) a method of stock valuation that assumes that the most recently purchased goods are withdrawn from stock first so that the cost of goods sold is based on the costs of the most recent purchases, while the value of closing stock is based on the oldest goods available.

lead time the time between placing an order or reorder and the goods being received into stores.

leaseback an arrangement which involves the selling of an asset by the owner to another person or company on condition that the asset is then leased (rented back) to the original owner for a specified period of time at an agreed rental.

ledger the accounting records that keep a note of a firm's day-to-day financial transactions with outside parties.

liability a claim on the resources of an individual or business in respect of monies borrowed. A liability is thus a form of debt (for example, a bank overdraft or loan).

limited company (Ltd) term carried by a private limited company after its name.

limited liability an arrangement that limits the maximum loss which a shareholder is liable for in the event of company failure.

liquidity ratio see **current ratio.**

loan capital or **debt capital** the money employed in a company that has been borrowed from external sources for fixed periods of time by the issue of fixed-interest financial securities such as debentures.

make-or-buy decision the strategic choice confronting the firm as to whether it purchases its raw materials and components requirements from outside suppliers or produces them for itself.

margin the difference between selling price and cost price of a product or financial security.

marginal cost the extra cost that is incurred by a firm in increasing output by one unit.

mean see **average.**

median a method of representing the middle of a set of numbers by a single number (ie, the value of the middle item when the items are arranged in increasing order of magnitude).

memorandum of association a legal document which must be filed with the registrar of companies before a company can be incorporated, and which governs the external relationship between the company and third parties.

method study an aspect of work study which involves the systematic recording and analysis of the way in which a job is performed, with a view to developing and applying easier and more efficient methods of performing the task.

mode a method of representing a set of numbers by a single number which is the value which occurs most often, that is, the one with the highest frequency.

monopoly a market structure characterized by a single supplier and high barriers to entry.

net current assets see **working capital.**

net profit the difference between a firm's sales revenue and all costs.

network analysis or **programme evaluation and review technique (PERT)** a method of planning, scheduling and controlling projects involving interrelated but distinct elements of work, or *activities*.

opportunity cost when a decision is made in favour of one choice, the opportunity cost of that decision is the benefit that would have been gained from the next best alternative.

ordinary shares or **equity** a financial security issued to those individuals and institutions who provide long-term finance for companies. Ordinary shareholders are entitled to any net profits made by their company after all expenses (including interest charges and tax) have been paid and they generally receive some or all of these profits in the form of dividends.

overdraft a financial facility for advancing money to an individual or business (the borrower) by a commercial bank, savings bank, etc (the lender).

pie chart a chart that portrays data in pictorial form, showing the relative share of each category in a total by means of the relative size of its 'slice' of a circular 'pie'.

portfolio a collection of financial securities held by an investor.

private limited company (Ltd) a limited company that does not issue shares for public subscription.

probability the likelihood of a particular uncertain event occurring, measured on a scale from 0.0 (the event is impossible) to 1.0 (the event is certain to occur).

process chart see **activity chart.**

production control the coordination and monitoring of production programmes and targets.

profit the difference that arises when a firm's sales revenue is greater than its total costs.

profit and loss account an accounting statement that shows a firm's sales revenue generated over a trading period and all the relevant costs experienced in earning that revenue.

profit centre an organizational subunit of a firm given responsibility for minimizing costs and maximizing revenue within its limited sphere of operations.

program see **computer program.**

range the differences between the largest observation and the smallest observation within a group of numerical observations.

rate of return the profits earned by a business, measured as a percentage of the assets employed in the business.

ratio analysis the calculation and use of accounting ratios to analyse the trading performance, liquidity and financial security of a company over time and by comparison with other firms.

raw materials basic materials, such as iron ore, bauxite, wheat and coffee, which are converted into finished goods or components in the production process.

reorder level a predetermined level for a particular item to which stocks must fall before an order for more of the item is placed.

replacement cost the cost of replacing a fixed asset (such as an item of machinery) or stock.

reserves revenue reserves arise when some after-tax profit is retained in the business to finance the acquisition of extra assets, rather than being paid out as dividends.

retail co-operative an organization that is owned by its consumers.

return on capital employed an accounting measure of a firm's profitability, which expresses the firm's profits for an accounting period as a percentage of its capital employed.

revaluation an administered increase in the exchange rate of a currency against other currencies under a fixed exchange rate system.

risk capital any business capital subscribed by an individual entrepreneur or group of ordinary shareholders which entails some risk of loss in the event of the enterprise failing.

sample, 1. part of a total population that can be analysed to make inferences about the whole population.

2. a small amount of raw material or finished product whose quality or performance can be tested as a guide to the quality or performance of a whole batch of material or product.

sampling the selection of part of a total population of consumers or products whose behaviour or performance can be analysed, in order to make inferences about the behaviour or performance of the total population, without the difficulty and expense of undertaking a complete census of the whole population.

share capital the money employed in a company that has been subscribed by the shareholders of the company in the form of ordinary shares (equity) and preference shares, and which will remain as a permanent source of finance as long as the company remains in existence.

share certificate a document which is issued to a shareholder in a company, which serves as proof of ownership of shares in the company.

software the programs or instructions that make a computer system perform particular data-processing tasks.

standard cost an estimated product cost, prepared in advance of production, that shows what a product ought to cost given reasonably efficient working.

statistics, 1. methods of collecting and analysing numerical data.

2. a group of data.

stock, 1. the part of a firm's assets that are held in the form of raw materials, work in progress and finished goods.

2. a financial security issued by a company or by the government as a means of raising long-term capital.

stock control the process of controlling stocks of finished products, work in progress and raw materials, in order to minimize warehousing and other stockholding costs, while maintaining an adequate level of stock to meet usage requirements.

stock-turnover ratio a measure of a firm's stock-holdings that expresses the firm's sales revenue as a ratio of its period-end stock, to show how many times stocks are turned over in sales during a period's trading.

transfer price the internal price at which raw materials, components and final products are transacted between the divisions or subsidiaries of a firm.

unit cost see **average cost.**

value added the difference between the value of a firm's (or industry's) *output* (ie, the total revenues received from selling that output) and the cost of the *input* materials, components or services bought in to produce that output.

venture capital money subscribed in the form of share capital and loan capital to finance new firms and activities which are considered to be of an especially risky nature and hence unable to attract finance from more conventional sources.

visual display unit (VDU) a means of displaying computer output, usually on a television-style screen or liquid crystal display unit.

work in progress any goods that are still in the process of being made up into their final form.

work study an area of production management concerned with ensuring the best possible use of human and material resources in carrying out a specified activity.

working capital or **net current assets** an accounting term denoting a firm's short-term current assets which are turned over fairly quickly in the course of business. They include raw materials, work in progress and finished goods stocks, debtors and cash, less short-term current liabilities.

yield the return on a financial security, expressed in money terms, related to the current market price of that security, to show the percentage return of the investment.

Suggested Answers to Essays

Chapter Two

Essay 1

The reasons why a public limited liability company (plc) might revert to private limited (Ltd) status are:

a The founder of the firm may wish to regain total control and limit the distribution of shares to selected people (for example, the family).
b The founder may feel than an autocratic chief executive can act more decisively in a recessionary period, unfettered by other directors elected by institutional investors.
c The founder may know something about future market operations which encourage him or her to increase their shareholding very rapidly.
d It may be that the very strict rules on financial dealings insisted by the Stock Exchange over public companies are felt to be counterproductive to the future well-being of the company. The Stock Exchange has no control over private companies.
e The cost of maintaining a shareholders register is very high for large companies. There is always the risk that, in spite of a register, there may be a hostile take over bid from 'a dawn raid' on shares. In a private company the rules over share transfer prevent unwelcome 'take over' bids.

Note: In many examples of recent movements from public to actual or desired private status, the public company has had one or two individuals with very high private investments already – for example, Sir John Webber (The Really Useful Company) and Alan Sugar (Amstrad).

Essay 2

The particular problems posed for a country by the existence of a multinational firm are:

a Multinational firms can contribute a significant part of the host country's earnings and thus domestic policies might be dictated by foreign investors.
b Multinationals can minimize tax obligation in a high tax country and maximize them in a low tax rate country.
c Local people seldom reach the chief executive level of the multinational, and therefore local policies are seldom considered.
d The sudden 'demise' of a multinational due to problems elsewhere can cause severe problems for the host country.
e The host country's security is threatened if a significant part of the multinational is located in an 'enemy' country.
f Some of the best brains in the host country employed by the multinational can be drawn away to foreign locations of the multinational.
g The multinational may have universal wage and employee agreements which are implemented but are distinctly different from those of other businesses in the host country. This can cause serious industrial relations problems.

Chapter Three

Essay 1

A medium-sized business can raise funds in a variety of ways:

a Internal sources of funds are obtained from:

- Profits generated but not distributed to the owners
- Selling assets no longer required
- Factoring debts to improve cash flow
- Delaying payments to creditors to acceptable periods
- Reducing stock levels or even eliminating them completely
- Acquiring new assets on lease rather than by purchase
- Selling assets and leasing them back
- Giving shareholders more shares rather than paying a dividend

b External sources of funds are available by:

- Asking existing shareholders to buy more shares
- Issuing more shares to new shareholders
- Issuing a debenture to the public
- Requesting a bank loan

Increasing the debt capital (the long-term loans) increases the gearing of the business and means a regular drain on profits to pay interest charges. Equity capital from shareholders means paying low dividends in bad years but high dividends in good years. There is more flexibility with more equity capital, but it also increases the risk of greater institutional control by the election of nominated directors.

Essay 2

A shareholder is sent a copy of the company report and financial accounts each year. Unfortunately, the details shown in the accounts give only the barest information as to the strengths and weaknesses of the business. In some reports the complexity of the accounting system results in incomprehensible accounts except to highly trained people. It is also true that many reports are presented to show the business in the most favourable light possible and this has been the subject of much comment in the UK business press in recent years.

In general, the shareholder can make a rough assessment of what his or her investment was worth some months after the period of the accounts by calculating selected ratios such as the gearing, the current ratio, the interest cover and so on. However, all these figures are very much out of date and the shrewd investor will carefully read up-to-date, informed press comment in order to evaluate the current state of the investment.

Chapter Four

Essay 1

Opinion polls relate to a certain situation at a certain time. The publication of the results of the poll can itself change the results of a repeated poll, and this is why the publication of polls near to an election is banned in France. In addition, in a moving state of public opinion which may be strongly connected with media presentations, a poll can be rapidly out of date by the time that it is published.

The statistical error in polls is always present since a sample cannot give a precise indication of the total population's views. However, many UK pollsters use samples of several thousand, resulting in low sampling errors of around plus or minus 1 per cent. But if two major political parties are 'neck and neck', the sampling error can give the wrong winner.

Essay 2

Many people are not trained to understand numbers in tables or in text, and a picture is a very important way of conveying information. You will note that the tabloid press rarely publishes number information in any format except as pictograms or simple bar charts. Many people are just too busy to spend much time on analysing numbers. This is especially true when conveying information on the differences between two sets of numbers.

Chapter Five

Essay 1

The Just in Time (JIT) technique is used to highlight the fact that stocks cost money to hold and therefore there is a waste of money. However, there must be a full examination of the total system operations and costs before advocating a zero-stock holding policy. The whole operation must be clearly thought through unless high 'stock out' costs result. JIT depends on low-cost (computer-based) information control systems to organize materials to arrive on time even though these materials might themselves be the result of a separate manufacturing system where JIT is present.

Stock control theory examines total system costs and it may be that JIT is not possible because of the cost of ordering materials. However, JIT is an objective, and one which is shown to have noticeable improvements on the profit performance of businesses.

Essay 2

Critical path analysis is a method of project management and has applications in any project. A project is defined as a job with a planned start time and a planned finish time. In large projects, formal CPA methods are used to optimize the use of resources and to minimize waste. A computer-based system of CPA planning and control is essential in order to provide accurate, up-to-date information. In smaller projects, the concepts of CPA are just as important but a computer may not be required. CPA is important in all sizes of project in order to ensure that the logical and most efficient method for completing the project is undertaken.

Chapter Six

Essay 1

Absorption costing 'absorbs' both the fixed and variable overheads and adds them to the direct costs of the products on a pre-agreed basis. Usually this basis is time-dependent since most overheads are themselves time-dependent. The common method is to apportion overheads on the basis of the direct operator hours allocated to the product.

Variable costing only includes those costs which vary with output. Some of the variable costs are direct costs; others are indirect costs, or overheads.

In periods of low sales and high production, with a consequent build up of stock levels, absorption costing methods will indicate much higher profits than variable costing methods since a high proportion of the fixed production overhead is capitalized in stock. This can be misleading.

Absorption costing methods are generally acceptable for past activities since the overhead is known and can be apportioned and allocated to products reasonably accurately. Managers have an indication of how all the costs are covered by the product types. However, absorption costing can only be approximated for future operations based on expected overheads and plant capacity.

There is a danger that variable costing methods might lead to underestimates of the full cost of the product since fixed production costs are not included.

Variable costing methods are most useful for forward planning, especially when combined with the contribution approach to profit planning. Calculations on determining the best mix of products to offer can only be sensibly achieved by variable costing methods.

Essay 2

Depreciation is a fair charge on the user of an asset for the loss in value of the asset during the period of use. There can be no logical reason why such a charge can be avoided even though estimates of the depreciation provision might be inaccurate.

Confusion arises over depreciation calculations when inflation is high and depreciation is related to the replacement of an asset.

The National Health Service in the UK avoided the depreciation cost as part of the accounting system up to 1991. The presumption was that costs related to wages and materials and that the government would replace plant and buildings as the need arose from their own capital budgets. Now that hospitals, for example, are more responsible for total costs, depreciation is included. This increases the 'caring costs' considerably, but new buildings and plant can be planned more realistically.

Chapter Seven

Essay 1

Financial ratios must be regarded as 'thermometers' measuring the temperature of different business activities. The only use for a temperature measurement is to compare the value with another value. A ratio by itself is meaningless.

Financial ratios among different organizations, such as 'production costs as a percentage of total costs', are only helpful if all organizations calculate their costs in the same way. The advantage in using the same type of ratio within the same organization is that the method of calculating cost is known precisely. Ratios for measuring trends are most important.

Sometimes ratios are calculated for groups of costs where the percentages must add up to 100 per cent. It is foolish to compare such ratios with others on the basis that some ratios increase whereas others decrease. If two ratios add to 100 per cent there are no degrees of freedom; as one increases, the other must decrease.

Problems also arise when examining a ratio of a cost which has a significant fixed element in addition to a variable element. Production costs are typical examples. The ratio of 'production costs to sales revenue' must decrease with increasing sales since the fixed part remains constant.

However, as a rapid and easily understood technique, ratio analysis is extremely important. It locates problem areas quickly and forces a deeper analysis in spite of satisfactory superficial results. For example, the 'production costs to sales' ratio might be acceptable, but the deeper analysis of, say, 'material costs to sales' can indicate significant problems arising.

Essay 2

Break even analysis shows how profits are related to output. The break even point calculation and comparison with current output give a measure of the risks in the business. As businesses consider more automation, the fixed element of costs increases and the variable element decreases. The effects of these changes can be clearly shown on a break even chart, and decisions can be taken on the suitability of some investments in relation to the likely increases in output volumes.

Essay 3

Small businesses usually ignore discounted cash flow investment criterion because the calculations look superficially complex, and some managerial training is low or non-existent. However, there are other factors involved. Although DCF is useful, in times of recession or high risk other emotional factors are present and there is always a strong desire to minimize losses. Payback is an investment criterion which helps to minimize losses either by demanding excessively high investment (for example, by demanding that an investment pays back within six months) or by knowing that after a few years any return must be profitable, whatever the return rate.

Chapter Eight

Essay 1

Computer aided bankruptcy occurs when a small business initially purchases a computer, then selects some sort of software to run it, and finally tries to find an application to apply the system. This is in exactly the wrong order. Unfortunately, small businesses feel that computers must be involved in business systems because bigger firms seem to use them efficiently. The dilemma with small firms is the inadequacy of the design of information systems. In most cases, information is stored in people's heads rather than being freely accessible, and most employees are doing several jobs at the same time. There is often in small firms a lack of good planning and anyone who has been involved with computer systems will know that computers need good data to process. The old adage of 'garbage in, garbage out' is most applicable. Small firms involved in complex business systems, such as publishing, need expert advice to design appropriate computer systems and they are reluctant to pay the going rate for a specialist. The disaster occurs when the small business employs an unskilled person to design the computer system in order to save money.

Essay 2

Communications within a business tends to grow with the business. Information channels follow all sorts of routes, including several called 'grapevines'. Gossip, rumour and facts abound in most offices and it is often difficult to find the truth. In spite of this, many people in family-type businesses do have reasonable communications.

When information technology is introduced into a business, many of the old 'unofficial' communication systems are abandoned and there is often an unrealistic reliance on the computer. This is misplaced since what is also needed is a redesign of the whole information and communication process, not just the substitution of computers for people. Some people, without adequate training, feel that computers put them into a 'straight jacket', and do not allow them to be creative. The secret is to use the computer system to create new ways of working which are more efficient and more effective than the old ways, and yet still retain the human relationships within the business. This is indeed a hard task for most managers.

Index

References to Dictionary bear the suffix D.